DORSET DAYS

Rhodes James and Macfarlanes, Broadstone, Dorset,1951
Alan's parents with maternal grandparents and family,
Alan, seated on ground

DORSET DAYS

AN UPBRINGING
IN THE 1940S AND EARLY 1950S

BY
ALAN MACFARLANE

For Fiona and Anne

who shared those Dorset Days

The Village
Digital Press

The Orchard Glasshouse, South Willingham, Market Rasen LN8 6NG UK

The Village Digital Press is an imprint of Courseware4Trainers Ltd. It works with proactive writers in the scientific, academic and business communities as well as the emerging field of socio-economic family history. The writers are the copyright holders and are responsible for all aspects of the book's preparation up to printing and distribution.

First published in the UK by The Village Digital Press in 2012

© Alan Macfarlane 2012

ISBN 978-0-85718-198-5

Printed in the village of South Willingham by

Courseware4Trainers Ltd

The book is set in Baskerville Old Face. It is printed on Xerox Colour Impressions 80gsm paper using a Xerox DC260 printer and bound using a FKS PrintBind KB200.

CONTENTS

PREFACE AND ACKNOWLEDGEMENTS

There are four questions behind this account of my childhood. One concerns who I was and how I came to be as I am. So this is the autobiographical quest for personal roots and identity. I hope to throw some light on the wider nature of an experience which is not confined to me – the evolution of a certain sort of middle-class, English, male in the middle of the twentieth century.

A second question concerns my family and its history. It seems that I come from a well-documented and interesting family whose tentacles spread across the world and can be traced in detail from the later seventeenth century. In particular, there are sets of letters and memoranda which give an insight into the inner dynamics of colonial family life. Not the least of these are my mother's letters and other writings which I hope to reassemble and expand. This is the genealogical quest.

A third question concerns England and Britain. I came back from India when I was six and encountered a new land. I needed to start to understand its distinctive history and culture. This is an exploration I have engaged in since, both as a historian and an anthropologist. The theme here is 'the peculiarity of the English (or British)', and what its causes and effects have been. From 'The Origins of English Individualism' written in 1977, through to my latest book in 2009 on 'Reflections on Cambridge', much of my work has been exploring the bundle of contradictions and strange cultural pattern of this small island. Through examining my family, and myself I hope to throw further light on this.

My final question concerns the British Empire. Britain was just the small hub of a great empire for more than a century. The British created this empire, but equally it created Britain. It has a very distinctive character which makes it different from other empires in the way it worked and imagined itself. I am particularly interested in what held it together and how the identity of those who were involved with it, such as my ancestors, was constructed. This knits together the three previous questions – my own education for empire, the experience of my far-flung family, the peculiarity of their British home, and how all this was shaped by, and shaped, the British Empire.

*

I seem to have been interested in the evocation of memory from a relatively early period in my life. This partly explains why I have been reluctant to throw anything away. From my teens I had the idea that I would try to construct an 'archive' of my life and perhaps that of my relatives. So I hoarded toys, photographs, letters, writings, anything I could. This desire to hold on to the past is shown in an essay that I wrote when I was eighteen entitled 'The past'. I shall just include the first paragraph to show my awareness, even then, of the importance of memory.

'People often find tremendous pleasure in reliving the pleasures of past events, partly as I have already explained, because they are surveying it from a safe peak of knowledge. It is only when we are not fully conscious, however that we can be truly transported there again and feel every emotion that we once felt. We must not worship the past. It is dangerous to idealise it, and useless to live continually in it. It can be utilized as a springboard to the future, and for those who have had an unhappy life it may be the dim backcloth to the glorious future, but that is all.'

There is a comment by my teacher in red ink at the end: 'One angle left out – the aged. What does it feel like, I wonder when all the major experiences of one's life lie in the past? The sole adventure left, death.' As I read this fifty years later it seems a pertinent remark.

*

In constructing this book I first wrote down everything I thought I could remember about this period when I was aged six to thirteen. I then checked this against the diaries, letters and school reports. This has thrown some light on the way in which my memory works. It shows that for this period, or at least before I was ten, without supporting documentation almost everything would be irretrievable. There would be just a very few lightning flashes of memory, usually moments of high excitement or pain or effort. A.C. Benson beautifully describes these isolated moments.

'Early impressions are like glimpses seen through the window by night when lightning is about. The flash leaps out without visible cause or warning, and the blackness lifts for a second revealing the scene, the criss-cross of the rods of rain, the trees shining with moisture.... So it is with memory; my early blinks are exceedingly vivid, but they are sundered, and though the passage of time does not dim them, as it dims the more fading impressions of later life, they do not form part of a continuous picture.'[1]

A second thing I have found is how faulty memory is, not usually in the experience itself, but in the surrounding details of when or where the event occurred or who was involved. I have re-contextualized many memories, when I caught my first fish at Oxford, when I learnt to cycle, when I stole from my grandfather. I have also had to revise my whole assessment of the degree to which I was unhappy at the Dragon School.

What I regret is that even with the detail in the documents, so little new memory has been triggered. I have sometimes managed to capture again the ambient smells, sounds and feelings surrounding a photograph or a letter. Yet very often I

---

[1] A.C. Benson, *As We Were: a Victorian Peepshow* (Penguin edn., 2001), 67.

feel I may be forcing or imposing memories now that I know an event happened. For, on the whole, I can recall very little of even major events of that time, like going to India for my eleventh birthday holiday, or singing in 'Iolanthe' when I was twelve.

Yet gazing at my past as it unrolls in photos and comments it seems mainly to be the life of a slightly familiar stranger. I feel a little affinity, some ghostly overlap. Yet mostly it seems to be a different person. I recognize the little boy as someone I knew a very long time ago but have almost now forgotten. The past is not just a foreign country where they do things differently; it is inhabited by half-familiar ghosts of one's younger self who seem disconnected strangers, yet are also part of oneself

This again emphasizes the good fortune of having the photographs, letters and other documents. There are clearly some people who seem to be able to remember their early years in vivid detail – Lord Berners, Roald Dahl, W.H. Hudson, Naomi Mitchison, Muriel Spark to name but a few. I cannot do this and would never have felt it worth attempting this study of a growing boy if it had not been for the chance survival of these documents, the 'paper trail' as it is now called in our audit-ridden culture.

Without the contemporary photographs, letters, diaries, school reports and other materials, I would be like an anthropologist who had done fieldwork in another society some sixty years ago and had destroyed all the fieldnotes. It would be an impossible task to write the ethnographic and anthropological account without the primary materials.

Yet even with these sources, one needs constantly to remember that each of them is biased. Just to take one example, an over-riding first impression is of how insular the letters were. While Indian Independence and its aftermath rocked India, the Cold War and the Korean War rekindled fears of nuclear war in the late 1940s and early 1950s. These events, let alone the two elections which took place in Britain, there is only a small amount in the documents suggesting that they impinged on us.

Yet I soon realized that, along with a slightly head-in-the-sand attitude which my mother admits to, there were also good reasons for this. Personal letters and diaries are not usually where you will find discussion of international or national politics or events – unless they directly impinge on plans. This is worth remembering. The sources I have, like all historical documents, create a bias - in this case away from the general to the particular.

Another bias lies in the letters that I wrote to my parents and grandparents. Addressing an adult, especially when one is still learning to control language, can lead into a kind of writing which conceals as much as it shows. How much of my own views and voice comes out of the letters, especially those written within the scrutiny of the Dragon? I don't notice much difference in my letters from home and from school to my parents.

*

This account is a small part of a more general autobiographical and biographical account. The period before we came back to England will be dealt with in a volume provisionally titled 'Indian Infancy'. The parallel life at my preparatory boarding school between 1950 and 1955 is published in Jamie Bruce Lockhart and Alan Macfarlane 'Dragon Days'. I hope to continue the story through my years at Sedbergh and Oxford in later volumes. What happened to me after the experience recounted here is sketched in briefly at the end of this book.

I have currently divided the book into text and illustrations. Some may like to look at the relevant photographs before reading a chapter, others may wish to do so afterwards or not at all.

*

I am grateful to those who have read drafts of this account and commented, especially Inge Harrison, Loulou Brown and

Jamie Bruce Lockhart. And in particular I am grateful to my wife Sarah, who has shared this, like many other journeys, and has always been encouraging, as well as eagle-eyed. My other deep debt is to my mother and father, whose letters and love are the bed-rock of this account, and to my close family, in particular my sisters, uncles and my daughter, who have helped in so many ways.

CHRONOLOGY AND SOURCES

1. ASSAM AND INDIA: 1940–MARCH 1947
All the family in India 1940-1945.
My grandmother returned to England in 1945 and my grandfather in 1946.

There is not a great deal for this period, except some letters and the odd diary reference and poems. There are quite a few photos.

This period will be dealt with in a separate volume on 'Indian Infancy'

2. OXFORD AND CHARMOUTH: APRIL 1947–JANUARY 1948
Iris, Mac, Alan, Fiona and Anne arrive on 16 April 1947 in England. They live together in a house in north Oxford. Father returns to India by early December 1947.
All the family, apart from father, including grandparents, go for about a month to 'Stonebarrow', Charmouth, December 1947 and early January 1948.

There is not much material for this period since my parents were together and I was too young to remember much.

3. DORSET WITH IRIS AT HOME: JANUARY 1948–OCTOBER 1948
Grandparents, Iris and children all move to 'By the Way', Dorset, January 1948
Iris leaves with Anne for India, c.18 October 1948.

This is one of the richest periods for materials since my mother was writing very frequently to my father who was away for the last nine months of her leave.

4. DORSET - IRIS, ANNE AND MAC IN INDIA: OCT. 1948–OCT. 1950

Alan and Fiona living with grandparents and go to day school.
Alan goes to Dragon in September 1950.
Iris returns with Anne from India, October 1950 to 'By the Way', Dorset.

There is a limited amount of materials, letters from my parents to grandparents and one or two from me, school reports etc.

5. SECOND LEAVE: 'PINECOT'– OCTOBER 1950 – JANUARY 1952

Iris and girls move to Pinecot, Broadstone, 1 February 1951.
Mac returns from India, June 30 1951.
Iris, Mac, Fiona and Anne go to India, January 1952

This is another very rich period for materials since my mother was writing very frequently to my father, who was away for the first nine months of her leave.

6. DORSET WITH REST OF FAMILY IN INDIA: JANUARY 1952–JUNE 1954

Alan trip to Assam, December 1952.
Iris, Fiona and Anne return to England June 1954 to By the Way.

A considerable number of letters, photographs etc.

7. THIRD LEAVE: MOVE TO THE LAKES - JUNE 1954– SEPTEMBER 1955

Iris, Fiona and Anne to England, June 1954.
Iris, Fiona and Anne move to Beck House, Windermere, October 1954.
Grandparents join them at Beck House, November 1954.
Mac returns to England, April 1955.
Mac, Iris and girls move to Field Head, Hawkshead, April 1955.
Alan leaves Dragon School in July 1955

This is another very rich period for materials since my mother was writing very frequently to my father, who was away for the first nine months of her leave.

1. COMING HOME

The Steam Ship 'Scythia' arrived at Liverpool on 16 April 1947 from Colombo. One of the families on board was the Macfarlanes who had embarked at Bombay. They were listed as follows.

Donald Macfarlane, aged 30, Tea Planter
    Iris Macfarlane, aged 30 [actually she was 24]
    Alan Macfarlane, aged 5
    Fiona Macfarlane, aged 3
    Anne Macfarlane, aged 9 months

Address: 25 St Margaret's Road Oxford

Country of Intended Permanent Residence
    Donald and Iris – Other Parts of the British Empire,
    The three children – England

The following day, my grandmother's diary notes our arrival on April 17 at 25 St Margaret's Road, Oxford.

My memories of the next nine months or so before we went to Dorset when I was are slight. I wrote what I could remember in an essay at the age of eighteen entitled 'Confessions of a schoolboy'.

'We went to live first at Oxford with my grandparents and aunt. The house was too small for us really, but I spent most of my time down fishing in the little canal. One day much to the surprise of everyone, including myself, I caught a fish. My sister rather disappointed me by not going into

1

ecstasies over the bony, five inch fish which I said I would let her have specially for supper. The only other two events which I remember were equally insignificant. One was that I intensely annoyed my young uncle (then about 14) by throwing his best metal airoplane out of the 3rd story in the hope that it would fly. The other event I remember was a row between my Aunt and her son Leigh. He insisted on taking his dog into the air force with him, and apparently his mother disliked this idea. Anyway on a walk I was dragged through the main streets of Oxford while these two cursed each other in violent language!'

We then all moved to a pleasant house on a steep hill above Charmouth. The hill was very steep and was superb track for my little jeep; and much to the terror of the other dwellers in Charmouth a friend (on a scooter) and I (on the jeep) used to scream down the main road. The only other things I remember were that we once had a Turkey too large for the oven, that there was an old derelict shed in our garden, which I cleaned out, and that there was a nice man living at the top of the hill who had a strange castle, which was designed for rolling marbles down. I went to my first school in Charmouth, which was ably looked after by two bearded ladies.'

Apart from a few photographs and half a dozen entries in my grandmother's diary, I have found nothing else for this period. The diary entries for 1947 are:

Wed July 2	Iris and Mac returned. Up to Cumnor
July 14	Snow White and the 7 dwarfs
July 20	Bill reports in town/tour
July 29	Robert returns
Sunday August 3	Anne's christening
September 15	Robert. Dentist

At the end of the diary are various train times to Broadstone, where we would move in early 1948.

As I recall the period now, there is not much to add. We settled in number 25 St Margaret's Road. The house itself is a blank in my memory. I have revisited it and it is like many of those tall brick north Oxford houses with a small front garden, a half-submerged basement flat, and three floors above. The back garden had brick walls around it – as I see from a photograph of my father and uncle in it – and over the back wall was another house where, so I seem to remember later being told, T.E. Lawrence was writing 'The Seven Pillars of Wisdom'. I remember it as cold, but this may be from stories about the grim winter of 1946-7 which had only just ended in the March before we returned.

The area is filled in for me by a number of later periods in North Oxford at School and university. It is tree-filled and affluent, with the Parks, where cricketers played, canals and rivers with boats and fish. It has a special ambience, unique in the world, filled with the quintessence of donnish life and private education of various kinds. It entered my blood at that time and then again when I returned to live half a mile away at the Dragon School in Bardwell Road.

I think I still remember the particular terrible row – the incandescent rage of my aunt, the screaming, slamming of doors, a dog, banishment. I still vaguely remember going down to the canal and fishing and catching my first small fish. I also think I remember going to the Cherwell, near where I would go to school at the Dragon, with a rubber dinghy with a sail and to swimming in the relatively icy waters.

My grandmother came back to England with Robert in January 1945 and went to stay with her sister Margery in St Margaret's Road, Oxford. My grandfather finally left India in December 1945 and they were together on 28 December. A month later my grandparents went to live at the vicarage at Cumnor where they seem to have stayed for eleven months before returning to St Margaret's road on 12 December 1946.

So, apart from the terrible row between Margery and Leigh, the swimming, the bottling of soft fruits, some studio photographs of Fiona, Anne and myself from Ramsay and

Muspratt, there is, as yet, very little in the way of memories of this period.

I seem to have been too young to be going to school at Oxford, though somehow I fitted in a term and a half at a kindergarten (unnamed) ending in a report in February 1948.

My father returned to India before Christmas 1948 as my first letter was sent to him from Charmouth, according to my mother's hand in December 1947. It is a paper with picture of juggling clown: *Dear Daddy, I hope you are very well. I hope you have a nice time at Xmas. Lots of love Alan*

*

What I did not really realize until I started this study was that my return was a tiny fragment in an ancient drama, in which my family was a microcosm within the British Empire over the last four hundred years.

My ancestors seem to have been at the outward edge of many of the waves of predatory expansion of the British Empire. My tenth generation James ancestors were among the first to settle in Jamaica, and Colonel Richard James was apparently the first English child to be born there in 1655. The James family prospered on Jamaica and still owned an estate there until the 1920s. My own fourth generation great grandfather was a Chancery lawyer in Jamaica. He finally left for England in 1837, three years after the abolition of slavery, his children having been sent home to be educated in England.

He invested for his three sons in the new colony in south Australia. One of his grandsons went to India, where my grandfather, William Rhodes James, was born in 1886 in Coonor amidst the Nilgiri coffee estates. After school in England and Sandhurst, my grandfather was commissioned into the Indian Army. By the time he met my grandmother Violet Swinhoe he was working as an intelligence officer on the Burma-China frontier.

The Swinhoe branch was reputedly descended from Viking raiders into Northumbria, where there is a village of that name. We have traced them back to the eighteenth century when they were lawyers in Calcutta. I have visited their impressive graves in the old Park Street cemetery in Calcutta and seen the street named after them in that city. One distant cousin went to China in the middle of the nineteenth century and a Chinese pheasant is named after him. In the later nineteenth century Rodway Swinhoe discovered a potentially lucrative niche in a new frontier of Empire, upper Burma, where he practised as a lawyer in Mandalay for over thirty years. It was there that my grandmother was born in 1896.

Much of British life from the eighteenth to twentieth centuries was essentially a system of what anthropologists might call cyclical nomadic predation. This depended on two poles. England (and Scotland and Ireland) was the base, the emotional, social and political core, and the family home. Here the children were sent to school and perhaps on to university or at least some kind of finishing and training institution. Here those from the colonies would retire and become grandparents and carers for the young sent home from abroad. Going abroad was a stage. Some 'stayed on' in remote hill stations and elsewhere, but the great majority came back to what they considered to be their real home.

In such a cyclical movement, the boarding school became an essential mechanism. Such schools were part of an internal system for encouraging social mobility by converting money into status and training the middle classes for professions within Britain. They were also a mechanism for indoctrinating, disciplining and training those who would become the colonizers to make their fortunes around the world. My extended family participated in this pattern from the seventeenth century onwards, various branches sending their children home to school to learn how to be English.

*

I was born in Shillong, Assam in December 1941. My first five years were spent in India as the Second World War rolled to the edges of Assam and I ended my time in India for a few brief months on a tea estate. In an autobiographical essay I commented that 'My first recollections are of a slightly unhappy childhood. My parents were in India, my father in the army, and so we did not live a settled life. There always seemed to be something wrong with my tummy and once I broke my arm. At the age of five I came home to England, and then I did not remember much, except that I was seasick most of the way home, and that my youngest sister was given a little stove for her birthday.' My mother later told me that I formed a strong friendship with the sweeper's son but the Urdu and ability to swim were to vanish almost immediately I returned to England.

The warmth, both physical and emotional, the brilliance of the landscape and the freedom which I think I remember from those first five years made the shock of coming home to North Oxford at the end of the coldest winter of the twentieth century, with wartime rationing and very limited coal supplies, all the greater. My mother stayed in England for eighteen months and then left me and my elder sister Fiona at home when I was aged six and three quarters.

I remember that parting – the delight I felt as I woke the morning after my mother had kissed me to sleep and discovered a small present at the foot of the bed quickly evaporating into a desperate feeling of loneliness and separation which has remained with me ever since. This pattern continued. My mother returned at the end of 1950, towards the end of my first term at the Dragon School, a boarding preparatory school in Oxford. I scarcely recognized her and the meeting was painful on both sides. She remained for just over a year, being joined by my father half way through the period. They then all disappeared again, this time taking my sister Fiona as well, at the start of 1952. I was alone with my grandparents until my mother returned in the summer of 1954. The absence was broken, however, when I flew out to Assam for the winter holidays of 1952.

When my mother returned in 1954 we started to look for an alternative home to the house in Dorset to which we had moved in 1948. We rented accommodation in the Lake District in the north of England and moved into the first home we owned in the summer of 1955 just as I was leaving the

Dragon School. The shape of this experience, laid out in the chronology at the start of this book, is thus of three periods with my mother at home, and two long absences. It was a rhythm of life at boarding school and holidays mainly spent in Dorset, with some visits to Scotland. The main actors in the tiny drama at home were my maternal relatives, to whom I shall now turn.

*

There is a photograph [reproduced on the cover, as well as in the photo essay] taken in our Dorset home in the summer of 1951, when I was aged nine and a half, which includes all of my closer family. These were the people who shaped much of my home life during these first eight years in England.

At the core of my life, the central relationship was with my mother Iris, seated with Anne on her knee. She will appear a great deal in her own voice in the narrative, and many of her attitudes and feelings are revealed throughout this account. I didn't really separate myself from her – in other words see her as an autonomous person, different from me, until the time she returned as a stranger in November 1950 to visit me at my boarding school.

My mother had been born in Quetta, now in Pakistan, in 1922 and was sent home very young. She was small, with a polio-damaged leg, good-looking and highly gifted. She was sent to six or seven schools before the age of sixteen. She won an open scholarship to Oxford when she was in her last school but was not allowed to take it up and was sent out to India. There, at the age of eighteen, she met and soon married my father. She was an excellent poet, novelist, philosopher and a reasonable painter.

My mother's intense love and protectiveness cocooned me in Assam and even when she left me for those first two times, in 1948 and 1951 I never really doubted that she loved me intensely. My mother wrote at length and with the greatest warmth, and though I missed her enormously, I knew she was there.

Finally, it is worth noting something I shall elaborate on later, which is that while I loved my mother intensely, it is clear that in the year or so leading up to her first departure to India I was quite troubled – rude, bullying, making her worried. Whether this would have happened if I had not known she was going to leave me, I don't know. But this was a low point in our relationship. And it is clear that she began to lose her confidence in me. Yet over the next twenty years we worked back together to a close, ideas-based, relationship. I admired her enormously and to a large extent my dreams, hopes, even style and world view, were shaped by her Buddhist, poetic, socialist and concerned attitude to life.

*

Then there is my father, seated on the right at the back, just above my mother. Again I never really 'saw' him until he had been away. Our relationship at this time is made more difficult to assess because later, when I went to Oxford, there was a certain awkwardness caused by the fact that our experiences had diverged so much.

My father Donald was born in El Paso, Texas, in 1916. He had been sent back to boarding school at Dollar in Scotland at the age of 12 and had been miserably homesick for his first two years. He never took to the school, despite being a first-rate athlete and rugger player, and left without any 'Highers' to be apprenticed to the engineering firm of John Brown on the Clyde. At the age of about twenty he was sent out to be an engineer on a Tea Plantation in Assam. During the war he joined the Assam Rifles and raised troops to fight against the Japanese. He met my mother when he was twenty-four and very soon married her.

Mac was clearly an intelligent and sensitive man. He was an excellent sportsman, strong, handsome, friendly and enormously popular. He was clearly an excellent and loved manager of the Tea Estates and a good crofter in his retirement. Yet there was also a shyness, overcome sometimes by a drink, so that we occasionally found it difficult to know what to talk about to each other.

The depths of his love for Iris was evident in their daily interactions and I could see how mutually dependent they were on each other. This may have been a slight cause of the tension between us – as my mother observed in her letters – because both of us (and my sisters) were competing for her love. In most families this would be less obvious because the family would be living in the same house. But the fact that my mother was constantly torn and having to decide whether she should be with her children or her husband was an enormous burden both on her and on all of us as we assessed what it meant for our relationships.

I do remember several wonderful times with my father when he was the boyish generous and adventurous man who so delighted many of the young children (my various cousins, for example, and my own daughter and step-daughters) who loved him so. I remember when he came to meet me in Calcutta on my first trip to Assam and gave me all the change from every transaction. Or when we went on fishing expeditions and a fishing holiday together in my teens. And I remember wonderful days on the Croft in the Hebrides.

When Mac died suddenly, at the age of 60, I felt as if a great protective tree had suddenly blown down and there was nothing above me. Yet I did not weep. The more I read the letters and think back, however, including my own letters to him, the warmer I feel, and the more I realize that he was a remarkable man and in many ways ideal for my mother. The letters of their first few years, married yet separated by war, are heart-breaking and I wish more of his to her had been kept. He had defects – especially a loathing of thinking too much about money, which my mother also had. This meant that they had to think about it almost all the time since they were always broke!

He never hit or bullied me in any way; he always encouraged me and showed pride in my small achievements; and he gave my mother great love and support. I absorbed a strong feeling of my Scottish identity from him, and this warmth and pride I think is another sign that our relationship was, on the whole, very positive.

*

After my mother and father, the strongest emotional (and probably intellectual) influence on my life was Violet, my mother's mother, seated second from left in the middle row. She had been through the same misery as many of my forebears – sent home young from the Empire (Burma), schooling in England, then out again to get married and have children. It is all described in my mother's book 'Daughters of the Empire'.

A remark of Saki's can perhaps preface a description. 'Romance at short notice was her speciality'. She was a pretty and charming girl and her teenage diaries reflect a number of her romances, a strand which continues throughout her life. Her physical attractiveness was greatly enhanced by her mind – a very good memory, natural logical ability, curiosity, sharp wit, love of poetry and art, as well as her personality – huge self-confidence, optimism, energy and a desire to change the world around her. Much of my mother's abilities came from her and in another time and place Violet would have ended up high in some profession – Prime Minister, head of the Civil Service, an acclaimed artist. Yet her energies and abilities were soon forced into domestic spheres. So like some Jane Austen matriarch she spent her life organizing and galvanizing those around her. Among those whom she ruled was my grandfather, Will, and her sons and Iris. This elemental force and her strong opinions seriously bruised them, but I was at just the right distance to get the benefits of her personality, and suffered from few of the costs.

I felt her constant care, attention, love and concern from the time I was looked after by her in my infancy. So when I was left with her and the family at the age of six it was not like the appalling experience of Rudyard Kipling. It was a continuation of a strong, but grandmotherly, relation which I felt happy about until the day she died aged over 90. The advantage of alternate generations, the love but only some of the responsibility for discipline which I have experienced in my own relations with grandchildren, was present. She acted as a quasi-mother, but had none of the guilt, insecurities and hangups which my mother's letters show. She had brought up five children in India and ran a complex household which was constantly on the move. Our small problems and logistics were relatively trifling and I felt completely safe in her firm hands.

Above all, with her zest for life, energy and humour, she made life fun – zippy, zesty, full of people, parties, good food and, despite rationing, a glimpse into richer worlds. She was not so good with my sisters, especially Fiona in her teens. But she liked boys and treated me fairly, kindly, as if I was the little boy, Monty, whom she had tragically lost – a younger brother to her own son Robert. It was no doubt largely because of her that Robert was so good with me, never feeling (or showing) jealousy or competitiveness. And because she had seen Robert (and his brothers) through Sedbergh, and Richard through a history degree at Oxford, it was easier for her to treat me as another of her offspring through my educational years.

My rosy picture of her has been confirmed by reading the letters – both hers to me and those between her and my mother. It is clear that the relations between all three of us were pretty good and that we respected, supported and encouraged each other. My mother had seen Violet in action with children and knew of her flightiness and roving eye. But she also knew what a capable, warm and invigorating woman she was.

The excitement Violet generated and her surplus energy was applied to externals – particularly animals – horses, dogs and chickens in particular. She was also a keen gardener and an excellent cook. I think that for her and my grandfather it must have been a happiness to have young people growing up after their own children had gone. This was a second chance, without some of the strain. Her self-confidence, love of hoarding and saving and contact with the Raj influenced me greatly.

*

Alongside my grandmother was my beloved grandfather, William or Will as she called him. I say 'beloved' because I never felt less than deep affection for him, even though he was not as strong a shaping influence as Violet. Partly his character suffered in comparison to my grandmother. She was obviously boss and though she treated him with love, she nearly always won their arguments, usually matters of exasperation rather than real scenes and shouting. He was a clever man, extremely good at languages, a lover of books and poetry.

He was also a brave soldier being awarded a Military Cross and later an O.B.E. He had had a distinguished career, rising in rank to that of colonel and was loved and respected. However, I think that he would have been happier as an academic or teacher like two of his sons. Yet he made the most of his job, learnt the languages and took an interest in the places to which he was posted.

When Will retired I think he hoped to get another job, a school bursar, or some minor teaching job, to keep his active mind busy. Yet it never happened, so he put his energies into crosswords (he was keen on the *Telegraph* crossword), walking, betting on the football Pools (at times he had up to three firms involved and assiduously noted his small gains and losses), reading (particularly poetry, war memoirs and detective stories) and, above all, gardening. His diaries are full of references to where the manure or leaf mould was to be deposited or what he was planting and harvesting. I spent a lot of time with him in the garden or on walks, and later in exchanging favourite poems. He was particularly fond of nature poetry and I have found several poems, particularly Laurie Lee's 'April Rise' copied out in his diary – a poem I remember him reciting to me.

My grandfather was seriously involved in the British Legion and was at one time secretary of the local branch. My grandmother also attended meetings of the British Legion at Corfe Mullen. He also spent a good deal of time, though not as much as my grandmother, working on the family pedigree, exchanging letters with distant relatives, seeking out family trees. For example, on 14 March 1952 he notes in his diary that he 'made out pedigree to date for College of Arms' and the next day he sent the pedigree to the College of Arms. He also painted a little, noting efforts at watercolour paintings when he moved to the Lake District and commenting admiringly on several of the local watercolour artists whose studios he visited.

Will was a very comfortable, stable, untidy, somewhat Worzel Gummidge like figure. I think my preference for old clothes may partly come from him, as does my love of trees and for certain poems. It is clear that he wrote to me a lot at school, particularly in the few months after my mother left for India in 1952, and noted our activities in his diaries with concern and pleasure. He nearly always jotted down our birthdays and frequently wrote to my sisters in India.

As I look out at the falling rain I think of his watch, which I still have, of the smell of tobacco that wafted round him, of his large gum-boots, of his old hats and macs, and of the wise advice he would from time to time give me ('Always go into a room with a smile on your face and go up to strangers with confidence').

*

Throughout the history of my family and its imperial entanglements, there has always been the structural problem when children were sent home as to where they would stay, either full-time or during holidays from the boarding schools to which they were sent. Quite often this problem was dealt with by handing the young children to newly retired grandparents, themselves perhaps having gone through this process. In my case, my mother's mother and father became surrogate parents and looked after me between the age of seven and seventeen more than my own parents.

This was a very good practical solution but it was not necessarily easy, particularly if there was a shortage of money and of space. The normal tensions between a mother and her daughter could well be exacerbated if the two couples lived together, and there were often serious differences about child-rearing methods. This makes the surviving letters between my mother and her own mother (and father) particularly interesting. They reveal that, given the likely tensions, and the very different temperaments of my mother and grandmother, as well as their different views on many matters, they lived in amazing harmony. There are hardly any signs of tension and many indications of affection and a common purpose.

The practical support which my grandmother could give in emergencies, for example, is well shown in a letter on 12th May 1948 written by my mother to my father when I was sick in bed with measles and my sister still recovering from a tonsils operation. *I don't know how I should cope without Mummy who is marvellous on these occasions and calm as calm.*

My mother had relied on my grandparents in India, where they had looked after me for periods. Then from 1948 until my parents retired in the mid-1960s they more or less lived together when my parents were home on leave. So, unlike the normal English nuclear-family structure of separate residence, this was an extended household which shared much of its economy, its culture and its child rearing.

*

It is perhaps strange that I should put my sisters after my grandparents, but up to 1955 I was with my grandparents continuously, whereas my sisters went back to Assam for a couple of years in the middle of my time at the Dragon, so were only partly around. Yet they were immensely important to me. Fiona (seated in the front row with her doll), two years younger than me, was closer in age and more of a playfellow. I have always admired her greatly. She was brighter at school than I was, and more imaginative and gifted artistically. She was also obstinate, self-confident, and great fun. For much of the time we got on very well, as I recall, though there was a period when I was about eight when I bullied her.

Yet on the whole right up to our late twenties we were good friends and I greatly admired and enjoyed her company. We helped each other later on in various ways and I know that I have been enormously influenced by her. She was the

14

companion of many games, shared toys and expeditions, friendships and the nice nature which my mother notes in her letters shone through. I was certainly lucky to have such a lively and talented younger sister, and lucky that as the oldest and first (and a boy) her greater natural abilities did not crush me because the two years gave me just enough advantage.

Annie (on my mother's lap in the photograph) is four years younger than I am and this gap meant that there was less rivalry, but also perhaps less closeness. And she was away for two periods in Assam, during the first of which, from 1948–1950, Fiona and I were together on our own. Again, my mother mentions a stage of bullying and others of admiration on her part. I mostly liked and got on with her well, but our temperaments and particularly our attitudes to intellectual matters, were rather different. She was more like my father – loving horses, television, and practical things. The character of the two sisters is well portrayed when they were about eleven and nine in Assam in my mother's book based on them, *The Children of Bird God Hill,* where Phillida (Fiona) and Annabelle (Anne) are described in considerable detail.

One thing worth noting is that women – grandmother, mother, and sisters – dominated my life. This more than counter-balanced the fact of spending ten years at single-sex boys' boarding schools. I have never been shy of women and have always enjoyed their warmth, affection, subtlety, depth and holistic view of life.

*

Also within this inner ring was one other person: my uncle Robert (top left). Because I had grown up with him when staying with my grandmother in India, and then shared a house with him for ten years as he went through Sedbergh and Oxford, we were very close. He was only eight years older than me, and closer in age to me than his older siblings were to him. He treated me as a younger brother. We shared numerous games of cricket and football and he coached me assiduously. He socialized me – teaching me how to lose at games. He enthused me with a love of American musicals and Gilbert and Sullivan. He encouraged some of my main reading, especially *Just William* and the books by Arthur Ransome. He played many imaginative games with me. So I entered the particularly rich fantasy world of this brilliant and rather lonely boy.

Robert was a role model both for my Sedbergh years (in the same house, the same history sixth form and teacher), and later at Oxford (the same College, the same tutor in the same subject). I was hanging on his coat tails, which made the moves through these otherwise difficult transitions easier. He seemed so clever, imaginative, successful with girl-friends, that I felt twinges of envy, but also admiration. From very early on, although he was older, his blindness in one eye and rather weak physique meant that I was more or less able to keep up with him in our endless friendly competitions.

*

My mother's brother Richard (back row, middle), then unmarried and spending some of his holidays away from Haileybury where he taught, was the next most important influence. He was unmarried, and five years younger than my father and so could be a proper uncle and had a considerable influence in several ways. One was that he had a car – and also some money. My grandfather's diary records in some detail the purchase of his first car in January 1951, a Morris 8 which he bought from a Miss Pontifex. It may be a new car that he bought on 10 April 1954 where I am pictured at the wheel. With Richard's car, some of the more exciting expeditions to horse races, the seaside and elsewhere were made possible.

Secondly he was prepared to enter into some of the sports and games which Robert and I devised. Later we would go on long walks in the Lake District and discuss writing and life. He was a firm evangelical Christian and as such was an Officer at the Christian boy's camps.

The junior version of these camps was at Swanage and through him I spent two summer periods of ten days there. It is probably the case that his evangelical Christianity acted strongly, alongside my mother's more philosophical search for 'the meaning of life', to start to plant an interest in religious-type questions which has been a theme all my life. Richard was also somewhat like my grandfather in temperament: gentle, a little shy, gruffly affectionate and supportive. I owe him a great deal as an example and role model and the daring war record in his book 'Chindit', and the humorous individual who comes out of his autobiography, 'The Road From Mandalay', was a strong inspiration.

I seldom saw his older brother Billy (middle row, second from right), though he appears in some of the family photos. There is a good deal about his army career – he was, like Richard, also in the Gurkhas.

*

The picture I have painted more or less reflects the widening rings of the English kinship system. Yet the normal pattern was distorted to a certain extent by the Indian links, so that my grandparents and their children, especially Robert, became more important than they would be in many families. Even so it was still a very English, middle-class, family. It was neither markedly upwardly nor downwardly mobile – roughly bobbing along as it had for some centuries in that broad belt of the middle upper-middle-class – schoolteachers, army, universities, and planters.

From the evidence of the letters it was clearly also a functional family. There were undertones of bitterness, jealousy and anger at times, but on the whole there was a great deal of mutual tolerance, support and love. I have absolutely no grounds for complaint. My relatives treated me with great kindness, respect and encouraged and sheltered me. This was especially necessary given the traumas and strains which we were all subjected to. There was the difficulty of keeping a foot in different worlds – India, England and also the fact that though they were respectable professionals, they were always struggling for money.

*

As for other relatives, my father's parents, Archibald (Archie) and Florence, had an influence on me on the two holidays my sister Fiona and I spent with them when I was aged seven and eight. It was there that I caught my first trout and I remember Florence as a very intelligent and sweet lady, a little like my sister Fiona. Archie's part was in teaching us to fish, though I don't remember much else about him. They both died before I left the Dragon.

Other Scottish relatives were important. My father's younger brother Alan and his wife Jean at Wishaw, and my 'aunt' (my mother's oldest friend from India, and then my godmother) Pat Cowan and her husband Alan. I spent several holidays with each of them and liked them all. My real uncle Alan, a surgeon, was a younger, more intellectual version of my father, and Jean, his wife, a wonderfully warm and gentle nurse. Their infant children, much younger than me, were just arriving. My aunt Pat was pretty and vivacious and her husband rather forbidding and austere, as I remember. Their daughters Nicola and Felicity and son Richard were later to become good friends.

The final ring of the family were a number of relatives of my grandparents, among whom were Aunt Margery, the irascible and unpredictable lady with whom we stayed when we first returned from Assam, and just a dim memory of my great-grandmother Annie – surrounded by her beautiful Burmese trophies. She influenced me indirectly by preserving so many of the treasures from my long-deceased great-grandfather Rodway Swinhoe. Then there were various second cousins, of whom the best remembered were the Mermagens. This was largely because they had also been at the Dragon School. Robert and Tim were there before me and Jonny (or Jake as he now calls himself) was one of my best friends there.

*

My real friendships began at the Dragon, which I write about in a companion volume. These were nearly all little boys, but it is clear that from a very early age I liked little girls as well, including my sisters and cousins.

My first recollection of a girlfriend was at a holiday camp on the south coast when I was about seven; I remember being desperately in love with a little girl with freckles whom I think was called Pat. On 18 March 1948, when I was only a little over six, I went to a party and my mother described the scene: *They have a lovely house (he is a surgeon) and had asked lots of little girls of eight and nine who tore round the house on bicycles and Alan was really rather out of it, but panted round after them, apparently blissfully happy.* It is not clear whether my bliss came from the beauty of my young companions. A couple of months later, on 6 May 1948, at my first proper school, Southlands, my mother describes how *Alan is still enjoying school, his "best-friend" is a little girl called Iona whom he tries to sit next to at prayers but hasn't yet actually spoken to I gather!* Sadly I do not remember Iona or whether I ever plucked up courage to talk to her.

Later I was to go through the usual *Just William* phase of being sarcastic and stand-offish with girls, just at the time I attained sexual maturity. My mother describes this attitude around my thirteenth birthday in a letter on 27 December 1954.

Alan stayed in bed a full week with a temperature that wouldn't go down, but came down to the drawing room on the afternoon of his birthday and we pulled a few crackers, he was up for the whole day on the 22 which was the day of our party. I had rustled up a few of the girls' friends and fortunately Alan has a Dragon friend living nearby and the girls brought along one brother so we had ten children together. The three boys retired into corners and made scornful remarks but otherwise it was a success I think, quite an effort getting the food collected but the only flop was the birthday cake which looked lovely but when cut turned out to be completely raw in the middle, fortunately the guests were all too full to want any. We played the usual games including Murder which consisted of everybody including the murderer rushing screaming downstairs every two minutes saying it was much too frightening but they insisted on going on playing! Alan had spent the previous two days saying that he didn't want a party and he was going out for the afternoon and what did I want to go and ask a lot of fleb girls for, but when it came to the point enjoyed it though it was rather a hectic beginning for him.

Yet, on the whole, I seem not really to have noticed girls and do not recall anything special about the few girls who were at the Dragon in my time. Perhaps it is a common fault of memory to keep our past innocent and perhaps all the time I appreciated beauty (in boys as well as girls). Friendship could sometimes have a sensual, as well as an emotional and intellectual content even in early days.

*

Of course there were many other important people, friends and neighbours, teachers and tradesmen; almost every day one is being influenced by those around us. All I shall do here is to describe one neighbour who, probably unbeknown to him, helped me by his kindness and left a mark on my mother as well. He can temporarily stand for the host of small kindnesses with which I was surrounded.

I dimly remember Old Mr Crapper, the retired dentist who lived next to us at 'By the Way'. My mother introduces him to my father in a letter on 2 March 1948.

On Sunday we went next door to try a bicycle that the owners said they would lend me. Some people called Crapper live there, a couple and their son, who is a dentist. The old man has fearsome false teeth, and a dewdrop on the end of his nose that collects itself and falls with the regularity of a dripping tap, it is fascinating. He is also stone deaf but quite a character and very kind. He has lots of sheds full of model boats, trains etc. which the children loved. Nobody here is under 70. I don't mind for myself but would like to find companionship for the children.

Three weeks later on the 25 she wrote *I enclose a couple of snaps of my own taking – not very good, they were developed by the old man next door and he is very old and I think his dew-drop must have got mixed up with the developing mixture.* When my mother left me for the first time, in October 1948 when I was six and three quarters, my grandmother wrote that same morning of 18 October to my mother in Assam. She mentioned that the next door neighbours had mended the jeep and we were sand-papering it in preparation for painting it. I commented in this letter about my pleasure at repainting the jeep. Clearly they helped at a difficult time. And I dimly remember that in the worst Christmas of my life, a couple of months after my mother had left me, Mr Crapper made and painted a little wooden fort for me. I have it still and it gave me great joy.

Relations remained amicable, if at times dangerous. My grandfather wrote to my mother on 19 September 1952 *Your hose pipe has been so useful – it came in handy 2 days ago when your mother accidentally set fire to the jungle in the Crappers garden... Crapper keeps giving me books on how to win at the Pools so I hope for the best.* Then when my mother returned in June 1954, one of the first things she did was to visit her old neighbour. On 21 June she wrote *I went into see the Crappers yesterday. She is just the same, he is practically stone deaf and more insanitary than ever but very bright and loaded me up with books I had already read.* The deafness was perhaps a blessing, for when I obtained my first airgun a few months later, my mother described on 16 August how *we set up targets and he knocked down tin after tin while I spattered the Crappers garden with gunshot.*

A couple of months later old Mr Crapper died. My mother described his death in two ways. First in a letter on 10 October she wrote to my father,

A sad thing happened last Sunday, old Mr Crapper died. He'd been looking like death for several months, but they only sent him to hospital on the Saturday. I got the phone message to say that the ambulance was coming and went over to tell Mrs Crapper and she snapped my head off. I was very fond of the old man, he was so kind the way he used to wander over with butter-scotch for the children, and so uncomplaining at the end, shut off in his deafness and feeling so ill. I've even been inspired to write a poem on the subject, if you like I'll send it to you. He had cancer apparently.

The poem she wrote was included at the end of a letter she sent to my father on 10 of December.

I am so happy for you that you are dead
(Free of the deaf-aids and the teeth that hurt you)
So glad that without warning
You need not face this morning
And the stained waistcoat waiting for you by your bed.

We have the winter to face. The grass is whitening,
(The candles of broom are lighted on the heath)
But you with knowledge and reason
Discarded our dead season
And stepped into the singing summer of death.

I hope you will find the adventure that you wanted
(Golden deserts to cross, and jade green seas)
I am sure God will provide
Horses of flame to ride
And as in the old life, so in the new, you will be undaunted.

I am only sorry that somehow I did not convey
(Piercing with patience the dark veil of deafness)
How light you made the labour
Of love towards my neighbour
Nor shake your trembling hands before you went away.

2. HOME

In the first weeks of 1948, when I was just six, my mother, grandparents and their youngest son Robert moved to a house called 'By the Way', near Broadstone in Dorset. There I was to remain for most of the period until I was almost thirteen. It is clear that after the war it was not easy to find accommodation. 'By the Way' was owned by Aunt Nell, the second wife of one of my grandfather's uncles. She had moved with her son to Canada after the war and so the house was vacant.

Upon arriving my mother wrote to my father at the end of January.

> *Well here we are, with the snow thick all round us and it's a great relief to be here with the packing and clearing of Stonebarrow* [Charmouth] *behind me. The last week was a nightmare and the house seemed to get dirtier and more damaged every minute. We eventually packed ourselves into a station wagon and quite how I don't know, you would have had a fit at all the 'bits' I insisted on bringing and got here in just over an hour which was pretty good going. It was bitter weather (that was yesterday actually, it seems days ago) and we were all cold and tired by the evening.*

Let me start here by situating the house. The nearest small town was Broadstone, where I would go to my first proper school. Broadstone was situated beside a Roman road (now covered with tarmac) and a railway station (disappeared). The main roads from Broadstone went in various directions, one of them winding uphill through woods and fields to Corfe Mullen, a smaller village which was also important to us.

The journey to and from Broadstone involved going down a short bit of the flint-strewn and unpaved Roman road, and then along a private road, Corfe Mullen road. On the right was a house with a small 'farm' where the Warrens lived and from where we got milk and other produce. The track went through some trees and then on the bend was our rented house. The road wound on up the hill and across a common where I used to cycle for my weekly sweets. In other directions from Broadstone were the bigger town of Poole and the city of Bournemouth.

The countryside around us was still very beautiful, on the edge of Thomas Hardy's 'Egdon Heath'. It was an ancient landscape with Corfe Castle, Maiden Castle, Bradbury Rings and many old sites and buildings. Although it was not precisely the Sussex described by Kipling, it still had the feeling of ancient civilizations evoked in 'Puck of Pook's Hill'. At that time it had not been built up and there were some beautiful woods, rivers and gorse heaths.

Something of the beauty is caught in two of my mother's letters to my father describing expeditions. On 24 April 1951 she wrote:

> *This afternoon Richard drove us all to a river at a place called Wimborne near here and we had a picnic tea. It was a divine spot, a bridge and a church tower and a field of cows opposite and green fields and hills all round and a warm but not baking sun. We looked for birds' nests and picked flowers and tried to catch minnows and saw a swan and a kingfisher and after tea Alan and Robert found an old deserted boat which they unearthed from the mud and have great plans for. I just drank it all in and tried to store it up as usual, a golden afternoon. I would like you and I to go there one summer evening, you could make a lovely painting of it.*

The following month, on 15 May, she wrote at the end of a busy day:

*went out on my bike into a golden afternoon and found
a lovely wood full of bluebells, primroses, violets and every
other wild flower you can imagine. A heavenly place and we
picked a bunch of flowers and went back very content.*

The house itself was a substantial brick building constructed
in about 1925. It was set within about an acre of woods and
lawns. My mother described it to my father soon after we
arrived. The dimensions of each of the rooms comes from a
note in my grandfather's address book.

*This is such a nice house. I cant possibly make a plan of
it for you, but its got quite a lot of smallish, nicely furnished,
well-carpeted rooms and seems so clean and bright after
Stonebarrow. There is a tiny kitchen with an Aga and then a
room off it with an ideal boiler which we eat in (really part
of the kitchen) (both rooms together 16' x 10'). Off the hall
is the children's nursery – a lovely room with a stove and
thick carpet, which I'm writing in now [described as a
Dining Room by my grandfather, measuring 14'3" x 9'6"].
Then there's the drawing-room, small but pleasant,
[described as a Lounge and measuring 14' x 13'] and
upstairs two big bedrooms, [15'6" x 11'3" and 13' x 11'6"]
one small one [10' x 7'] and a dressing room where Anne
sleeps. Fiona and Alan take it in turns to share my room!
The cooking and fires are gas and far simpler and warmer
and the hot-water system is excellent. Altogether it's an
easier house to run and keep clean. There's a big garden,
mostly lawn and orchard which will be fun for the kids
when the weather improves.*

One lightning flash of memory, which partly illuminates the
problem of the dining room, was when we were having lunch
and my grandfather looked out and mildly observed that the
cloud drifting outside the window was obscuring the garden.
We suddenly realized it was not a cloud but smoke and that
the heath was on fire, which quite often happened. Much

excitement and ringing of fire bells – but nothing of ours was destroyed.

I don't remember much about the furniture in the house. The one outstanding piece of furniture I think I remember from this time was an imposing wardrobe with many deep drawers called 'The Georgian Gentleman'. This belonged to my grandmother and was important for it was, in effect, the archives office. Letters, photo albums, etc. were safely kept in it, and they survived to end up with me.

The garage was where we kept our bikes, the back was filled with much junk and the ceiling with tobacco leaves. For most of the time it had no car in it. My uncle Richard had a car and would visit us and when my father came on leave he hired a car, but they never bothered to use the garage.

*

My memory of the house and garden was refreshed by a visit in 2009, when the current owners were kind enough let me look around. Unlike many other attempts to go back in time, I was relieved to find that much remained as I remembered it.

One entered the garden down the drive with trees on both side and bushes on which I used to swing. On the left was a wood with large trees, good for Cowboys and Indians. The bigger wood on the right with a path through it was fairly wild. I had forgotten the tree on the corner of the large lawn, or that the chicken houses were not only in the main pen but also in a number of buildings throughout the grounds.

I seem to remember that there were dwarf apple trees between the lawn and the chickens The fruit net was very big, and the vegetable patch was also large. There was a gate out on to the heath.

The wildness of the garden is shown by entries in my grandfather's diaries. He several times mentions periodic cutting and clearing along the overgrown boundaries and, as someone who had spent much of his life in Burma and India on military expeditions, clearly felt some echo of those days. On 29 May 1952 he noted, 'Cleared part of jungle along Willis boundary'. The following day he 'Cleaned part of garden near drive', and on 2 June 'Cleared boundary of jungle'. Other clearing followed on 7 when he 'Cut down blackberry hedge' and two days later 'Dug up roots of blackberries'.

The difficulty was that in the struggle of the post-war years on too small a pension, my grandparents tried to do a lot with the garden. It had an extensive lawn and a large area of fruit cage. I still remember the tiny pearls of red, black and white currants, each breaking in the mouth with a very different flavour, as well as the strawberries and raspberries which my grandmother, to my mother's dismay, used to serve with dollops of expensive cream.

There were other areas with fruit trees – I particularly remember dwarf apples of varieties I now grow – Cox, James Grieve and various Worcesters. There was an extensive vegetable garden. For the middle part of my life, for ten years or so, I kept a similar area of near allotment size under vegetables and it is indeed hard work.

My grandfather also grew his own tobacco and this seemed to require quite a lot of work. There are various descriptions of this process – the harvesting, the leaves drying like bats hanging in the garage, then further drying and the use of some application of honey or sugar as I recall. It finally ended up in my grandfather's pipe which went out every few minutes, but was seldom out of his mouth. I don't know if he sold any tobacco, though he does seem to have sent packets of it away as presents – for example, to my father in India. Yet he certainly produced large quantities, an activity which stopped when we moved to the Lakes.

The entries from his diary for the year 1951 give a flavour of one of the main background features of those years.

10 January:	Ordered Tobacco Seed
4 April:	Prepared pots for tobacco plants
12 May:	Planted out 32 tobacco plants.
13 July:	Wrote for tobacco home curing cabinet

15 July:	Picked first tobacco leaves and hung them up
2 August:	Tobacco all hung up except line nearest cage (6 plants)
21 August:	Treated tobacco leaves with Formic Acid
18 September:	Bulb in tobacco curer fused
22 September:	Packed tobacco in drawer

Two or three flashes in my mind relating to the garden at 'By the Way' remain. One is the excitement of the two little woods on the property, the smell of the pine, the mystery and the explorations. Another was that when we were searching for a missing arrow, I discovered a deep ditch behind the brambles on the side away from the Crapper's. I decided to continue to clean this out and for weeks I found I had a secret tunnel, invisible to the outside world. This is something I have tried to replicate later in my life in the long tunnel through fruit trees in our present garden. My sister shared this pleasure with me, and on 16 June 1954 my mother notes *Fiona is very happy pottering round the garden making 'secret places', she climbed a tree and tore a large hole in a new jersey ...*

A third flash is of going out to collect wild fruit. This must have happened at Broadstone. But my chief memories were in the Lake District. Particularly in September we drove out with baskets to collect wild blackberries near Elterwater. We had noted the best places and came back with red, pricked, fingers and buckets of blackberries – and once so many that they mouldered in the bath. I remember the pantries of both houses were filled with kilner jars of fruits. I remember the smell of jam and marmalade making, the cutting and bottling of the fruit, the crusty remains of the testing in the saucers which we were allowed to spread on our toast.

The autumn fruits, particularly blackberries, are a sad memory for this was an immanent sign of my parents' departure for Assam – something that happened twice at Broadstone and twice when I went on to my school at Sedbergh. I still find picking blackberries in our garden a delight – fat, glistening and spangled with spider's webs – but also melancholic.

*

The fullest account of life in the garden comes in my mother's letters in the first summer of 1948. Here, aged six-and-a-half, I obviously developed a craze for gardening, much stimulated by my grandfather.

In the early spring, on 2 March my mother noted:

> *'Alan is fit, touch wood. He has a newly acquired passion for gardening and trails round all day persuading Daddy to light bonfires he doesn't really want. ... Daddy spends all day in it [the garden], and maddens Mummy by plodding into the kitchen in muddy boots and mixing fertilizers in the washing-up bowl. We've had perfect spring weather lately, the children have been in shirt-sleeves and the birds and buds and spring breezes have been enchanting.*

The wonderful spring continued and on 25 March my mother gave a further description.

> *Spring in the country is very exciting after so long... The children are pink and freckled as they spend all day in the garden... We have planted cabbages, but though we scan the seed-box with a microscope almost hourly we cant see them. All our activities are concerned with growth and yours too I suppose.*

Unusually the good weather continued and on 13th April she wrote: *The weather is divine though which makes such a difference as I can just turn the family into the garden all day and don't have to bother to take them for organised exercise.*

After a lovely spring, the large netted fruit garden began to yield up its prizes – obviously it had existed when we arrived and my grandfather just continued to cultivate it. On 29 May my mother wrote:

We picked 6 and a half lbs of gooseberries to-day, the first, and ate two of our own strawberries yesterday! Soft fruit is the easiest thing to grow and about the most profitable. Alan and I planted out our cabbages with great ceremony, twenty-one of them have passed the final test and survived the neglect of long weeks. Alan is getting quite knowledgeable in garden matters and talks about aphis and compost in a very grand way. He is an interesting creature, full of fun, but exasperating.

Two weeks later on 15 Jun: *We're getting peas, beans, strawberries, raspberries and gooseberries from the garden now with lots more to come. Not very fair of me to dwell on this with you living on ladies fingers, poor pet.* A week later on 22 June my mother writes again, noting my short attention span, *Most of our time is spent in and around the garden, the fruit is all coming on and the children pick it – or rather Fiona does, Anne eats and has to be removed and Alan loses interest after five minutes.*

The wide variety of fruits which my grandfather grew are mentioned throughout his diaries – they included loganberries, gooseberries, blackcurrants, raspberries, strawberries and several varieties of apples. Just to give one example of his work, on January 6 1952 he mentioned, 'Sprayed Blackcurrants Gooseberries Red currants Plums and Pear with Shell Universal wash (D.N.C.)'. Many of these were eaten by birds so my grandfather spent a good deal of time setting up (and taking down and cleaning beneath) the large fruit cage.

The vegetables included all the regulars – peas, broad beans, runner beans, French beans, spinach, cauliflowers, cabbages, broccoli, tomatoes, carrots, but also very large numbers of kale, sweet corn and sunflowers to feed to the birds. For example my grandfather notes in his diary on 24 January 1953, 'Sowed Peas, Sweet Peas, Cabbage, Cauli, Sprouts and Broad Beans in boxes and pots'. These vegetables were constantly eaten by rabbits, and there is a long period in February and March 1951 when my grandfather is busy making a rabbit-proof fence.

The garden was also full of flowers, for example on 11 April 1952 he mentions; 'Sowed sweet Sultan pansy Antirrunums and Sweet William'. On 24 October he notes 'Planted Wallflower and Forget-me-not in bed where Lily of Valley was'. At the end of the year on 8 December 'Got Mich daises, Can bells and ereigerous from Mrs Dangibau [a neighbour]. Put first two in ground'. There were also climbing roses which my grandfather pruned.

An indication of the ancillary tasks around this gardening is shown in the preliminary notes at the start and end of 1951 in his gardener's diary. Just before the year began he wrote a list:

> Concentrate on
> > Perpetual Spinach
> > Winter greens and Tobacco
> > With some Peas, Beans, Beet and Lettuce
> > New site for Tomatoes
> > War against slugs
> > Bracken for composting

At the end of the year he wrote:

> > Perpetual spinach for hens
> > Covered shed for sawdust and tools
> > Greenhouse drains
> > Tiles house and garage
> > Pipe water to garden
> > Cover for compost

Apart from the variety of fruit and vegetables the garden provided, it also fed into a widespread English love – the desire to compete in local shows for the best turnip, carrot, apples or whatever was appropriate. Thus, for example, my grandfather mentions on 18 August 1951, 'Went to Broadstone to put in entries for Show' and on Wednesday 22 'Broadstone Fruit and Flower Show'. I don't remember that my grandfather ever received first prize. He had presumably learnt to garden during his retirement. My grandmother, on the other hand, was an active member of the poultry club and on at least one occasion, on 14 January 1952, he notes 'V goes to Poultry club and wins 1 for egg'.

From India, my mother reported the state of her garden in Assam from time to time so we could compare notes. For example on 24 November she wrote from Assam, *I'm struggling on with my gardening and have one baby cauliflower appearing, which we all go and peer at every morning. Everything looks better for the rain – oh yes, I've got one flower out too!*

Much of my life at home was spent in this garden, playing football, practising cricket, finding secret paths, swinging on the branches, playing with small pets or helping with the chickens. But it was clearly difficult to maintain and towards the end my mother noted that it was getting out of hand. Whether my grandfather just lost heart or because he was getting older, or because we were intent on moving house so the huge effort did not seem worthwhile, is not clear. But on 16 June 1954 my mother wrote *Mummy and Daddy are very fit, but the house and garden incredibly shabby and dilapidated, can hardly walk in the latter for grass which is waist high, am longing to get scything but my hay fever reduces me to pulp every time I go out!* Just before we left, on 10 October, she wrote *We have had quite a few people to see it, but nobody's decided to buy it, the garden is so terribly out of hand I think most people feel its too much to pull it round. Actually its too big a garden for one person to cope with and I think puts people off.*

*

There is quite a bit of evidence in my mother's letters that we went for many walks and expeditions out of the back gate of 'By the Way'. I remember the little wooden gate – which on our return in 2009 was still there. This took us straight out on to 'Egdon Heath' of Hardy fame, a gorse and clay-pit immensity as it seemed to me then. On 2 of March 1948 she described a walk to my father.

The house opens onto a heath at the back and we went for a walk there the other day. Anne and I took one path, Alan and Fiona another, and when we were well separated by half a mile of gorse and thistles they suddenly came face to face with 3 enormous goats, which proceeded to chase them, playfully, into the thickest thicket. I was torn between a desire to rescue them, and uncertainty as to whether to leave Anne open to attack from the rear. Fiona was screaming herself into a fit of hysterics, and when eventually I came face to face with the goats I could understand it, they were huge and horned and stood on their hind-legs and pranced round me until I felt as brave as a bullfighter except that I was scared to death. Of course when I shook a leaf at them and said 'Shoo' they fled, but the walk was ruined!

I do not remember this, but I do remember the heat, the smell of gorse and heath plants, the yellow flowers surrounded by bees, the cobalt blue of the disused clay pits where we used to sail our model boats, the picnics up in the pine woods and beside streams.

It seems in my recollection to be beautiful walking country where we could find many treasures. There was a Roman road, for example, on the border of Broadstone and our walk up to 'By the Way' went along this for a few hundred yards. It was not paved in those days and we constantly scanned it for Roman coins and I think found one or two things, as well as numerous interesting looking flints. The road, still called 'Roman road' is now covered in tarmac but the conker trees along it are still there.

More widely, the walking and expeditions led through the enchanted landscape described by Hardy and were not dissimilar to that evoked in all its magic further down the coast in Sussex by Rudyard Kipling in one of the favourite books of this period, namely 'Puck of Pook's Hill'. With its evocation of ancient spirits, Romans and fairies, it helped me to people this landscape and bring it into imaginative games.

When we visited ancient ruins such as Corfe Castle, or Maiden Castle, or Banbury Rings, we felt part of an ancient landscape, and this again may have seeped into me and be one of the threads that finally led me into my love of history and feeling of connection with Anglo-Saxon and earlier history. At the time it did not really feel like 'history'; it was living in an old country where past and present were not separated.

The walks also had something of 'Winnie the Pooh' and other children's books about them – playing at Pooh Sticks and searches for the heffalump. My mother was constantly dreaming up adventures for us. The picnics, sometimes by placid rivers, also had echoes of 'Wind in the Willows' and indeed, looking back from our crowded and opulent world now, it seems as if the 1950s were in many ways closer to Hardy and A.A. Milne than they are to us now.

3. DAILY LIFE

The landscape and the houses were the stage and scenery. The actions were further determined by the physical constraints of life in the decade after the Second World War. 1947 to 1955 was the really low period after the War, an age of austerity. It is difficult to remember now how bleak those days were – perhaps as bleak as the war itself, but without any excitement. It appears that England was even in a grimmer situation than France in this period and there was full rationing.

This was compounded by the fact that my parents and grandparents were living at the edge of their income. Both were sending their children to private schools and trying to live a middle class life, while they did not really have the income for this. They struggled at every turn, with bills and expenses. With too little food and fuel, and in an environment which was usually filled with the kinds of disease which now seem mostly to have vanished, This was a material world which seems to be as distant now as Elizabethan England.

Looking back from a world where National Health doctors and dentists, ubiquitous cars and planes, supermarkets and advanced agriculture, plastics, central heating, television, computers and the internet, surround us, I find it difficult to recapture a world where all this was yet to occur.

*

If we turn first to food, when we came back in April 1947 it was to a Spartan existence. This was owing to two things. One was the extreme niggardliness and puritanical attitude of my Aunt Margery – of the 'either butter or jam but not both' brigade – which is described by my mother. I think there were a number of rows over food. Secondly, it was the period of real shortages and food rationing, so things such as meat, butter, and so on were very scarce. Even by 1950-1 my mother's account of food (especially meat) shortages are a reminder of what it was like. But I don't remember being hungry, just the pleasure of the gradual increase of chocolate and sweets, the days of bull's eyes and liquorice allsorts and the kind of sweets and sweetshops, immortalized in 'Just William'. I was also cushioned because my grandmother both loved food and was a good cook.

Somehow we never seemed to be especially short at home. We had plenty of cockerels and chickens, fish was not rationed, and there were rabbits. I especially remember the amount of butter, cream with puddings, and of condensed milk (how to choose between the last scraping of thick, sweet cream at the bottom of the tin, or the crusty sugary substance at the top and on the lid?). My mother comments on my grandmother's extravagance and we certainly seemed to have great feasts, where the rich puddings made from our Bramleys, rhubarb, raspberries, redcurrants were topped with cream, or baked in wonderful pies. My grandmother was a great pie maker – I still remember the little 'blackbirds' which supported the crust.

Then, of course, the big vegetable patch produced quantities of peas, beans, cauliflowers, and so on. The problem was, in the days before deep freezing, how to store the large harvests for the winter. This takes us to rows of kilner jars in the pantry – a tradition that continued up to the Lake District. I remember that the pantry or larder lay off the kitchen and had long shelves receding into the darkness. My mother in a letter of 30 April 1948 describes how, *She (Anne) flooded the bathroom the other day and the ceiling underneath fell down, it was the larder ceiling and we have been picking it out of our food ever since, telling each other with sickly smiles how good all this lime will be for us.*

The accounts of rationing and its effects are infrequent in the letters. On 11 February 1951 my mother wrote to my father:

> *You should have seen our meat ration this week, it was a thin slice of beef less big than this paper – for the three of us. I grilled it for lunch to-day and it was delicious and that's that! Of course there's always fish and I'm well up for eggs and actually I don't mind at all, but will find you a bit of a problem – alright I know darling, but you can't live on herrings.*

The following week she wrote again:

> *I feel much better and the girls are looking pretty well and eating like a couple of mules, the meat ration lasts one meal now and the rest of the week we string along on fish and rabbit, but I must say the kids are a joy to cook for as they greet everything with screams of delight – my proudest moment was when Fiona finished her third pancake and said in thick and rapturous tones 'Oh Mummy, you do cook lovely lunches'. I fear you'll be more critical darling, but I shall be more practised by then and they really were nice pancakes.*

In fact 1951 seems to have been a real low point on account of a conjunction of a number of factors which my mother describes. On 1 February she wrote:

> *The deepest gloom has settled over England lately, a combination of less meat less coal and the weather and the news, but except when my immediate family are concerned it doesn't affect me much. I selfishly plan our leave and potter on disregarding it all. The cost of living is a bit shattering and forces itself on my notice quite frequently – but at least you get value for your money here and don't pour it all down the hatch!*

A month later on 1 March she wrote again that:

> *the poor Labour government are having a bad spell what with the peanuts and poultry farms and the meat ration and the fuel crisis, the Railway Strike nearly stopped me getting to London last Monday but luckily they resumed work that day. Everyone moans and curses and is quite cheerful though the women do look pretty drab and tired (myself included).*

When I went out to India for Christmas 1952 I went to a world without rationing and with food in plenty for a tea manager's family. Even on the plane I seem to have moved out of austerity, writing on a postcard on 19 December *Dear Granny this is the Argonaught I am flying in it is very comfortable and we get wonderful food.* This turn for the better began to spread in England with growing economic prosperity.

When rationing ended, my grandmother was in her element as my mother (back in England again) wrote caustically on 3 July 1954, *Mummy and Daddy both eat far more than I do! There is no rationing now so it is joint nearly every day...*
On 15 December she wrote to my father:

> *The children's appetites are enormous, we get through a loaf at every meal on top of the usual courses! It's nice to see them so hungry but I'm at my wits end to collect enough sustenance, but I shall get into the swing of it.* The following year on 27 March she wrote *There isn't much to report from here, the girls eat enormously and my constant problem is to collect enough food for them all – but they are both helpful in the kitchen and make their beds and at the moment there are no fights.*

Finally, on 7 April 1955 she wrote again about the problem of housekeeping.

*I don't feel too exhausted either, the only chore I really
hate is shopping, we seem to get through such mounds of
food I'm for ever trailing round with laden shopping baskets
and over Easter with all the shops shutting for days and
days, it has become too hectic for words. They descend on
the table like locusts 4 times a day, and Anne is at my heels
when I'm cooking to lick all available saucepans, but of
course I wouldn't have it otherwise.*

She even describes how she found my grandfather chewing
the stale bread from the bird table.

A special occasion, of course, was Christmas and we used to
have either a chicken or a turkey. We had rich Christmas
puddings with small Victorian sixpences wrapped in greased
paper, which one unwrapped and exchanged for modern coins
so that they could be used again. There were crackers and
games, presents and a tree (perhaps cut from the garden).

There were picnics on the heath, in nearby woods, at the
seaside and later in the Lake District. My mother would throw
together sandwiches, crisps, fruit and perhaps a little chocolate
and we might even make a fire and cook a sausage or a sliver of
bacon. I remember them with pleasure.

There are scattered references to sweets in the letters, but
not many. In a letter to Father Xmas on 25 November 1949,
shortly before my eighth birthday, I asked for an ambitious list
of things, including 'sum sweets'. I wrote in a letter from school
in early March 1951, *Thank you very much for the lovely
sweets you sent me.* This looks like a special present. My
mother, however, was economizing on such things and in
outlining her expenses in a letter to my father on 15 May of
that year she mentions, *Sweets. One ration book (I never use
all three).*

Yet we seem to have managed. For example, there is
mention of the large amounts of chocolate we ate when we
went to the pantomime on 11 January 1951, even when
rationing was still present: *We got home eventually over-tired,
over-excited and stuffed with chocolate in the time-honoured
fashion.*

I don't remember much emphasis on drink at this time. My grandparents, older uncles and parents drank sherry, beer, wine and ginger wine and I suppose gin and whisky. But none were addicted to drink, though my father had to fight back the demons as my mother mentions in several letters. We children, I suppose, drank mainly water, with some milk and perhaps squash of some kind. Whether we had hot drinks, certainly not coffee, but perhaps a little tea, ovaltine, Bovril and such drinks I am not sure. Certainly the family benefited to a certain extent from presents of tea from my father's tea plantation, for even tea was incredibly expensive. The pressure of rationing faded out so that by the time we went to the Lakes at the end of 1954 the main constraint was cost, for my parents always seemed short of money.

I don't remember any other foods beyond the rabbits of which we ate a lot. Our eating out at this time is occasionally recorded by my mother, especially when we went to the cinema in Bournemouth, but seems to have been a mournful affair of being reduced to over-expensive tacky cafés with awful food – were there any Lyons Corner Houses? I wonder whether my parents ever went out to country pubs.

*

Something I do remember of those years is the cold. Perhaps this was exacerbated in my case by the contrast with my infancy in Assam. I imagine we all wore as many layers as possible, but this did not stop the cold as we huddled round fires and radiators. I don't remember the house at 'By the Way' as particularly cold, however, though my mother does comment on it. I expect that, as with food, my grandmother did not stint on coal and coke. In my grandfather's diary on 12th December 1952 there is mention of the arrival of a ton of anthracite, and less than a month later on 8 January 1953 half a ton of 'Nutty Slack' [a form of long-burning coal]. The bliss of a hot bath (we had no showers in those days at home) was all the greater against this background.

There is evidence that in all the houses we lived in, the open fire, lit in several different rooms, was the focus of social life in the cold weather. At 'By the Way', when my mother arrived she noted in early February 1948 that, *The cooking and fires are gas and far simpler and warmer and the hot-water system is excellent.* In fact, there were open fires as well, for a month later on 2 March she wrote to my father, *My fires nearly out and I must bath to-night.* Then in October 1949 I wrote to my parents *There is an awful gale blowing and we have been roasting chestnuts by the fire.* On 1 January 1951 it becomes clear that there was also a fire in the nursery, to which my mother alludes. When my mother rented the small house in Broadstone, she wrote on 1 February 1951, *Well as you see we're here - just! We moved to-day and now its 8.30 p.m and I'm sitting in front of my bedroom fire in my pyjamas ...*

When we moved for a few months to the house in Windermere, my mother wrote to my father on 26 September 1954, *It has central heating.* Yet the pleasure of the open fire continued and my mother recognized its symbolism. On 1 November my mother wrote that, *we bought a bag of chestnuts which we roasted on the fire after tea. It was lovely to have my family round me again but I did wish the menfolk could have been there! ... Wish you were here to sit by our own fireside...* Then on 26 November she wrote, *it was raining so hard and we sat by the fire and played Mah Jong instead.... They played outside for a bit and then came in by the fire and did Jig-saws...* There was clearly also a coke boiler, for on 3 January 1955 my mother wrote *we then washed it up for half an hour while Robert sat by the fire and Daddy coped with the boiler which had gone out.*

The solution to some of the coldness was clothing. We wore pyjamas, and I dimly recall bed-socks at home and sometimes a sweater in bed. So what else did we wear? Here I obviously have to distinguish home clothes and school uniforms. My clothing at home is illustrated by the sets of photographs - for instance, my mackintosh and sou'wester, my clothes for special photos, my first school uniform on going to my kindergarten and to the Dragon, my playing clothes at 'By the Way'. Even my shoes and galoshes are open to inspection.

*

Now with widespread car ownership and reasonable public transport it is difficult to remember how much of an effort it was for a family living in the countryside without a car to manage. A good deal of the regular foodstuffs, coal and other things were delivered, but for shopping of other kinds, entertainment, doctors and dentists, it was obviously exhausting for my mother with three small children to move from place to place – perhaps aggravated by the fact that she limped after having had polio as a child and the tendons in her foot caused her pain.

One example of the complexities of a local journey is in an undated letter of February 1948.

> On Tuesday I had a hectic day, as I took Fiona in to see the throat specialist in Bournemouth (and Alan too.). This involved getting a lift to Poole, taking a bus halfway to Bournemouth and finding Peggy Wades house, spending one and half hours with her, catching another bus on, changing into a tram and finally finding the doctors house and then reversing the whole process. All on a bitter day with snow deep on the ground. Actually it all worked out very well and we just flung ourselves into suitable buses in time in every case.

Two months later she decided to take me to the cinema, leaving my sisters with my grandparents. She wrote on 7 April 1948 that:

> To-day has been hectic beyond belief as I decided to take Alan into "Bambi" in Bournemouth which involved the most minute preparations from early dawn and even then was a rush. We had lunch at 12.30, hurled Anne and Fiona into bed, left the house at quarter to one and got to

the Cinema at quarter to three. Alan and I came out at 5, had tea and a pink ice while waiting for the bus and got back here at 7 p.m!

A particular regret of my mother was that although we lived only about ten miles from the sea, it was really difficult to get us down there without a car. On 17 May she wrote, *I do so wish we could get down to the sea but its just too far alas. I might rise to a taxi one of these days.*

She took the plunge the following month and described on 15 June how *On Sunday we hired a taxi and went to Sandbanks ... Altogether it was lovely. I wish we were a little closer, I hate taking the children in crowded buses, and taxis are the devil.*

Journeys by train usually involved many changes and sometimes some odd companions. In an undated letter in August 1948 my mother went to Oxford with the three of us and described how *We left Broadstone at 8.30 and got to Reading at 12 a.m. where we were met by Noreen and taken out to her place for lunch and tea, and caught the 4.30 train onto Oxford. The journey was easy except for endless changes, and during one spell we all had to sit on the floor of the guards van in the company of 50 or so sailors! – but on the whole it was simple.*

There were occasionally cars, as when my uncle Richard stayed with us, or when my father was on leave. But the absence of a car, which clearly my mother compared to many of her richer friends, continued to weary her throughout the following years. On 11th July 1954 she wrote, *I wish we had a car and could go to the sea but moving about by bus on a Sunday is murder and I bicycled all yesterday and am on strike as far as that's concerned!*

*

As for longer journeys to holiday in Scotland, these were complex events, especially when combined with trying to get all of us to boarding schools. Thus on 30 August 1954 she wrote to my father about a trip to Scotland, *we are going up on the 9 and staying till the end of the holidays, and I'll drop the girls at Ambleside on my way back, haven't quite worked out how I shall manage Alan who is due back at school on the same day but I daresay something will occur to me. It is all very complicated really as I hadn't bargained on getting their school clothes ready so quickly and I feel the organising of their trunks is almost as involved as establishing camps on Everest!*

The journey to Glasgow to visit my father's brother Alan and his wife Jean, is described in a letter of about the 12 of September in some detail.

We came up here on Thursday, starting at 2.30 p.m from Broadstone and arriving in Glasgow at 6 a.m. the following morning, almost as long as it takes to reach Calcutta! We had a mass of trunks, suitcases, fishing rods, guns and packets of sandwiches which had to be manoeuvred in and out of trains and taxis, augmented as we went along by comics and chewing gum but managed to arrive without losing any of them though the fishing rod did a certain amount of damage among the ladies hats as Anne swept past. We had nearly two hours wait at Euston before getting into our sleeper, but it was a very sunny little cabin and we were relieved to be able to put our feet up and relieve ourselves of some of our sandwiches. Alan and Fiona took the top bunk and Anne and I the bottom and I for one didn't sleep a wink all night but at least it was restful and the kids managed to sleep quite a bit – for two it would have been lovely but Anne kicked me in the ribs all night, when I complained next day she said 'Well it wasn't very nice for me either having your stinky feet in my face!' We hurried out into the raw morning at Glasgow and sat on our cases till 8 waiting for Alan, then gave him up and got a train to Wishaw and from there a taxi, it was pouring with rain and very cold and we arrived white and battered to find Alan had just returned from Glasgow, he had run out of petrol and mistaken the time of the train! Jean had a fire and breakfast waiting which saved our lives.

The journey back on her own, having sent us off to school, was equally tiring, as she had decided to come down from the Lake District by bus in order to save money. A journey by bus which would nowadays take six to eight hours at the most, took three times as long. She wrote on 30 September:

I arrived back yesterday afternoon after 18 hours in the bus - 12 hours to London and 6 on here with only an hours rest. Not my idea of how to enjoy a journey but certainly simple and cheap - the only snag was arriving at Broadstone with my Rev. robe weighing a ton and not being able to find a taxi to take me the last mile. I was enquiring at the garage when Birch-Reynardson rolled up so he obliged ...

Visiting me at school at the Dragon from the Lake District, to which she had just moved, was now particularly difficult, especially as my mother was trying to economize and travelled down by bus. On 14 November she described;

To start at the beginning I came down by bus to Birmingham on Thursday, it was raining in a monsoonish sort of way when I left Windermere, and the bus splashed along happily for the first couple of hours, but we arrived only 10 minutes late - left at 8.30 a.m and got to Birmingham at 4.15 p.m!

A week later on the 21 she described part of the journey back:

'on Monday I went on to Huntingdon to the Wenham's - its quite close but most complicated to get to and I couldn't get a train till 2.30 so decided to leave the hotel and have a snack at the station. I ordered tea and buns and sat down and suddenly felt terribly ill - sick and palpitating all over - thought I was getting 'flu or worse and spent a

miserable hour in a cold sweat, and got onto the train and fell into a deep sleep. Fortunately I woke up feeling perfectly alright before my change, but had to wait about a lot and got to Huntingdon at 6 p.m.

On 3 December she described another journey north to Scotland.

I came up by bus on Monday, it was a lovely day and I didn't find the 8 hours too bad, the only excitement was when we were batting along that road beyond Carlisle at a fair pace, it was dark and suddenly a huge grey cow loomed in the middle of the road, the bus just swerved round it but we all got quite a turn – it was the most astonishing sight on a main road in England. I got to Edinburgh at 10 p.m and hoped the Cowans might meet me, but they didn't, so I took a taxi. I spent two days in Edinburgh, which I enjoyed as it was restful ... I came over here [Wishaw, near Glasgow] by bus on Thursday afternoon, slung around with fishing rods and Thermos flasks and a case that was brimming over with the clothes that I'd left behind with Pat in the summer, I had some difficulty in getting off the bus with it all and fell in a heap at Alan's feet, I was very glad to see him as I was afraid he mightn't be able to meet me.

*

I do not think I was consciously aware of how great a strain my mother found it to run a household, but the constant background of her tiredness and anxieties must clearly have affected me considerably.

The difficulty was the product of various factors. One was the contrast with Assam. In India she had had a reasonable income, things were cheap, there were servants aplenty, there were large houses and gardens, transport was reasonable. In the back of her mind as she struggled during the periods she was on leave must always have been the comparison with how easy it was in Assam.

Another difficulty was the absence of my father for much of
the time. During the approximately four years during which my
mother was at home with us between January 1947 and
September 1955, my father was around for less than one third
of the time. She missed him in many practical ways in sharing
the burden of bringing up three young children. There was also
the anguish of constant long-distance moves back and forth to
India with one or more of us. Furthermore, the houses she
lived in were all rented until the very end, which added to the
strain since major improvements were not worthwhile and
there were landlords and the care of their properties to be
thought of.

She did, however, have one considerable advantage, though
this also had its difficulties. For three out of the four years she
was at home we lived with our grandparents, her mother and
father. It is obvious from the letters that it was when she was on
her own in a small rented house in Broadstone 1951 that she
found it most difficult. This was compounded by the fact that it
was one of the bleakest years of the post-war period – much
illness, awful weather, political uncertainties and the threat of
atomic war. Yet it is worth noting that when she lived with my
grandmother, still a relatively young and immensely capable
and energetic woman, and my grandfather, a keen gardener
and willing helper, with the occasional presence of her brothers
with cars, a telephone (which she did not have at Pinecot),
there was then an enormous amount of support. Expenses
could be shared, for example, heating and lighting, and the
burden of looking after children was lessened.

The following account of the practical life of a middle-class
colonial family after the war may seem somewhat prosaic. Yet it
is unusual to have such a full account of some of the constraints
of a world on the eve of modern affluence. It illustrates once
again, both for my mother and also her parents, the very
widespread experience of moving between worlds. In India my
grandparents had lived well, with high status, large houses, cars
and as many servants as they needed. When they returned they
could not for a long time afford to buy a house, had no servants

and could not afford a car. They lived in two worlds, just as I lived in the two worlds of home and boarding school.

*

In the first letter from 'By the Way' in late January 1948, my mother refers to something which has changed utterly, namely the problem of keeping clothes clean in an age before the washing machine or even laundrettes. She wrote how at the end of a day she, *usually had the prospect of a big wash in front of me.*

Shopping with very little money, no car and three small children she also found a nightmare. Two months later on 25 March she wrote

> *We all went into Poole yesterday to do bits of shopping and look at the park which has a bit of the harbour in it and boats some of which are for children. They weren't working unfortunately, but should be fun later. Poole is a frightful place but has very good shops. I only bought two pairs of pyjamas for Alan and a cotton dress for Fiona but it was an exhausting business. I loathe shops now, I never can find what I want and end by buying something I don't at twice the price I meant to pay.*

The result was that she never seemed to have any time – aggravated by cooking and the endless washing up. In the same letter she described how,

> *People round here are very sociable we find, but really there is no time to be hospitable back. I get up in the morning and do a bit of washing and squeeze some oranges and its lunch time and before the washing-up is finished its time to think of tea and so the days melt away. A sign of old age creeping on!*

The strain of keeping three small children occupied, especially in bad weather, is described in her next letter on about 1 April. *The weather has broken and we're being treated to March gales and April showers together, horrid although we can't really complain. I can't make up my mind which is worse, staying in all day with the children getting bored and irritable or battling our way through slashing wind and rain in an effort to be hearty.*

Shopping in the local town of Poole, about five miles away, was bad enough. But going to the bigger city of Bournemouth, and especially London, was even more of a nightmare. Here are two vignettes of such trips.

She described in a letter of 23 April a visit to see the doctor in London (about possible family planning advice) where she also met rich friends.

> *Afterwards we shopped or rather they did, I didn't get any further than asking the price! It was most exhausting and I finally tottered into Waterloo in a bruised and battered condition from having got involved in the "Rush hour". I arrived back here at 10.30 p.m. London is really rather awful, I've decided, and I don't ever want to go there again.*

On 29 July 1951 she described how,

> *On Monday I went into Bournemouth to see a dentist and thought I'd make a day of it, have my hair done and do some shopping and enjoy (?) myself. It turned into a boiling day and Bournemouth the hottest place in England! Having been steamed gently in the hairdresser all morning I snatched a quick lunch and then started tramping the shops. By 4 my feet were burning, my temper fraying and my money vanishing at an appalling rate. Bournemouth is full of the most fearful people, just a heaving mass of hot humanity and one can hardly force oneself along the pavements. I staggered into the dentist half an hour late after having caught the wrong bus ... I eventually got back to Broadstone at 7, more dead than alive.*

This nine months of living with my grandparents was not the worst period, however. Not only did she have the support and housekeeping skills of my grandmother, but it was the one time when, briefly, she hired a part-time woman to help look after us for a few months. This seems to have happened in the first part of the year and as there are only references in March and April it may not have lasted long. On 9 March my mother wrote, *The "girl" turned up the day before yesterday to look after them for a couple of hours – she is a nice little thing, and they all seem to like her, even Anne who is firm about who she goes out with.*

Yet my mother does not seem to have found it a very satisfactory arrangement for on 7 April she wrote:

> *Eileen (the girl who sometimes turns up to help)* **did** *turn up, fortunately and coped at home. She is a very nice girl, but rather spineless and the children do exactly what they like with her. I went in the other day at tea-time and found Anne walking about on the table tramping bread and butter into the cloth, while Fiona spilt cup after cup of milk and Alan spat orange pips at all and sundry.*

The problem was that she was very irregular, as well as young, and it is difficult to see how she could have disciplined us when our own mother despaired of doing so. This was in contrast to some friends' children who had proper nurses. My mother wrote on 29 July, *Last Saturday Betty Deane took us in her car to the beach ... Betty's children are very sweet and so well-behaved compared to mine! She has always had nurses for them and strict ones at that which explains it.*

*

When my mother returned to England towards the end of 1950 and shortly moved into a separate house, she faced the greatest difficulty. Short of money, with no car or telephone, much sickness and bad weather, she clearly struggled to cope.

While she was still with my grandmother she wrote moderately cheerfully on 24 January 1951.

> *I've forgotten all about Assamese shrubs and the little I knew about butterfly wings, but I'm beginning to find out quite a lot about making soup and pastry and I made a really wonderful sponge cake the other day - honestly darling! ... I'm due to go in 4 days time, but so far haven't had time to do anything but stir round the children's toys - with the cooking and carting Fiona to and fro from school and invalid trays there hasn't been a great deal of time. However it won't be hard as I can throw everything pell mell into the lorry, and fling it out the other end. I've signed a formidable document from the Agents full of "heretofores" and "inasmuch as" es and am still a little vague as to what it was all about but the house is going to be ours and that's all I care about. I'm going to try to make it a real home and plant sweet-peas and maybe buy a cat to sit by the fire (do I hear you groan?) and Dig In as if it was going to be for ever. After all time is only relative and we can stretch a year to fit our needs the way things are we may have to fit ourself into...[damaged]. Anyway all these high minded notions apart we'll have a wonderful time.*

By this time I was at boarding school. She goes on in the same letter to describe her domestic life in some detail.

> *There isn't an awful lot of news as my week has been purely domestic get up, cook breakfast and eat it, pot children and dress them, collect them, put them and self onto our respective bikes and go off to school. I get back at 10.30 or so. And after a swift flapping round of dusters and cleaning of clinkers I get cracking on the potatoes Anne is being most awfully good and amuses herself scribbling hieroglyphics and ripping used stamps off old envelopes and handing me endless "letters" which I have to read when I'm in the middle of stirring something very vital or have my head and shoulders in the oven. She did look at me rather*

*sadly this morning and say "You always work now" but
really its very good practise for both of us, and we're both
coming out of it quite well... After we've washed up lunch I
sit by the fire with her for half an hour, and then we get
ready to go down for Fiona again. As soon as we get back
there is tea to be got for us all, the children get something
cooked, and then its just about bath time. When I've put
the kids to bed at 7 I have to come down and cook a 2-
course supper for us all, this is a bore and I shall stop it
when I'm on my own. Actually it'll be far easier in my new
home and specially with you to help. In spite of the way it
sounds it isn't drudgery. I love it, even the potatoes, I love
seeing the dirty brown skin slide away and leave a hard
white path behind it. I think I'm a bit infantile in some ways.
Anne and Fiona suddenly got an urge to "help" over the
week-end, they draped enormous aprons round themselves
and washed up everything I put down for a second, by the
time I'd finished tripping over them and they over their
aprons it was questionable whether they were actually
helping a lot.*

As soon as she arrived in the new house, however, the
enormity of the task facing her began to dawn. On the first of
February she wrote,

*This place seems a lot smaller now we're in it and
various snags appearing – such as lack of cupboard space
and nowhere to put empty boxes – its full of large round
tables and wash hand-stands, quite useless and take up all
the room, however no doubt we'll shake down. The hot-
water system is rather terrifying, you climb on a chair and
open a little door in a cistern and turn on a tap and put a
match inside the door, at which there's a deafening
explosion and huge blue flames roar out and burn your
hand. I haven't worked out how long the water takes to heat
or what you do when it is, blow the flames out and start
again I suppose. Those are the sort of things I'd like to
leave to you, but I got a hot bath anyway, the only thing that*

went wrong there was that when I pulled out the plug the sponge went down the hole and has blocked the pipe and I haven't got one of those suction things – ah well, I shall learn.

So she wrote on 19 February that, *time is my chief problem, I only have a couple of hours after the children are in bed and theres so much I want to do and make and read.* Ten days later, on 1 of March, she laments,

You should see my hands darling, I've burnt them with fat and scorched them on the iron and chopped and sliced and chapped them and rubbed all the knuckles off with the washing – serves me right for being proud of them – I've only got my ears now and I'm having those pierced soon!

The frantic routine is described again on the 20 of the same month.

To-morrow is going to be one of those hectic days, getting Anne to school, feeding my bantams, buying fish, rushing back to cook lunch here and some food for Daddy for next day, going down to collect Anne and after lunch packing and carting ourselves and our belongings back home again. Come to think of it, most days are like that, it seems to come naturally to most people but not to me! I have to keep running over what I must do and in what order and repeating it like a dirge until its done – or isnt.

If she went out, work piled up. On 24 April, she arrived back at 'Pinecot' where she found my grandfather baby-sitting.

I arrived back at 12 to find unwashed breakfast dishes, unmade beds and Anne and Grandpa shut into a room with a blazing fire and reeking of home-made tobacco and felt a little depressed. However it sorted itself out in the end. My biggest problem is washing and ironing, there just doesn't seem time for it and it piles up in corners till I feel quite dizzy. This week I've got to get Alan cleaned and mended up for school and his trunk off in advance quite when I don't know!'

Visitors were an added strain. On 6 May she wrote that,

We got back here at 12.15 and I threw a lunch together and then threw myself and Anne into my double bed and went fast asleep – to be woken after ten minutes by a ring at the front door. This, I may say, is the first time I'd gone to bed in the afternoon but for some reason I felt completely cooked. Anyway I crawled down in my stockings to find Sheila and Noel Lawn on the doorstep (Aunt Margery's daughter do you remember them?) the house was in a perfect ferment, fires unswept, beds unmade and I only had some broken biscuits for tea – but here they sat until 6 p.m. Fiona came in looking a bit green and said she had a headache and felt cold and I wanted to put her to bed with a bottle – but still they sat. Very nice of them but they couldn't have chosen a worse day.

The shortage of money meant that she added to the normal tasks by trying to sew and mend. On 23 May she wrote that,

I've just kicked the inkbottle over the carpet and have been rushing to and fro with salt and hot water. I can't see by this light whether I've got it out but I don't expect so, I can't see us getting out of this place without a couple of lawsuits. Ah me! I've been making curtains to-day, I don't know if they'll "hang" right, I doubt it, my ignorance about those sort of things horrifies me, what have I been doing all these years, loving you and being thousands of miles away from you mostly it seems to me. Not a good excuse for not knowing how to make curtains. All the same, I've just made myself a sack-like skirt, but still it's the first effort, I will improve. With the price of clothes now, I shall be depending entirely on home-made sacks from now on.

The final letter on this theme on 30 May describes the stress on her body and particularly notes the difficulty of coping with the house and small garden without my father's help.

I must write to Alan to-night and already its 10.30, don't know where the time goes but these light evenings I don't get the kids bedded down till after eight. The light has gone and I've had to unplug the wireless and plug in a table lamp. Oh for a man! You will have a pile of jobs waiting for you, lawn mowing, hedge-clipping, bicycle-mending and greasing and lots more, so be prepared – and a wife who wants to be made love to every available minute, work-worn and smelling slightly of onion as she is! I'm afraid I haven't been able to put on much weight if any, I've come to the conclusion I'm the Thin type – do you think so darling?

*

A responsibility which largely fell on my mother's shoulders was to organize schools for myself and my two sisters. As soon as our family moved into 'By the Way' my mother was faced with deciding about our schooling. In her first letter at the end of January 1948 she wrote, *I've got to get cracking over school and how to get them there.* The latter point was important too. I was accepted by Southlands School, but this was in the centre of Broadstone, more than a mile from 'By the Way'. Much of the pressure to get bicycles, and for me to learn to ride came from this. There was no bus, no car, and the only other alternative was a thirty minute walk each way every day.

My mother obviously hoped that my sister Fiona, two years younger than me, would be able to join me at the same school in due course. But on 14 July she wrote:

I'm a bit taken aback as the school I had arranged to send her [Fiona] to now doesn't know if they can have her. If I can't fit her in I think I will have to bring her out with me, and send her up to the convent in Shillong. I don't think Mummy is

55

*keen to have her at a loose end – and I know you don't want
me to bring her out, it's a bit of a problem. I know you feel that
I will give all my time to the children if I bring them out – but I
will try not to darling. Anyway it's not to be decided for a
couple of weeks.*

It appears that it was resolved, for my sister was left in
England on this occasion when my mother returned to Assam
with my younger sister Anne in October 1948. As for my
longer-term education, she noted in the same letter of 14 July:

*Before I forget, the Dragon School has definitely accepted
Alan for September 1950, when he'll be 8 and three quarters.*

*

My mother returned to England with both my sisters in
June 1954 and it was now her job to find a boarding school for
me after the Dragon, and boarding schools for my sisters.
There seems to have been little doubt that I would follow my
three uncles, Billy, Richard and Robert, and go to Sedbergh
School in Yorkshire. A revealing insight into how I was
accepted there is given in a letter of 3 July 1954.

*About Sedbergh, Mummy wrote to a master she knows
well and he has "fixed" it, but Alan is to go to Lupton
instead as they have a new housemaster who is a good type
apparently ... I wrote a very cool letter to Mr Ward –
apparently they didn't "realize Alan was connected with the
Rhodes-Jameses" – an eye-opener on how to get into a
Public School. She added that I had a letter from Mr Ward
from Sedbergh this morning, very apologetic and said that
so many applications were not reliable – I think he might
have found out first!*

My mother continued to teach my sisters for a while when
they returned from India in 1954, but could not really find the
time or inclination to go on for long. Instead, she arranged

them to go to a P.N.E.U. school in Ambleside, where they started as boarders in the Christmas term of 1954. She admitted that it was a relatively cheap school, without the amenities of the Dragon, but on the whole approved of its approach. This settled all the school business – apart from the task of equipping us for each of these schools and paying for them.

*

Although my mother shared the tasks with my grandparents during the last leave from June 1954, she still found herself exhausted by household tasks, exacerbated by the large move from Dorset to Westmorland. On the 3 of July 1954 she wrote:

> *I couldn't finish this yesterday after all as I'd left it till after dinner and then had one of those queer hot and cold turns and had to go to bed, slept for 12 hours and feel fine this morning. I think I got over-tired as I washed, ironed, gardened (most energetically with shears cutting myself and the grass about equally) and had a couple of kids to tea with all the extra washing-up involved.*

The full force of all the energy she had to exert in housekeeping hit her when my grandparents were away house-hunting. Thus she wrote on 30 August:

> *The kids and I and Robert looked after the hens in their absence and I found it tiring as everything seemed to devolve on me, on Saturday I was nearly dead at the end of a day cleaning, cooking, hens, taking the girls to a show at Poole, and finally a fuse when I was about to get my supper, with Robert out with the only torch.*

Moving around the country in search of a new house and new schools for my sisters added to the strain of getting the three of us off to school. About the 23 September she wrote from the Lake District,

Poor you I've neglected you and this is at least 3 days late – I'm so sorry darling but this last 10 days has been terribly exhausting and I began to feel I'd never get the children's clothes named and sorted and ironed – there were so many little last minute things like nail-brushes and garters and Pat [Cowan] and I spent so much time talking that I was up till 3 a.m. the last night – it was much complicated by having Fiona's trunk downstairs and mine and Anne's 3 flights up! I had to see Alan off on the night train at 10.20 p.m. and then return to the fray and felt quite sick with nerves and anxiety.

When the move to the house in Windermere took place there were further crises. Thus on 26 November she wrote,

Mummy arrived on Thursday evening and it's been black as night ever since, except for a brief spell this morning when a pale sun broke through. Added to that my Calor Gas has been playing up again and our meals for the last couple of days have been most haphazard and uncertain, didn't think we were going to get any lunch to-day but the man arrived just in time for me to hurl everything into the oven and produce a rather peculiar lunch for the girls who were coming out.

The last months before my father arrived were also a strain, though the work could be shared with my grandparents. On 6 February 1955 she wrote,

Nothing of interest this week darling, am lying very low and without help in the house I necessarily spend a good deal of my time on scrubbing – my hands are becoming horribly work-worn and ingrained with potato stains but no doubt they will recover and you will love me still?!'

Twelve days later on 18 of February she wrote on the same theme.

*I shall enjoy cooking for you darling, but frankly I find it
rather a bore continually breaking off to get meals for M & D it
seems to fritter my precious time away and splits the days up
into little bits when it isn't worth settling down to anything. If I
were on my own I'd live on fruit and eggs, the eternal chopping
and peeling and piling up of dirty dishes seems such a waste of
time – I suppose because I don't really like cooking much or
put my soul into it. But I will for you darling, I look at piles of
tripe every time I go to the butcher to get myself immune to it
in preparation for you!*

I have included as much on these humdrum worries and
efforts as I can find since they are the usually unrecorded tasks
which fell mainly to women. My mother wrote some of them
down, but the huge bulk of the daily grind of cooking, cleaning,
maintaining warmth, stocking the house, went on all the time,
day by day. Anyone with three children will know what this
means.

Of course my mother was relatively fortunate in having
strong and capable parents to hand, and a loving and
reasonably paid husband in India. In the period when she lived
separately from her parents she struggled even harder, and
when they lived together there were inevitably some tensions.
Meanwhile I enjoyed my childhood hobbies and imaginative
world and did not, as I recall, give much thought to what efforts
she and my grandparents were making to look after me.

*

A letter from my mother when she returned to India in
October 1948, leaving me at home with my sister Fiona, sets
out some of the practical and financial details of the
arrangement. It is an undated letter of late October from
Deopani Tea Estate.

*Darling Mummy,
Well here we are at last, back to "aloo chops" and rusty
bathwater but safe and well which is the main thing... I feel*

disembodied and quite unreal suddenly finding myself so isolated but will enjoy it once Anne has settled down I think. She is still liverish and bemused most of the time, a surfeit of bananas I shouldn't be surprised, they hang around in hundreds and she has one every time she passes. I have decided not to have an Aya for her as I really don't know what I should do with myself if I didn't have her to keep me busy. There are quite a few children around for her to play with when it gets a bit cooler. [end of typed part]

I was so pleased to get your letter yesterday and hear that the children weren't upset. I hope they're not demanding too much of your time and continue to behave reasonably. Mac is as keen as I am about Canada so we hope Heather [Chesney, a cousin] will really stick to her word, and let us have the prospects. I miss the children every minute tho' I know they're better off in every way at home. Mac's commission (a good one of £380) has gone into the bank which will pay off our overdraft and I enclose a cheque for £100 for you for the children. Would 5 guineas a week be enough for their food and board – we feel you should make some profit out of them so don't hesitate to say if that's not enough! The 10 shillings family allowance could go towards Mrs Hayly and extras like clothes and shoes and buses and medecines would be separate of course. Do say what you really feel about this. If you can possibly hang on for 6 months I'm sure we shall have found some way out of Assam! Don't forget to pay yourself back for what I owed you. ...

The next letter was a birthday one written by my grandmother to my father. Their relationship might have been difficult – living under the shadow of my powerful grandmother and often sharing a house is not easy for a son-in-law. The letter, however is pretty positive, and again show affection and care for all concerned. It is dated 24 October 1948.

Dear Donald – I will add a few lines of birthday wishes to the children's ... Fiona watched Daddie dressing this morning very thoughtfully and when he put on his tattered, buttonless garden coat she brightened up and said "Ah – now you look like Grandpa"! Poppa misses Anne very much – as do I and am sure you are delighted with her. We are looking forward very much to Iris' first letter telling us of her "flight" and I was very glad to get the cable. To-day has been absolutely perfect and finished up with a glorious sunset which Alan insisted on my going out to see but we hear we are in for a cold spell (... news of the cockerels etc...) Both Mrs Byas and Mrs Deane have asked the children and Mrs Fairhurst Alan and I like her very much. Much love and best wishes from us both, lots of love to Iris and Anne your loving Mother.

The only other surviving letter of mine I have found during this first absence was written in early February 1950. It is on the back of one from my grandmother and my sister which suggest that we were happy. *Darling Mummy and Daddy Thank you very much for the lovely watch and letters. It is very windy and rainy here and we are playing schools and I am practising writing. I got a distinction last week. I hope you are all well lots of love Alan oooooooxxxxxxx*

There is added a short note from Fiona, *Darling Mummy and daddy, I got a distinction last week. I like school very much. My Best Freind at school is Susan Burry. Hope you are all very well lots of love Fiona xxxxoooo*

The letter from my grandmother clearly refers to a visit we made after Christmas in January 1950 to Exeter to stay with my Aunt Margery and great-grandmother, Annie Swinhoe. Annie's diary contains the following:

Monday 2 Jan. Margery went to Exeter to meet Alan and Fiona.
Sat 14 Violet and Alan and Fiona left.

Clearly there was a negative response from Aunt Margery, which she conveyed in a letter to my mother.

My grandmother wrote the following outraged letter.

Darling Iris – I have been so dancing mad all the week at A.M's [Aunt Margery] *letter to you that I have not dared put pen to paper in case I burnt it up. – I did write to her yesterday and said as little as poss: and that I was not sending the kids again. I don't know how she can say those things about Fiona over eating. The kids have very definite ideas on food and there are lots of things they don't care for and so I let them tuck into the things they do. You must not feel they are nuisances to us as they are a constant interest and Daddy is completely wrapped up in them – my rôle is more domestic and disciplinary I fear. You must do exactly what you think best about Fiona going out and there is plenty of time yet. I am so sorry you have had to send to Calcutta for jerseys etc and I should never have worried you. The weather is awful and the garden one big muddy watercourse and the only happy people are the ducks. Fiona and I have colds and 'flu is rampaging everywhere. I do hope you are better and that the bilious attack is not going to be Anne's Christmas present!! ... Have written to Florence* [paternal grandmother] *in case arrangements can be made for another Scottish holiday. I lost 4 lbs last fortnight and hope for more this spell. Forgive scribble. All love Mummy.*

The observation that my grandfather was totally wrapped up in us, which comes through in other letters, and my grandmother's assured realization of what her role was, as well as her stout and angry defence of us are revealing. In fact, though there was clearly a cooling of relations, I note from later references that we did go back to Exeter with my mother – she was enormously fond of Annie, her grandmother, who had played an important part in negotiating the difficulties of her own childhood – and seeing Margery, whom she always found very unpredictable, was an acceptable cost for a visit.

There are no further surviving letters between my grandparents and parents during this first absence. The next one from my grandmother, attached to one of mine, was written on 12th August 1952 some seven months after my parents and both sisters left for India on the second absence. It again tried to keep my mother up to date in a cheerful and positive way.

Alan is full of beans and stick-em-up and he is very happy with his 2 uncles. I can't cope with going to the Marsdens [tea planter friends] *before Alan goes to Scotland so I rang her up and we will hope to go over for the day later. Still no definite news about Alan's sleeping berth on Friday which I find agitating but I have his ticket and the Traffic Manager sure a berth would be available. I arranged for him to go up a week before going to Patty* [Cowan, god-mother] *as Florence* [grandmother] *had wanted him for a day or two but now she is in hospital and I hope a week won't be too much for Jean* [Macfarlane – father's brother's wife]. *The chickens I have are Indian Game x L.S.* [Light Sussex] *hens and are the cockerels for Christmas and apparently this crossing produces very big and very plump birds. I've lost one which was very weak. We had to finally use a blow lamp on the litter house which really seems to have rid the house of them (red mite). My egg count for this year was 9,663 which seems quite good ... I hope the floods are not round your way too much. I will send those tools by Alan* [going out to Assam for Christmas] *and hope they won't make his weight too much. I shall also send outgrown pyjamas etc in case you can use them for F and A. Lots and lots of love, Mummie.*

My grandfather also wrote to my parents, though only one or two letters, appended to letters from me, survive.) One is dated 19 September 1952.

We are very sorry indeed to hear about the dog incident and that the injections had such a bad effect on you and we do hope you are better now. Alan is very fit indeed and very cheery. Robert is very good at keeping him amused and they play a lot of soccer. Alan should develop into a good player with all this practice. He goes to school [Dragon School] on Monday 22 and his box has been packed and is waiting to be collected by the railway. ... We have had a wonderful summer and autumn. It will not be long now before you get the cold weather which you must be longing for. Sept in India is the worst month of all. I am so glad Fiona is doing so well at her work. How does Anne compare with her I wonder in intelligence. Richard went back to Haileybury 3 days go. He was very good about taking us about in his car. Shepherd the cricketer was at his camp at Iwerne Minster. I think he is going in the church. Alan is musical and he and Robert are great Gilbert and Sullivan fans. Richard and Robert have been to several concerts at the Winter Gardens Bournemouth ... My tomatoes have been very successful this year and the Apples are very good and it is good to see Alan tucking into them.... I hope Mac is fit and that the tea prices are better. Best love Daddy

Another, again appended to one of mine, is dated 30 April 1953 and was written by my grandmother.

*Darlings – I feel very guilty at writing so seldom but I seem to be **very** busy and by the evening can't write a line. I have bought the watch and cricket bat with the money I got from selling your bits and pieces and a final 24 shilling for Alan's suit. I had meant to buy saving certs: but I thought these things were as essential and save you the cash! The school fees came to £94 odd and I've had to buy a few odds and ends of clothes so am £9 short as I had some in hand before and I should like to book Alan for the 2 periods at Swanage – which will be £11 but if he goes to Scotland they will refund me for the period he doesn't go. He comes back from school so mute and quiet but returns [to] his own cheery – even cheeky – self and he does look grand. The*

Marsdens took him for 3 days and returned him to me at the Point to Point at Bradbury Rings. She is a nice untidy creature and looks as if another infant were on the way but it may be just natural! ... "Kidnapped" is on and I find it difficult to concentrate. Lots and lots of love, Mummy.

The final surviving letter between England and Assam is dated 30 August 1953 and was written by my grandmother. Having explained about how I had dealt with difficult dental treatment with some courage, she ended by commenting that she had bought me a Padda set as a consolation for the pain.

He gave a derisive guffaw when I said I would play with him but found Granny was much better than he thought possible and in fact could beat him! – The Mermagans are coming to Parkstones for 10 days from Saturday so I shall try to contact them and hope Alan will be able to bathe with them. Billy, Julia and Caroline are coming here tomorrow. Daddy's birthday and staying the night – thank you very much for the cheque and I'm glad there will be no expenses over Alan's op: Lots of love, Mummy

The other insight into their relations and discussion of future joint living arrangements occurs as the move to the Lake District is being planned. My mother, in England, wrote to my father in a letter dated 30 September 1954.

Anyway I seem to have got a bit off the point. I returned to find a state of upheaval here. I don't know if I told you about a row in progress with aunt Nell over blankets, it has ended in her more or less giving M & D notice to leave, saying anyway that she was going to sell "in the near future" so the outcome is that they are coming up to live with me! I'm a bit undecided about this – I had a happy dream of a house to myself and a job and utter peace – but it will help me financially and of course I want them to live up there and it will be a good opportunity for them to look for a house. I am only rather worried about the mountains of stuff they are preparing to take as the Kirwins have let me have the house on the understanding that I look after it very carefully and Mummy's ideas of "squeezing in" her large bits of furniture alarm me rather! But after all they've done for me I can hardly refuse to have them. I daresay it'll work out alright and it was a nice dream while it lasted!

It is clear that my mother was aware that my father would be as ambivalent as she was about living with his in-laws. This is reflected in a letter dated 25 October 1954.

The idea is that Mummy and Daddy stay with us until next summer holidays – this will mean they will be there with you and I until July, but I don't think it will be too bad darling, because we shall be going out and about, maybe on a short tour, and the house is big enough for us not to fall over each other. As you know, I wanted the house as a home for us, but I couldn't very well turn them down after them having harboured me, and I think it will be a financial help for me to have them for the winter. There's no room for Robert or Richard in the house, at Christmas they'll have to stay in the pub down the road and I shall probably give them lunch, but I shan't kill myself over them – after that I don't know what they'll do and frankly don't care – but when you are here there certainly won't be any question of even the lunch. I do feel they should start to cope for themselves. Anyway Robert will be finishing at Oxford and getting a job in June. I do hope you agree with all this, I had to make so many snap decisions without consulting you, I could only hope you would feel as I did.

In the event, the fate of the two families continued to be locked together. This was at least partly because of financial considerations. My parents were only able to buy their first house because they shared the burden with my grandparents. Reciprocally, despite a successful career in the army, on a small pension and with no savings, my grandparents had sunk to the level of very dependent relatives. So they bought the house at Field Head, Hawkshead, together in the summer of 1955.

The arrangement was a continuation in another part of England of a pattern which had begun soon after my birth in India, whereby my grandparents were there to look after me and my sisters when needed. My parents were away for the majority of my time at Sedbergh and Oxford, and my grandparents looked after me and my sisters while my parents were in Assam. It obviously made sense that they shared a house – but when my parents came home now, they would move temporarily into rented accommodation nearby.

4. MONEY AND CHICKENS

When I was growing up I don't think I ever asked myself what sort of financial state my parents were in. If I had been asked, I would have said that they were reasonably well off. My father had a good job in tea, with bonuses from time to time. My grandparents had been successful in India and retired on a Lt. Colonel's pension. According to a note in my grandfather's address book, probably referring to the period soon after he returned, this was stated to be: Pension £793-19, Pokey Premium (whatever that was) £53-18-4; FP Fund £23-18-0. Thus they had under nine hundred pounds a year and shared expenses with my parents, but had no house.

Of course, everyone seemed hard-up in those austerity years after the Second World War. But the fact that they could afford to send me to an expensive boarding school costing nearly £300 a year, and later sent my sisters to boarding schools, albeit less expensive, and me to Sedbergh, would have made me think that they were well off. They must have been in the top quarter of the population in terms of income.

Yet when I come to examine the details I am surprised at how much my parents struggled financially. There were several contributory factors. Two were relative. In India the costs were low and subsidized through housing, food and other perks. In England everything seemed very expensive and the standard at which they could live, in material terms, was much lower. Secondly, a lot of my grandparents' and parents' friends seem to have been better off – as my mother often described. They swept up in smart cars or went out to expensive shops and restaurants, neither of which my parents could afford.

It also seems that, like many families even today, they never saved much and always lived just beyond their means, thus accumulating debts. The temptation to borrow was exacerbated because in India the tea planters could easily borrow from local financiers, professional Marwari moneylenders. Company law prohibited this, for it could lead to pressure from these same Marwaris who supplied many things to the Tea Gardens. My mother was worried about this and I know that at certain times my father did borrow in this way – no doubt at high interest.

Another expense was drink – my mother refers in a letter to wasting money on drink and commends my father for trying to cut this down. From memory, my father did drink a certain amount – and certainly in the Club and Assam generally, drink was often socially required and a way of forgetting miseries.

There was another, structural reason for the difficulty they faced, which they shared with my grandparents and many other middle-class families at this time. It is described by David Kynaston who notes that while the standard of living of average working-class families increased by about ten percent between 1938–1948, that of an average salary earner had decreased by about 20 per cent.[1]

A tea planter's income, less magnificent than it was alleged to be in an earlier period, was not enough to keep my parents in the upper-middle-class style to which they were accustomed to in India, and which the family in earlier generations aspired to. Despite sending us to boarding schools they were sinking and by the end of their lives both my sets of grandparents, as well as my mother, were in difficulties.

So my parents and grandparents considered themselves to be Gentle Folk, or in the older parlance, Sahibs. Yet the externals – by which the English have always judged this – were difficult to procure. Buying a house, as we shall see, was an enormous struggle. And the constant nagging refrain to in my mother's letters, is shortage of money and anxiety about this. As much as ill-health, the insecurities of how to deal with her

---

[1] David Kynaston, *Smoke in the Valley; Austerity Britain 1948–51* (2007), 49.

children, the loneliness and fear of being apart for long periods from my father, the ache of being separated from us, there was the constant anxiety about money.

The irony was that by trying not to think about money, and if possible not to talk about it, they became trapped and hence obsessed by money. It is one of those very English paradoxes. Families who talk about money openly and treat it rationally alongside other things worry much less about it than the many families where the subject of money becomes almost taboo.

My parents were constantly making half-hearted efforts to sort out their finances. But it was all piecemeal. Not only did this mean that they never seem to have worked out what they could afford, but it makes it difficult to reconstruct their total income and expenditure over the period. As yet I have not been able to find out what my father's annual income was.

While all this makes for another sad strand in their lives, and the fact that everything we bought was an effort – from bicycles to special meals – it also had several good effects. It meant that I had to save carefully for toys or other treats, and in many ways to live quite austerely – walk to shops, keep clothes for a long time, make do and mend in general. Now living in a world where I can afford almost anything, it is still a luxurious treat to make a long phone call, to travel in a taxi, to have a bottle of good wine.

Secondly, it cemented the tie between my parents and grandparents; they really had to operate a joint economy and this was undoubtedly to my benefit as I was always part of a loving household. Thirdly, for the historical record, it provides interesting insights into the cost of certain items and what a downwardly mobile, or at least seriously struggling, middle-class family thought it needed and could afford.

*

My mother lived with my grandparents from January to October 1948. She was living in a shared house in which there was a telephone but no car. Simultaneously my father was running the household on a tea estate in India. In fact the first letter is about my father's purchase of a jeep in Assam. In an undated letter in February, she wrote, *I'm glad the jeep is a success. Have you paid for it? I expect you'll get a lot of fun taking it to pieces and putting it together again...* In the same letter she mentioned a recurring theme in the letters, the cost of medical care in England, this time for my sisters. *The throat specialist said Fiona has chronic tonsillitis ... Poor wee thing, she'll be miserable about it all. So will we when we get the bill!*

The next evidence, in a letter dated 18 March, concerns the cost of travelling back and forth to India, including insurance.

> *I've been making enquiries about passages through Grindlays and they say they will let me know as soon as they hear of a boat going to Calcutta in October. Of course I'd like to travel with the Derbys but feel I'd go to any lengths to avoid that extra bit in the train. Does my passage have to be booked through the company? They do pay for it don't they? You'd be able to get to Calcutta to meet me wouldn't you? While we're on the subject, is your Insurance Policy in order? I never see anything about it on any Bank Statement and I hope its all alright? I think we should insure a few of our things and against fire – don't you?*

My mother continues in the same letter to express both lack of knowledge and anxiety about their finances. The fact that she felt so guilty, and had to defend at length the purchase of a child's bike for me, is revealing.

> *I don't know how our finances are at present. I've been wildly extravagant latterly and have bought, (or am about to buy) a bicycle for Alan, a dolls pram (for Fiona's birthday) a doll's house (because its such a bargain and we shan't be able to get another like it) a tea-set and coffee percolator (for us) and two beds and mattresses for the children (they had to have these as there were none in the house for them). On top of all this theres F's tonsils and Alan's schooling and uniform and summer clothes for all of them and so on and so on. Can we do it darling? I feel quite mad*

71

to have gone so spiv-ish suddenly, but nowadays one feels one must buy the things while they're there. Your jeep must have more than cleared us out – so please let me know if we are really in a bad way and I'll try to restrain myself. I myself have been given a bicycle by somebody down the road, and it only needs two new tyres. I feel that if Alan learns to ride we shall be able to take picnics out in the summer and its very flat and pleasant for biking round here. I must try and explain myself because I realise I've been very naughty – but I'm only going to have them for this summer and can't help being a little weak-minded darling... I went into Wimbourne on Monday to start another dentist orgy (one more expense, I forgot that.)

I started at my first proper kindergarten in April, and this was another expense. On 23 April my mother wrote *Alan starts school on Monday and I bought him his school uniform, a dream of a coat (£4.6.3!) a cap, tie, and belt, it made me feel very old to see him all dressed up.*

Some money arrived in May, and my mother wrote on 17 *£149 arrived in my account, thank you darling, don't send any more, that should see me through. I'm just about to send off cheques to all the doctors, wish I'd waited till after the Health Scheme had started!* [The NHS started on 5 July 1948]

For the moment our school fees were low, I imagine, but my mother saw expenses looming ahead and, ever hopeful, talked of saving towards them in a letter dated 14 July. *Before I forget, the Dragon School has definitely accepted Alan for September 1950, when he'll be 8 and three quarters. I'm glad about this, the only problem now is to pay the fees, but maybe we can save a bit towards it when I join you.*

The money which my father had sent turned out to be not enough, as my mother explained on 29 July.

I got my bank statement today and was rather shattered to find there was only £51 left in our account. As I owe Mummy for a month, and haven't yet paid Fiona's tonsils operation this isn't going to last very long. Could you please

*send another £50 as soon as possible? I'm afraid I've been
terribly extravagant and I won't get another thing, not even
curtain material. Money just vanishes as you look at it. I do
hate asking you for it, particularly as you probably haven't
got any! It should be better when we're together.*

In a letter dated 3 September she was still worrying about
the expense of the air flight out – more expensive than the
boat, but meaning that she would not be delayed in England
for an extra five months. She also notes that the tonsillitis
operation had cost £25, another blow. She also indicates that
she kept a little money separate from my father, presumably a
kind of dowry, and that she did not want him to borrow money
in India. The plan to make savings for my future school fees, as
far as I know, never materialized.

*About paying for our passages, if the company won't
play about advancing the money, I have £100 of my own
which I could use, and would use, you could always pay me
back if you wanted to darling, though what difference it
makes I can't imagine! I'd much rather that than get into
debt, in fact shall be very cross if you do (get into debt I
mean, over this). Thank you for your £50 by the way, half of
it went straight away to pay for Fiona's operation. We must
get our money matters on a basis when I come out. I
suggest we tell the company to put half your pay straight into
the bank at home, as Alan's prep school fees are going to be
something staggering I should think. Anyway we can work it
all out. I refuse to worry about such trifles when I shall be
seeing you in about 6 weeks time.*

The final indication comes in an undated letter from India
in late October. It has the valuable information about the
commission, and also some of the housekeeping expenses and
joint arrangements for the upkeep of myself and my sister. It
also mentions the overdraft – presumably from the bank. I am
not yet sure who Mrs Hayley was or what she did – perhaps
some kind of part-time home help? The only other reference

to her is in my grandmother's letter of 18 October, when she writes, *Mrs Hayley did not come to-day but I expect she was very busy getting straight in her next house.*

The anxieties tended to grow over time and during the next two periods in 1951 and 1954–5 when my parents were apart the letters are even more anxious and filled with monetary worries. I shall not include these here, or the worried accounts of my grandparents, also struggling. They belong to their story.

Enough has been shown here to indicate the constant background of difficulty which my expensive education at boarding schools made even more problematic. The question of my school fees came up several times in the term in letters. For example, on 19 July 1954 my mother wrote to my father, *I shall ask the Dragon to wait a bit for Alans next terms bill if we can't cope, rather than than you borrowing any more.* Then on 30 September she wrote to my father that she did not have enough money for my fees of £95. Three weeks later, on 22 October she wrote in some relief. *I got a letter from the Dragon School this morning, saying they would reduce Alan's fees by 10 gns a term and enclosing a cheque for that amount to square last terms account. I was most agreeably surprised and will now go and buy Alan's new coat, with the happy feeling that I'm not spending anything. You mustn't go and visit him in a large Bentley or it'll look fishy.* Actually, a large Bentley was the last thing we could afford.

In a letter of 10 October she spoke of the continued financial difficulty, this time of the school uniform. *I've had a series of letters from Alan's matron saying "Where is Alan's second coat?" "What about gumboots". I'd hoped to get away with not sending them as he needs new ones but shall have to do something now.* At the time, as far as I remember, I was largely unaware of any of this, but it no doubt coloured our life in numerous ways.

*

My parents and grandparents never had enough land or wealth to keep large livestock, as they had been accustomed to in India. They began to keep chickens. My grandmother specialized in White Sussex and Red Leghorns, and started in a modest way with a dozen or so. But as she found it made money, especially if she could glean corn for free or get scraps from her household and neighbours, her enormous energy and organizing skills turned it into a commercial exercise.

A considerable amount of work was involved and was rather unpleasant at times, especially in muddy winter weeks. We children were, of course, roped in, not normally for routine feeding or egg collection, though there was some of that, but in sudden 'purges'. On a particularly beautiful sunny day my grandmother would announce at breakfast that we would be moving a chicken house and run, or creosoting a shed or similar 'chore' which would take up the whole day – much to my indignation.

I still remember squashing, scorching and destroying vermin and the ragged chickens suffering from various diseases. In particular I remember an attack of the blood-sucking red mite which we had to clean out of the sheds with a blow lamp. My memory is obviously of an event which my grandfather mentions in his diary on 1 August 1952. 'Chickens badly affects by red mite. Sprayed house.' Then on the 4 'Got blow lamp from Warren. A[lan] and Robert cleaned two hen houses'.

Yet I also remember the delight of the newborn chicks, the excitement of seeing a nest-full of eggs, and the beauty of some of the cockerels. No doubt this activity channelled some of my grandmother's energy and hence made us freer, as well as better fed. I suspect my grandmother was part of a bartering network in which quite a lot of eggs went in exchange, for example for the milk of our neighbour down the road. The spirit of the war lived on.

Here is the account as it unfolds in my mother's and grandparent's letters of a small chicken business which played a significant part in the background to my childhood. My parents started to keep chickens in Assam around the same period as the venture started in England, but there it was at least possible to hire very cheap labour to look after them.

*

On 19 April 1948 my mother gave advice to my father:

> *I'm glad about the chickens darling – the main thing is to feed them – I suggest you keep a deshie* [large dish] *for scraps and see it every day, they must have one cooked meal a day with a bit of meat or fish if possible in with the rest, and some sort of "meal" mixed with it, and corn in the morning. You know all this of course, and plenty of water. I suppose tics are the chief menace, and an occasional dipping of each bird into disinfectant might be good. I shouldn't try to set any eggs for a bit – you do realize you need a cock around for that don't you?!*

This experiment was not only useful in itself, but my mother suggested that it might be a good thing to do when they left tea-planting, a dream which she constantly turned to. So on 6 May she wrote *When we retire we must have some fruit trees and currant bushes and bees and chickens – I'm thoroughly won over to a cabbage life and feel I would be perfectly happy to be caked in mud and manure for all my days.*

Five weeks later, on 15 June, she wrote encouragingly again, and gave a first glimpse of what would turn into a large enterprise by my grandmother.

> *I was so glad to hear from Alan's letter that your chicks hatched. I hope they're all thriving – you have to feed them 4 hours you know. Mummy gives them fine uncooked oatmeal, breadcrumbs and hardboiled egg, cooked porridge, milk and things like ground rice and barley. Lots of water too, and greenstuff after a fortnight. One of ours has died and another looks like it. Mummy now has 34 chickens altogether, I cant think why, she spends pounds and pounds on them and never stops cooking their messes, it seems silly to me when 6 hens would provide us with*

*enough eggs. As it is she has lots of people registered on us
and we really don't see many eggs ourselves.*[1]

There are signs of tension here which continues later as the
chickens multiplied. It was clearly, along with gambling on
horses, the main outlet for my grandmother, still quite a young
woman and used to running a large household for many years
in India. This experience was already modifying my mother's
dreams about chickens, though she was still able to write on 12
September, *I should love to have an orchard full of apples and
bees, and an enormous fruit-cage for soft fruit and a handful of
chickens.*

When my mother returned to India a month later she wrote
about the progress of the chickens, which was now becoming a
bond between Assam and Broadstone. On 30 November she
wrote to me about the ducks and chickens.

The following spring, on 15 April 1949 my mother
described how, *I'm going to have a cup of tea before I start on
the chickens, with the two broodies and the babies I find it
takes hours. I expect you help Granny with all hers don't you, I
hope so.* I am not sure how helpful I was at this stage, but later
I do remember the rather unwilling help I gave on special
occasions.

In May 1950, the chickens in Assam were a part of the
ritual of the day. *Every day is much the same now and I seem
to spend hours and hours standing about watching Anne feed
the horses or wandering backwards and forwards with scraps
for the chickens.* Filling time was a difficulty on a tea garden,
and animals helped for my mother.

When she returned to England in late 1950 my mother
found that my grandmother's chicken farming had expanded.
On 20 March 1951 she wrote to my father about looking after
the hens in my grandmother's absence:

---

[1] People had to register with suppliers to be able to use ration books,
so my grandmother must have been registered, allowing her to have
access to chicken meal. She could exchange egg coupons for chicken
food with neighbours.

The reason for the delay is just tiredness I'm afraid. I'm finding Mummy's hens a bit of a handful as it has rained solidly for two day (and intermittently for a week) and the garden is a quagmire. The 60 hens are divided into runs of about 6 each and each run is surrounded by a sea of mud through which I plod four times a day, my galoshes sucked off at every second step, clutching huge tins of food and baskets of eggs. As well there are 20 baby chicks who need constant attention and who are housed in a groggy arrangement of wire, sheets of tin and bits of sacking and surrounded by more mud and brambles. The only way to put their food into them is to lie on your stomach and lift the contraption bodily. My temper has been severely tried I'm afraid and it has made me vow never to keep hens on a large scale, not at home anyway. In between feeding these brutes I have to peddle down to Broadstone...

A week later on 28 she was equally irritated. *Well I'm back home [in Pinecot] and have been for nearly a week, it was nice to get back. I find Mummy's house very cold after this one and as for those hens!*

My mother's feelings and my grandmother's enthusiasm are again caught in a letter a few months later on 6 May. *Mummy is getting more and more chickens, she has 30 babies in the spare bedroom and the whole house stinks of them – she's having complaints from some of the neighbours as the cockerels crow at 4 in the morning. I really think she is over-doing it a bit, but she always does, when she starts anything in the animal line.*

Complaining neighbours were not the only problem, as my mother wrote two weeks later on 23 May. *Poor Mummy was feeling very upset as a fox got in last night and killed seven of her best hens which Daddy had forgotten to shut up. She takes these wretched fowls so seriously and has fought with everyone on the road over them. I don't get it!*

A week later my mother elaborated the picture. *Mummy has baby chicks and full-sized fox-mauled hens all over the house and spends her days pottering round feeding them spoonfuls of oil and milk. Don't know how she does it, the smell and the saucers of stale food and the droppings...!!*

The account of the fox and the first attempts to deal with it is in my grandfather's diary as follows:

Monday 21:	5 hens killed and 2 maimed by fox
Tuesday 22:	One hen on eggs taken by fox
	Fry lends me gun
Wednesday 23:	Sat up for fox, 4.30–6 No luck

My grandfather waited up again every night until the following Monday and then 'Waited up for fox and returned gun to Fry'. On 22 June he noted 'Fox nearly gets young RIRs' [Rhode Island Reds].

The problem with foxes obviously continued, for early the following year on 17 February 1952 I wrote from school to my grandmother *I hope the chickens are getting on okay and no more hens have been caught by fox.* My hopes were in vain, for my grandfather's diary continues the saga a few months later in May as follows.

Wednesday 7:	3 hens taken by fox. Fish monger took them away
	Fixed double wire netting round pullets run
Friday 9:	Ken sat up last night to shoot fox but had no luck
Saturday 10:	Ash set traps for fox

There are various entries about further strengthening of the wire of the chicken runs and then on Tuesday 13, 'Ash sets 2 more traps for fox'. Finally on Thursday 22, 'Caught Vixen in trap and shot it'. The next day he noted that 'George Chesney came and took his gun' (Chesney was a distant cousin, working in Parkstone, Dorset). There was obviously a further attempt at pest control for on Tuesday 10 March he noted, 'Put trap for fox with poisoned hen'. Unfortunately, two days later he wrote 'Caught hedgehog in trap and poisoned hen taken' and then on the 13 'Fox caught in trap but got away'. That seems to have been sufficient as we hear no more of foxes.

Fox or no fox, my grandfather, who struggled out in all weathers to feed chickens and collect eggs, also felt the strain. He wrote on 7 April to my mother in India: *The indoor hens continue to lay well. The 58 young ones will be 8 weeks old the day after tomorrow and are ok. There are 5 cocks among them though the batch is sex linked. It has been a job seeing them through all the bad weather we have had.*

The reference to 'indoor hens' denotes a move from chickens in an outside run to the several large deep-litter chicken houses which began to accumulate on the property, one being recorded as bought on 25 January 1952. (One of the houses was still there in summer 2009 as I remember it, when we visited the house again!).

It looks as if my mother enquired from India as to what kind my grandmother favoured and she replied on 12th August 1952. *The chickens I have are Indian Game x L.S. [Light Sussex] hens and are the cockerels for Christmas and apparently this crossing produces very big and very plump birds.*

A danger to the chickens is mentioned in my next letter on the subject in late February 1953 to my grandparents. *I hope the chickens are getting on allright and none of the chiks have died. I wonder wether any of the chicks have been caught by pudy yet or wether pudy has caught any mice yet.*

I seem to have been impressed when I came home on holiday at the ubiquitous chickens, writing to my mother on 25 March 1953 that: *Granny has got about 36 brown chickens in a big house where they stay all the time and 44 white ones wich are in the same kind of house and they layd 43 eggs. Also she has got 96 chicks in another big house and soon granny will have another sixty day olds.*

There was a hiccup, however, for my grandmother wrote to my mother on 30 April, *Have had a set back with the 2 week old chicks who developed coccydiosis and I've lost 13 but I hope the sulphmeyathine will have put a stop to it now.*

My grandfather's diaries frequently mention the cleaning, creosoting and moving of chicken houses and runs. For example on 7 January 1951 it was noted, 'Fixed up a new run for Leghorns; Old hens put into new quarters' and the next day, 'Cleaned out old and odd hen houses'. The arrival of mash, millet and chicken food is noted. The particular diseases from which the chicks and chickens died, included dropsy and on Friday 10 July 1953 'Coccidosis trouble with chicks'.

A specially unpleasant problem is mentioned on 29 January 1954 when, 'Barton came to advise on hen cannibalism'. The solution is perhaps surprising for on 6 February, 'Men came to put hen spectacles on' and six days later, 'Ballard comes to cut beaks and fit rest of specs'.

As the family contemplated the move away from 'By the Way', the chickens were suddenly swept away by my always impetuous grandmother. On 11th September my mother wrote about my Grandmother's disposal of all her chickens. And then on 30 September my mother wrote, *Things have settled down here and Mummy is back to her racing again and has sold all her hens and houses for £200 odd so is feeling happier.*

Never again would my grandparents try to make money from livestock, though I think we did have a few hens at one point when we bought our first house in the Lake District. But the eggs were strictly for the family.

*

Hens on this scale were a great strain, though I think that my grandparents needed the money and the eggs and the odd chicken to eat was a bonus. Even the half-sized bantams, as much pets as egg-layers, were not easy. I remember the very sweet tiny birds wandering under the apple trees at 'By the Way'. This was probably before they were sent down to my mother's rented house [Pinecot] in Broadstone. Just before we moved on 1 February 1951, my mother wrote, *the only thing that kept Fiona happy was having her pet bantam in bed with her so chicken droppings were added to the general mess.*

My mother writing on 11 February: *Mummy has sent down her 3 bantams and the cock for me to look after which pleases the girls no end, they've been running out with bowls of food for them all day but I don't know how long the enthusiasm will last. The bantams laid 2 eggs this evening in appreciation.* Later in the same letter she notes, *Have been out to see the bantams (Fiona shut them up for the night).*

Even looking after four bantams was a strain, however, alongside everything else. On 20 March my mother wrote *To-morrow is going to be one of those hectic days, getting Anne to school, feeding my bantams, buying fish, rushing back to cook lunch...* Two months later it was over. On 23 May she wrote *I've got rid of my bantams as there wasn't enough room for them here and if they were let out they went into the neighbours gardens and dug up their seeds.*

My grandparents dabbled briefly in two other forms of poultry. On 11 February 1951 my grandfather's diary mentions 'Fixed enclosure for ducks', but a little over two months later, on 14 April, 'Ducks sold yesterday'. There is no further mention of ducks. There is a reference on 17 January 1953 'Partridges light fused – Man came and put light right', and then the next day, 'Partridges have worms'. They may not have been worth the trouble; certainly nothing more is recorded of rearing partridges.

5. PAIN

Medically, the world of the late forties and early fifties seems a foreign country. The National Health Service was just being introduced and the antibiotic revolution and new methods of dentistry were just beginning. The picture I shall paint shows a society much more prone to debilitating pain than children would now be used to in moderately affluent middle class families in the west. This applied both to our home life in Dorset, and to boarding school at the Dragon, where I shall deal with another set of illnesses and pain (measles, chicken pox, mumps and others) which I mainly associate with school.

It is not clear that the absences from kindergarten all relate to illness, but some probably did. They suggest that at that stage there was quite a lot of illness about, and it affected me throughout my time there. The absences were described as 'Half Days'. The figures are as follows (NA = Not Available):

	1947–8	1948–9	1949–50
Winter	NA	3	0
Spring	NA	17	22
Summer	15	NA	12

The Spring term seems to have been the sickliest, and my last Spring I was especially illness-prone.

*

Although we were presumably vaccinated against that deadly disease of childhood, smallpox, there were also other injections, for example my mother mentions on 12th September 1948 before my younger sister went out to India, *I've fitted in a visit to the dentist and Anne's second T.A.B. injection.* And early next year my mother wrote to me on 16 February 1949, *Granpa wrote the other day and said you were going to have Whooping Cough injections but I don't think they are very nasty ones are they?* But for most sickness there was little that could be done in advance and treatment was still rudimentary.

One epidemic disease which struck me before I went to school was measles, which was far more widespread then. My mother wrote to my father on 12th May 1948,

> *The fact is, not a very cheerful one I'm afraid Alan has measles. A pretty nasty go of it too and the last two days have been pretty grim, his temperature yesterday hovering around 105 degrees all day. It came on very suddenly, though he had been off his food for a couple of days before, and his rash was out the first night. To-day his temperature has been down but he has a nasty wheezy sort of cough and as I write is moaning and gasping in his sleep in an alarming way and you know me on these occasions, my insides turn to water and I imagine all the worst possible complications. I'm certainly not looking forward to going through this with Fiona and Anne, they're bound to get it! Still other people do it, so I suppose we shall survive and it will merely be remembered as the first of the infectious diseases they all get. Alan must have picked it up at school as one other small boy came out with it on the same day. Its really the best time of year to indulge if one has to, and there are other consoling points, but on the whole I wish they could have waited until they were older. It is so difficult to get a small child to be philosophical!*

My mother's worries are further elaborated five days later on 17:

> *Darling, I'm afraid my last letter was rather morbid, but Alan was really very seedy and I thought he was getting*

pneumonia and a lot of other fatal diseases with it. Now he is up and about again, for short spells, and will soon pick up I'm sure. He's looking pretty skinny and knock-kneed at the moment! Anyway that is something over, but I feel I shall be in an asylum by the time all three have finished with it! Fiona still looks pale blue but is full of beans with a good appetite and should be fit enough resist going down too bad a crack with measles.

The rest of the family did, indeed, get measles and a week later on 24 May my mother wrote

Darling, I'm afraid I haven't written for a week – I expect you've guessed the reason. Anne and Fiona are both having measles! Anne went down with sickness and a temp last Tuesday, a week to-morrow, and Fiona started on Wednesday. Of course we knew at once what it was but it didn't make it any easier! They were in bed 4 days before the rash came out. Anne with the most desperate cold, and then really turned my insides round and round for 24 hours specially Anne, who lay and gasped in her cot with a roaring temperature and no pulse at all that I could feel. I sat up all one night with her, expecting every breath to be her last. That was yesterday actually, time seems to have stopped altogether this last week. To-day they are both better though feeling like wet rags and utterly fed up with beds. You can imagine what its been like trying to keep them both amused, Anne has been simply impossible poor little thing, and is looking dreadful and they've still got racking coughs but I think they'll pull up in a day or two. It's a good thing to have over but I wish they could have waited a year or two! I feel as if I had been through several bad illnesses myself, completely wrung out, as you know I fuss more than is really necessary. The doctor is very nice, though very young and has 3 small children of his own so was sympathetic. Alan is perfectly fit again, full of cheer although he has been left to his own resources completely since the others were taken ill.

I don't remember this illness at all.

*

Flu struck my family first in Assam from where my mother wrote to me on 22 August 1950:

> *This has been an awful week, starting with an earthquake and ending with flu! Actually neither the earthquake or the flu are quite finished, but I thought I must try and write a line or you might be worrying. .... on Saturday evening Anne and I started feeling coldy and miserable and were both in bed with flu on Sunday. To-day is Wednesday and I am feeling better for the first time since then, so altogether it has been a horrid time. The weather hasn't helped. It has rained almost without stopping since the quake and been very dark and gloomy and we still get shakes about twice a day and night – it seems as if everything has gone wrong and queer suddenly and I wish it would get back to normal. I felt awful with the flu until this morning, and Anne was streaming and coughing next to me poor wee thing, but didn't seem to feel ill and kept cheerful. I hope Daddy doesn't catch it.*

When she returned to England she encountered the serious epidemic of 1951 which caused a considerable mortality. My grandmother was the first to become ill. On 24 January 1951 my mother wrote:

> *Life has been very busy this week as Mummy arrived back from her 3 day holiday with flu and went straight to bed. She is up to-day (6 days later) but is still very wobbly and not able to do anything but sit by the fire. She felt very ill for 3 days, the same symptoms as I had, crashing head and sickness (due to sulpha chiefly) and for two days I felt rather queer myself but think mine was liver!*

The flu did spread and on 11 February, in the midst of moving house from 'By the Way' to Pinecot, my mother reports that she woke up to find both the children sick with it.

*

The constant background of minor irritations and pain, particularly skin complaints such as chaps, chilblains and impetigo, are dealt with in 'Dragon Days' as I principally associate them with schooldays. They are not often mentioned in letters or other sources, and it is easy to forget their constant debilitating effect. One complaint I have only just discovered is in a note in my grandfather's diary for 4 November 1951 when he writes (of my sisters), 'Children have ringworm'.

Likewise it is easy to forget the colds. These are only occasionally mentioned, but happened frequently. On 25 September 1948 my mother wrote to India. *He [Alan] had a sharp cold this week, lay in bed, very happy and pampered for one day. He got it from me.*

When my mother returned to India with my younger sister she wrote on 16 February 1949, *Anne gave us a fright by running a high temperature the day before yesterday, she woke up in the middle of the night and said "Oh my heads broken" and we found she had fever and it went on all day and the next night and then suddenly went again – we never discovered what it was but she was very miserable and very difficult to keep in bed.*

Also practically invisible in the records are numerous minor injuries and accidents as growing children. A few are recorded in my letters from the Dragon. At home the most serious I experienced was a broken arm which occurred before I came to England. Injuries in India were potentially more dangerous. Only one is mentioned, when on 9 August 1954 my mother wrote to my father. *I was so sorry to hear about your leg darling, I can imagine how miserable you must have been imagining that gangrene was setting in and it must have been very painful, I do hate to think of you not well when I'm not there, for goodness sake take care of yourself and don't go chasing tigers in gym shoes.*

There must have been endless small injuries, cuts, grazes and thorns. I do remember that our great salvation was 'Savlon' which must have just arrived as an antiseptic cream at this time; my grand-ather always swore by it and many a potentially septic sore was averted by its use.

My mother describes just one other example of the minor injuries on 28 March 1951.

Easter Monday was a horrid day, the weather was awful, gales and rain all day, and I had a very painful eye which got worse as the day wore on and was quite closed by the evening. I think I must have got something in it and formed a small abscess, I felt frightfully depressed and foresaw the worst as usual, glass eyes and lurid operations figuring largely in my mind, but in the morning it was much better and had subsided by evening!

The worst event was a potentially fatal running-over of my younger sister Anne. I still remember the corner of the street, the screeching car, my mother's panic. Her account of what nearly happened was written on 16 April 1951:

When we came out it was still raining and we had missed a bus so felt a bit let down and then Ann nearly got run over and I was very glad to get home. It still makes me sick to think of Anne's escape, she ran straight out into the road in front of a car, tried to stop and fell flat on her back and it pulled up within inches. It was my fault too because she had been straggling and I said "Come on Anne, we've got to cross" and started to walk towards the edge of the pavement. All the people standing round said loudly to each other "She told the child to come on didn't she" and glanced at me and I didn't know whether to hit them or to be sick. Anyway its taught me a lesson although I keep re-living it and breaking out into a cold sweat. Anne herself hasn't learnt anything I fear and has to be watched like a hawk.

*

Describing each disease in turn gives an impression of the background level of pain. What it does not do is to show much of the anxiety and desperation which an actual illness could cause to a small family. Some of this was buffered for my mother by having her parents at hand, so it is really at its most extreme when she was living on her own.

She wrote again to my father on 11th February 1951,

My dearest, As you will have gathered (I think Mummy wrote to you?) this has been a pretty awful week, but things are at last getting back to normal and I hope we'll all behave reasonably from now on! I think I last wrote on Friday, a depressed letter about Fiona – well on Saturday her temperature went on rising until it was 104 degrees by tea time – you can imagine my feelings, specially as the doctor said when he came that she had bronchitis. I was feeling pretty grim myself and when I'd got the children to bed felt so cold and miserable I lay on the floor in front of my bedroom fire and went to sleep – eventually woke up, took 2 aspirin and crawled into bed – but the next morning, oh dearie me! It was a frightful day, with gales and sleet beating against the window and I woke with 'flu full on me and two sick children to nurse – and no telephone! I collected them both into my bed, turning on the fire and collapsed back to bed. Fiona luckily was a bit better after M & B and Anne more or less alright, she had a mild attack. At 9 I crawled downstairs to give them some breakfast, awful this, I sat with my head between my knees while the eggs boiled and only just managed to get the tray upstairs again before I had a black-out – I was feeling quite desperate as I didn't think the family could possibly get down on such a day – at 11 there was a knock at the door and there was Daddy – I never was so pleased to see anyone in my life! After that everything eased up. Mummy came down with a suitcase to look after us, Fiona got better quite quickly and I got up on Thursday and yesterday (Saturday) I took over the house again. I really realised all along that I was bound to get the wretched thing and you probably realised by the cross and querulous letter I wrote on my arrival that I was getting it, but it was most frustrating that it should come when it did, and Fiona was a great worry.

As my mother noted, she was supported nobly by my grand-parents. We have a parallel account of the events in my grandfather's diary for these two months which shows what they were doing and the kind of support grandparents, albeit living a mile and a half away without a car, could give. The entries are as follows:

Friday 19:	Violet returns and went to bed with flu
Saturday 20:	V bad with flu, Iris also not well
Sunday 21:	V still in bed and feeling rotten
Wednesday 24:	V got up
Monday 29:	Fiona down with flu
Wednesday 31:	Dick Norman comes to see Fiona. Anne also down with flu
Friday 2 February:	Visited Iris at Pinecot – asked White to see her
Saturday 3:	V visits Iris
Sunday 4:	Went to see Iris who has flu Fiona has bronchitis Violet went to their house to stay and help
Tuesday 6:	Took milk to Pinecot
Wednesday 7:	Took milk to Pinecot
Thursday 8:	Took chicken to Pinecot

Friday 9:   Violet came here with Fiona
                   and Ann
Saturday 10:   Mrs Warren drives me to
                   Pinecot – Fiona has ear
                   trouble

The crisis was now over, though there were further visits to Iris noted over the next months.

Even three years later, without a car and a call-out service for the doctor, it was difficult for my mother. On 6 September 1954, just before she left for the Lakes, she wrote that Fiona, *said she had an awful pain in her side and could hardly move her leg. I rang up Dick who said we should bring her down, so off we set again (can't believe a bicycle ride would have done her much good if it had been an appendix but Dick didn't seem to think it mattered) and of course when we got there the pain had gone and she was as bright as a button and I felt rather a fool, it was only indigestion apparently.*

*

There is a good deal about the treatment of children's teeth in the letters. Here I shall only include mention of my teeth – which brings back those days of very painful and inefficient drills which seem suddenly to have given way in the 1960s to something much better.

The first reference is on 3 September 1948 when my mother mentions that I, *went to the dentist on Monday to have a tooth filled, it had been aching very badly on and off and we thought it would have to come out. However it didn't and Alan was marvellous, he never stirred in spite of a lot of drilling which must have been very painful. Fiona's first filling will be Something!*

My capacity to face physical pain, whether in the dentist's chair or on the rugger field, seems to have impressed others.

The next reference is not until 4 August 1953 when my grandfather mentions in his diary 'V. takes Alan to dentist, and then a week later, 'Alan sees dentist – walks home'. Clearly this was a local dentist, probably in Broadstone.

This was the prelude for further treatment, for on 23 of that month I wrote to my parents: *I am probably not going up to scotland as I have to have four teeth out soon. I have got a padder set and we have played one or two games so far. I have had an anethetic and I had four teeth out. I was a bit sick but I am alright now except for a horse throat and my cheek has swolen. Lots of love Alan.* It appears that the operation was in fact on the 25 for my grandfather wrote in his diary under that date 'Alan sees dentist'.

Attached to my letter was one from my grandmother, who wrote,

> *Well – thank goodness that op: is well and truly over and Alan was an absolute <u>brick</u> – I thought this visit to Preston was just to have 2 teeth out and the op: to be arranged for. I let Alan have some breakfast (8 a.m.) and of course I should not have given him anything but Preston and the anaesthetist thought if left till 12 o'clock he would be all right so we trailed out looking at shops. Alan was given an injection which made him very sleepy and contented so I went to see Mr Adney who is not going to bother to operate on me for the time being. Preston sought me out to say all was over and Alan would stay in hospital till the evening so I went home and had lunch and back to sit with Alan and we were brought back by ambulance at 7.30. Alan's face is very swollen but he looks much better to-day – I suggested to Patty, and she thinks it a good idea, that Alan should go up there for Christmas and so I've bought a Padda tennis set as a consolation and Alan is jolly good.*

Dentistry continued the following year for my grandfather mentions in his diary on 29 March 1953, '9.20 Alan dentist appointment' and then again on 7 April '9.40 am Alan dentist'. Then on 31 July my grandmother wrote *I have got to take Alan to the specialist to see about his plate and he will probably have to have another tooth out as his bottom ones are doing the same as the top.*

On 16 August she wrote *The dental man said that Alans plate had been a failure and the only thing now was to take out three teeth, two of them are baby teeth and one is permanent which means that he has now lost two permanent double teeth, a pity but cant be helped.*

A month later on 6 September she wrote again,

> *Thursday was a bad day, I took Alan down to the dentist in the morning and he had three teeth out, he was very nervous and miserable and of course had to have his whole mouth deadened, six injections altogether and then we had to bike back against a stiff wind, I gave him an aspirin and put him to bed. Alan actually had very little pain from his teeth so it all ended alright.*

This brings back the feeling of a plate, trying to get the sticky bits of left-over food out of the wires which held it in place, not to mention the pain. As Woody Allen joked, the one- word answer to those who cry that we should bring back the good old days is 'dentist'!

*

The particularly traumatic experience of this period was visits to the ear specialist in Poole. I inherited narrow and upturned ear channels which were difficult to clean and so it was thought, like my father, I needed to have special attention (though my sisters did not have this I believe). I am not sure when this began, for there is no mention before my mother's return at the end of 1950. I remember two or three sessions. They are again etched on my memory, sitting in a dentist's chair while a small man probed with wires and tweezers against my eardrums. It was terribly painful and I have always found George Orwell's account of the threat of rats eating into the brain in *1984* particularly horrible because of this memory.

As soon as we left for the Lake District the doctor said it was possible to use 'Cerumol' and it was not necessary to use these instruments. I have never really forgiven the ear specialist, whom I now discover was a published leading expert in the field and no doubt very expensive.

The first recorded visit, when I was just nine, is in my grandfather's diary on 21 April 1951: 'Alan to see specialist'. My mother's comment three days later suggests that this was not the first visit. *On Thursday morning I took him to the ear-specialist, a painful business. As he always sobs bitterly, and we missed the bus back and were half an hour late to meet some friends who were taking him to a "Point to Point"...*

I did not go again for three years. My mother mentions on 9 August 1954 that:

> *Thursday, had been a real summer effort, a speciality of this summer anyway, it rained and blew all day and as I had an appointment to take Alan to the ear specialist in the morning I decided I'd give them a treat and take them on to see a film in Bournemouth. We got the ear business over early, Mackenzie Ross was quite pleased with Alan's ears but said it was time he had them done after nearly three years and I have to take him back next week.*

It does not sound from the description a week later on 16 August that it was quite so bad. *Alan and I had to make another trip to Bournemouth, this time another ear appointment, but got it over early and we set off after lunch* [to a county show].

*

I am not sure when I had my tonsils out – perhaps in India. From a throwaway remark it sounds as if it was very painful and difficult, but I do not remember it except possibly the ice creams afterwards. But my mother's graphic accounts of the operation on my sisters' tonsils are worth including as they describe the sort of thing we went through with an operation which now seems not to affect young children. One wonders what has changed. This was also in the pre-Bowlby maternal deprivation days when part of the shock for the child was being abandoned.

The first reference is in an undated letter of February 1948 when my mother wrote to my father: *The throat specialist said Fiona has chronic tonsillitis and I arranged to have the bloody deed done on May 7 in a Bournemouth nursing home. Poor wee thing, she'll be miserable about it all. So will we when we get the bill!*

On 19 April my mother wrote:

I had a letter from the surgeon who is taking out Fiona's tonsils, saying he would like to do it next Wednesday, 21, so I'm taking her into the nursing home on Tuesday evening. Poor little thing, she is in a state of happy anticipation about it, particularly the train journey to Bournemouth, and quite unaware of what is in store for her! It's a good place I believe and there is to be another little girl in with her, so I don't think we can do better. I'm dreading leaving her at the hospital, but it couldn't be worse than Alan's affair. Honestly the misery children inflict on one! She is so fit at the moment I feel a brute.

Four days later she wrote on 23 April:

Dearest, A line to let you know Fiona had her tonsils out on Wednesday 21 and is alright. I took her into the Nursing Home on Tuesday evening and she was very pleased and important and didn't mind a bit my leaving her. There was another little girl with her and they were delighted with the whole set-up so I felt quite happy about it. A different picture when I went into see her this morning poor pet, she was looking like death and begged me to take her away and cried pitifully, it was horrid. The little things are left alone all the time and it must be terrible for them in a strange place and suffering too. I'm going to see if I can't take her out on Sunday, I can't bear it, I've been feeling wretched all day. By the time you get this she will be better so I feel I can let myself go! I suppose I shall go through all this with Anne again – but I won't put her into a hospital alone when she's so wee. I took Fiona in some beads to thread which cheered her up.

Three years later it was the turn of my younger sister Anne. On 20 April 1951 my grandfather noted in his diary 'Anne Tonsilitis' and then my mother wrote on 24 April that:

alas my family have chained me to the house again – Anne this time with tonsillitis. She wasn't really very ill and I was never very worried about her, but was feverish and feeling pretty miserable and stayed in bed for 5 days – till yesterday in fact – on sulpha and penicillin lozenges. She was looking the <u>picture</u> of health but is pale and thin now, however she'll pick up very quickly if this weather goes on. My doctor is not keen on taking out tonsils but is going to give a final verdict in a few days, she was completely clogged up with adenoids and we couldn't take her temperature as she went purple in the face and couldn't breathe! She was very good and slept most of the time, now she's up she feels worse I think and is very cross and convalescent, still I hope she'll pick up quickly.

Then on 6 May, *I took Anne to the doctor on Friday and he says her tonsils and adenoids are both very nasty. Do you think the company would fork up if I had them done at home? Burke did say they should come out, so would you ask him? The Health Scheme has a waiting list of 2 years! If the company won't pay I'll try and delay having it done till we come back.* This alludes to another aspect which is worth noting, namely the cost and how eagerly the National Health service was anticipated.

Ten days later on 15 May my mother gives a vignette of a consultation, along with further reflections on the cost of health care.

I had to take Anne to the throat specialist about her tonsils and spent a long time there, he said her tonsils needed coming out but not urgently, but he was very much against having them done in India, he said the standard there was inferior and he'd had to clean up after so much bad work done in India etc. I muttered about American mission doctors but he dismissed American surgery and swore that Britain was ahead of the world in every branch of medicine and quite carried me away until I began to think that Hughes and Hasselbad were a couple of quacks – on thinking it over it seemed a lot of fuss to make over a very small pair of tonsils. He is a diminutive Scotsman with a bad stammer and very aggressive as a result! When at the end of his tirade I mentioned the Health Scheme he didn't draw breath for a full twenty minutes, having run through the characters of the Labour Government, the Korean War, rubber from Hong Kong, General Macarthur and why the British were a nation of sheep. Eventually I did impress on him that we couldn't afford to have Anne's tonsils out without State Aid and he said he would fix it somehow – in September probably. He's really a very nice little man and an excellent surgeon.

It appears, however, that nothing could be arranged, for two years later my mother wrote from India on 5 June that *We are drawing to the end of our term now, two more weeks and then some exams and then two weeks holiday during which I hope to have Anne's tonsils out.* There is no further reference to this.

6. EDUCATION

My first two schools were kindergartens, pre-preparatory day schools. There are some telling photos of me in my new school cap and uniform going off to my first school. There is also a poem of my mother's which I believe refers to my first day at school with all the pain of the long-drawn separation which school entails.

First Parting

I would not hold you. Yet I know not why
I fear to let you wander from my side.
You are so small, I guard you selfishly
For all your hurts are mine, intensified.

But I have seen you off to school, and turned
And shut the door. I would not keep you back.
My grief for you is more than you have earned,
Mine is the sorrow, mine the only lack.

Yours is the world, your eyes can make it fair;
I would not cloud them with a mother's fears.
I only wish, my darling, I could share
Its newfound beauty with you, through my tears.

Ah no. I would not hold you. This is only
A passing weakness, weighing on my will.
And yet - I never knew a day as lonely
As this which you have left for me to fill.

*

I was just six when the first report on me was written on February 19 1948. I am puzzled as to where the school could have been since we were rather mobile, being in Oxford until late 1947 and then at Charmouth certainly over the Christmas of that year. We moved to Broadstone in late January or February 1948. Perhaps we were at Charmouth just long enough for the 'term and a half' (62 days) referred to in the report by Winifred Whittington, Class Mistress.

The report places me as second place in form 1. The subjects covered were recitation, reading, writing, arithmetic and tables, and art. I was 1 in class in recitation and arithmetic, and 2 in all other subjects. In the exams I got 20/20 in two exams, 18/20 in the other four. My term mark was A in all subjects except writing which was a B. The headmistress wrote that my conduct was 'Excellent'. In the General Remarks it stated: 'Alan has made good progress in the term and a half he has been with us. He is a favourite with the other children. We are very sorry he is going and feel sure he will do well wherever he is.'

This was just to have been a temporary arrangement, for on 9 March 1948 my mother wrote to my father:

> *Did I tell you that I went to see Alan's school the other day? I liked it very much, there was a friendly, "homey" sort of atmosphere and the headmaster was very pleasant and showed me all round. I was rather over-awed at having to interview an official school-master and tried to ask intelligent questions without appearing inquisitive – anyway he accepted Alan which was the main thing and he is starting at the end of April. Fiona will be able to go to a Nursery School just opposite in the autumn so it should work in. I try to teach them a little occasionally but somehow something else always crops up to divert us.*

A month later on 19 April my mother wrote again: *He starts school on Monday 26 in spite of best intentions I haven't mentioned the subject of sums or letters to him for weeks and*

I'm afraid he's going to be very backward at first. In a letter four days later on 23, my mother wrote again, *Alan starts school on Monday and I bought him his school uniform, a dream of a coat (£4.6.3!) a cap, tie, and belt, it made me feel very old to see him all dressed up.*

Only a week later there is a fuller account.

> *Alan is still enjoying school, they play games and have break and then stories and some singing, I don't quite know where the actual teaching comes in ... He is a problem Alan, he is getting so difficult and rowdy and sticks out his tongue at me if I tell him anything. I sometimes feel I just can't control him. In fact I feel it several times a day! I know a good thrashing would do him good but can't bring myself to it, thou' he gets cuffed all day long. I suppose he's a normal small boy, and though I wouldn't have him otherwise I am too tired really to appreciate the fact.*

I shall come back to my character later, but it is worth noting that within a week of going to school my aggression and self-confidence seems to have increased.

On 29 May my mother wrote about me to my father. *He is an interesting creature, full of fun, but exasperating. His headmistress said they were delighted with him at school, he was such a "keen worker."! I wish they could hear his comments about "that bloody school"!* I can't really believe that I swore in this way at the age of six, but still.

I had always thought that my Southlands Kindergarten was in Corfe Mullen, a small village half a mile from our house and there was some confirmation in the presence of a Southlands Road there. But there was no sign of a school when we visited it. But on re-reading my mother's comments I came across the following. On 2 June 1948 she wrote: *Guess who I met in Broadstone the other day – Betty Deane. This is her home and she lives just near Alan's school!* Since there is evidence that my sister went to the same school and we have located her school as opposite our Pinecot house, I began to wonder whether I went to the school there – in which case there are signs of a large, school-like, front.

Putting this new information into 'Google' I have come up with a Kelly's Directory which for 1939 gives the following commercial property: Southland School, York Road, Guy C. Barnard M.Sc and Mrs M.M. Barnard, Principals. This ties in exactly with the signatures of my headmistress from Summer Term 1948, which is that of M. Margery Barnard, High Cert. N.F.U. L.R.A.M. So this is the school. This means that instead of the short journey across the heath, I had to be taken over a mile each way to school and there was no bus service. How this was done, I am not sure, until I could bicycle. The bicycle came quite quickly, in fact, being bought in June and I was riding before the start of my second term at the school.

After less than two months at Southlands school, aged six-and-a-half, my mother had already despaired of me. Writing to my father on 22 June she reported that though I was dogged and courageous in learning to ride my newly purchased bicycle, I was not showing any academic progress. *He doesn't appear to be learning anything at school, except, I suppose, the ability to mix. He doesn't seem to want to learn to read, so I have abandoned all hopes of him being literary! Fiona will be brighter, I think and Anne who shows signs of a good memory too, she knows most Nursery Rhymes already.* If she conveyed any of this disappointment, or of her impending anxiety at the thought of leaving me three months later to return to India, then it is perhaps not surprising that there were problems.

In the same letter she commented on my short attention span in relation to fruit picking. This was the same defect which she emphasized when she wrote a month later to my father about my first school report from Southlands. On 22 July she wrote *It was Alan's last day at school and he brought back his report which I enclose. Not very brilliant, he is so hindered by his inability to concentrate on anything that is the least difficult. I hope he will get over it as he* **is** *intelligent. However as its his first term I don't think we need bother too much.*

I have the report beside me for this term. The form is 'Kindergarten' and I am aged six years and seven months, a month older than average. The assessments read as follows:

Reading	Good
Writing	Neat work but he is very slow
Spelling	Satisfactory work
English literature	Good. But could pay more attention
Arithmetic	Good, but not enough work
Handwork	Very slow
Art	Good
Singing	Quite good
Physical training	Good
Games	Good
General Conduct	Good, but he is inclined to dream

All but singing are signed by 'SAW', who taught me for my first two terms. The principal remarked on the report 'Alan has worked well. He is a shy but very pleasant little boy.'

My mother obviously hoped I would immediately show my brilliance, and the several references to 'very slow' or 'not enough work', and even dreaming, she interpreted in a bad light.

There were some brighter signs, however. The day before I returned for my second term at Southlands, 18 September, and shortly before leaving for India, my mother wrote to my father:

> *There is a small 6-year-old boy staying next door who lives with us to all intents and purposes – to my great joy he is actually smaller than Alan! A goes back to school to-morrow, which is a mixed blessing, he gets over-tired and doesn't look nearly as fit in the term time. He is beginning to read a little, but his arithmetic is really quite amazing I think – we asked him the one about a herring and a half costing one and a half pence and he got it straightaway with hardly a pause. He is my pride and despair alternatively. He can be so sweet and helpful and in between is a bully and a brute!*

A week later on 25 September my mother sent a letter which included something of mine which my mother proclaimed as *Alan's unaided work, especially for you*, but which is lost. She writes, with the knowledge that for the next two years our only form of communication would be through letters, *I wish Alan would learnt to write, he is really no further with either reading or writing and very backward in both, it is just lack of effort as he's quite intelligent otherwise... He is happy at school, but doesn't appear to gain much solid fact. Fiona will be catching him up in no time.* At this time Fiona had not even arrived at Southlands school. This is her last surviving letter before disappearing from my life in mid October for two years.

The only other reference in a letter is a year later on 16 August 1949 when my mother wrote to me and my sister that *We thought your reports were very good and are glad you are moving up Alan.*

There are five end-of-term reports surviving for the six terms while my mother was away in Assam. In order not to clutter the text with too much detail I shall summarize them, picking out one or two most salient points.

In Autumn term 1948, aged 7-0 I was still in the kindergarten and now nearly a year older than the form average. The reports were very positive. In reading 'Alan has worked hard. Excellent progress', in spelling I was 'very much improved', in story telling I was 'very keen' and 'most interested' in music. In other subjects I was very good – writing, arithmetic, handwork and physical training and good in English literature and games. My general conduct was 'Excellent. He is a very helpful little boy.' The headmistress wrote, 'Alan has made considerable progress this term he is a very able and a very attractive little boy.' This fits with my grandmother's assessment that my sister and I took my mother's departure stoically.

It was probably around this time that I made my first – and almost my last – appearance in a play. I have the programme for two school plays, with some holly and balloons on the outside which suggests that it was a Christmas performance.

'The Kindergarten Present' "The King and Queen's Daughter"'. Among the named actors is Alan Macfarlane who suitably for a future anthropologist plays the Red Indian Prince.

The spring report is missing, but that of Summer 1949 shows me still in the Kindergarten and still over a year older than others at 7 years 7 months. All reports speak of me as being 'good' and are now signed by another teacher. My general conduct was 'Excellent. Alan is always willing to assist quietly and cheerfully.' The Principal reported 'Alan has had a really good term and he has gained confidence. He will go to the Transition next term. He is a particularly nice little boy.'

Two terms later, in Autumn 1949, I was eight and in Transition, aged nearly six months older than the average. I was now being taught by at least three teachers and the reports were again good. I was 'Very good' in Arithmetic, where I worked 'intelligently' and in English literature and physical training. I was good in writing history, scripture, nature study, geography, handwork and games. I was 'fairly good' or 'fair' in reading and art. But in spelling I was 'much below average for his age' and 'a very slow worker' in composition. My general conduct was 'Good' and the principal wrote, 'Alan has improved very steadily this term. He has worked very keenly and well'.

One point needs to be made in relation to the wording of school reports which, though it comes out in the Dragon years, also applies to these kindergarten reports, and particularly to the frequent use of 'fair' or 'very fair'. I have often wondered whether these ratings meant 'pretty awful, but not terrible', or 'quite reasonably good'. I also wondered whether 'very fair' meant better than fair, or the reverse.

This is related to the wider difficulty of reading the deeper opinion of teachers. Their problem, as I have encountered it over the years as a teacher, is that one needs to be honest in pointing to deficiencies but also encouraging. In the Christmas 1953 issue of the *Draconian*, the school magazine of my preparatory school, the writer notes 'Staff made their way, appropriately, to the Silence Room, where report forms awaited them, to spend an hour or two in trying to think up some new and original euphemisms, before falling back once again on the old ones. And come to think of it, "Very fair" will do well enough as a report on this term, which if it never hit any very high spots, was nevertheless pleasant enough...' It is clear that 'very fair' was assumed to mean just that – alright, but not particularly good, and by implication, I think, 'very fair' was better than 'fair'. We have to think of weather reports, where 'very fair' and 'fair' mean reasonable days, but not really good.

In the Spring term of 1950, aged eight years and three months, and still almost half a year older than average, I was in form 1. I had obviously been ill as there were 22 days of absence, and this is referred to in the Principal's remarks. The report is much as before, with mainly good and very good. The Principal wrote 'Alan has worked well this term. With better health and steadier attendance he should do well.' Apart from one letter in which I mention a cold, however there is no indication of what was wrong with me.

The final report, when I was aged 8 years and 7 months and still over half a year older than average, and back in Transition (though for what reason I moved backwards, I do not know), was roughly the same. In spelling I was 'Good, much improvement this term', but in writing only 'fairly good', 'Alan persists in forming the letter "a" incorrectly'. In fact, I was clearly mildly dyslexic until I was about nine. For example, a letter I wrote from Scotland on July 14 1949, when I was seven-and-a-half, has 'I have a fishing rob', 'Scotlanb', 'anb', 'frienb'. No doubt I shall find the reversed 'a' as well. The Principal hoped well for me, though she clearly saw no stellar career ahead. 'A good term on the whole. Alan is a delightful little boy and quite capable. We wish him all success.'

What emerges from all this? The overall impression from the reports is that I enjoyed my school, tried reasonably hard, was generally liked, was enthusiastic, and not too miserable. There is no talk of any problems or sadness, and some of cheerfulness and helpfulness and popularity. This account needs to be placed alongside my mother's account of my temperament and character since this seems to be have been somewhat difficult at this stage. I was well behaved at school, and, I think, with my grandparents. But the last few months of my mother's time before she left was very mixed.

What is also clear is that in the two years of preparation for the Dragon I was covering quite a wide range of the subjects I would continue to study. It is also clear that I was just about average. The reports were moderately good, but I was always at least half a year older than the average, and seem to have stayed in transition – with a brief move up. Nor was the early sign of mathematical ability, which my mother hopefully noted, developed at this stage. My best subjects were really geography and nature study. My worst were, as my mother had noted, reading and writing.

*

In September 1950, aged eight and three-quarters, I was sent off to my first boarding school, the Dragon School in Oxford. The full account of my time there until July 1955 is given elsewhere. Here I will just write briefly about the intersection between home life and a boarding school.

The reasons for sending me away to boarding school are fairly obvious. First, it was a middle-class custom which had been going on in my family for many generations, from early days when my ancestors were sent home from Jamaica or India or Burma, down to my own parents. My father had been sent home from Mexico to Dollar Academy in Scotland, where, for part of the time, he had been miserable. My mother's parents in India had sent her to a succession of boarding schools. My mother's brothers had all been through boarding preparatory schools and then public boarding schools. It was what you did – there was no questioning it.

It was supposed to bring a number of virtues – self-confidence, toughness, resilience, team spirit, as well as teach you manners, middle-class ways of deportment and speech, the basics of reading, writing, arithmetic and other formal studies. Without getting on the first rung of the ladder and being toughened up to a certain degree, the next stages, boarding school and then perhaps university, would be extremely difficult. And without that experience, how would one learn about one's own culture and identity as an English gentleman, ready to return to the far-flung Empire which one was destined to rule? And girls needed to be sent home to be shaped into suitable spouses and daughters.

There were also strong practical reasons. For generations my family had been living in hot, unhealthy, remote parts of the world. When their children were sent home for education, someone had to look after them. There was only so much you could ask retired grandparents or aunts to do. They could look after them for the holidays, but it would be a huge burden if the children were not sent off to board. Furthermore, it was believed that the indulgence of home life would spoil the child. They needed the discipline of unrelated strangers, both teachers and other little boys, to bring them under control and temper the steel of their character.

Yet there were counter-arguments. My parents were miserable at their boarding schools and did not want to inflict on us. My mother desperately wanted to bring up her own children and made great efforts to do so – for example the system taking my sisters out to Assam when they were seven and five and educating them through a special scheme, PNEU (Parent's National Educational Union) for the next two-and-a-half years. This was just possible for girls, though she writes that, 'I was considered very eccentric for keeping the girls out in India till they were ten and eight'. Yet for a boy it was thought especially necessary that he go to a preparatory school in England, even though this cost my mother so very much.

So there was really no alternative, or so it seemed to my parents, even if it caused so much misery, as well as considerable expense in fees, clothes and other things.

As for why they chose the Dragon, as yet there is no particular evidence as yet. We had lived five minutes away from the school when we returned from India in 1947 and had bathed in the river by the school and watched cricket in the school grounds. So they knew something of it. My second cousins, the Mermagens, had sent two of their sons to the school already and a third, Jonny as I knew him, joined me there in my third year. These may have been factors. They must also have been aware of its reputation not only as one of the best preparatory schools in the country, but also as particularly liberal, tolerant and open. The only hint of this is when my mother noted in her 'Daughters of the Empire' (135) that the Dragon 'was a famous school and we thought we were doing the best thing possible for him.'

*

So I went off to the Dragon for my five years of preparation for adulthood. How children adapted to the tensions between their boarding school life and home in the holidays has not been examined much. It is difficult to find retrospective evidence on this. It is also difficult to get independent evidence on how I regarded going back to school, or returning for the holidays. More generally, there is usually only indirect evidence as to how happy or unhappy I was during these years at boarding school.

My own views on what I felt are distorted by time. It is clear, however, from this account and school reports on the absence of smiles and indirectly from the fact that I put on hardly any weight, that I was quite an anxious little boy – though intrepid on the sports field. It is also clear that I mostly enjoyed the school and looked forward to returning to it – especially during my last couple of years. This is borne out by the cheerful tone of my letters.

For the moment, here are the fragments from letters to suggest something of the interface between the boarding life and school holidays, and my parents, and grandparents, assessments of my physical and psychological state, mixed with a few comments of my own.

Let me start with the only evidence I have yet found of my feelings in advance of going to the Dragon. In a letter dated 8 July 1950, some ten weeks before I would go off to boarding school, I wrote to my parents, expressing both anticipation of the school and also my feelings about my parents' absence and return. I have left the atrocious spelling, as well as other indications of my hopes and dreams and activities.

> *Dear Momy and dady and Ann off corse. I hope you are all very well. I am looking forwod to when you are coming Back. I exspect I will like the dragen it sounds lovly. I wish dady could come too and we could have lovly fun. I am very keen on Airplans I think I will be a Airman. It is a exiting life. The deans have been very very kind [kinb – reversed b] nearly evry week they ask me to play. I have got the lovl pasel from you with your cloths in it. The day after tomorrow is exams day of July we have the exams it is a lovl day it is the 8 now Saturday July*
>
> *Lots of love alan I did it all by my self they don't now I have evon dunit Lots of love Fiona and Alan xxxxxxxxooooo*
>
> *Very many happy returns of your Birthday XO*

My mother returned on her own in November 1950, and her first visit is described in a letter to my father from the hotel in Oxford.

> *My heart sank rather at the completely silent little boy at my side – he has changed even more than Fiona and is no longer the "heart throb" of the family. Actually I didn't think he was looking very well, his face is much thinner and he has deep black lines under his eyes again and frowned a lot, however I hasten to add that he seems very happy at school and I expect after this first term (which is bound to be a strain) will probably lose that anxious expression. It must have been an ordeal meeting me again and he told me later he didn't recognise me. We had lunch here and he thawed a lot, and afterwards he taught me "knock-out Whist" a whizzo game that is the rage at school now.*

When I returned on holidays after my second term, my mother wrote on 16 April 1951, *Alan is becoming his usual non-prep school self again and is almost too much for me on*

109

occasions. His nagging of Fiona is absolutely incessant. This morning I lost my temper with him. This suggests that the school was already disciplining me in a way which, without my father, my mother found extremely difficult.

Yet two weeks later both her affection, and my enjoyment of the holidays are shown in a letter of 19 April.

> *I shall hate saying goodbye to Alan and he is already saying "Oh how fleb, the hols are almost over" every few minutes ("fleb" is his favourite expression, meaning everything that is awful, as opposed to "beefy" which is usual applied to himself!). I shall miss him so much, he is more of a companion to me than the girls are yet. And is a very affectionate little boy, although terribly irritating at times!*

Just after I left for my first summer term my mother wrote on 6 May *Alan went off on Tuesday, very cheerfully I was glad to see. I think he was quite looking forward to being among the "chaps" again.* The difficulty of imposing discipline, and the relief that someone else was doing this, a central reason the English sent their children to boarding schools, comes up in a comment in the same letter to my father, *Poor Alan, now of course I miss him terribly but really I think it was time for a bit more discipline. I hope I haven't given you the impression that he is an unpleasant character. He is a typical small boy I fancy who needs a good belting now and then and <u>definitely</u> a father?* There is also a revealing comment about the difference between how I seemed physically at home and on her two visits to see me in my first two terms. *He was looking so well when he left, fat rosy cheeks and his hair bright and curly. When I take him out from school he has dark lines under his eyes and the little hair they leave him is plastered to his head and he looks awful.*

During my first summer, she seemed to think I was happy. On 6 June she wrote, *I heard from Alan yesterday, six riddles and the startling news that they were wearing Aertex vests! He seems happy though.* Then my father returned and we were together until January 1952 when my parents went off to India with both my sisters. I was left with my grandparents and at the start of my second Easter term, on 20 January 1952 I wrote to my grandmother, *I am enjoying school Already and the days are much quicker now.*

I returned for the Easter holidays on 28 March and my grandfather wrote to my parents about me. On 7 April he reported that: *Alan's being a very good boy and his old self especially now that Robert is here.* Then, towards the end of the holidays on 30 April he wrote again. *Alan is very fit and looking grand. He seems to have enjoyed his time at Milford (a camp by the sea)... Alan has been as good as gold and is a dear boy. Robert and he have been good companions. Alan has never groused once and takes everything in his stride very philosophically.*

In the summer holidays my Grandmother wrote on 12 August, *Alan is full of beans ... and he is very happy with his 2 uncles.* Then on 19 of September my grandfather wrote to my mother that, *Alan is very fit indeed and very cheery. Robert is very good at keeping him amused and they play a lot of soccer. Alan should develop into a good player with all this practice. He goes to school on Monday 22 and his box has been packed and is waiting to be collected by the railway.*

Within a few days of the start of term, on 28 September, I wrote to my parents *Dear Mummy and Daddy. I am having a nice time. We are playing rugger now and I am in fourth game.* The next comment is six months later, at the end of my third Easter term when, on 25 March 1953 I wrote to my parents from our house 'By the Way' as follows. *Dear Mummy and Daddy, It was nice getting back to By-the-way after a very pleasant term.* My grandparents gave me love, food and entertainment so that at the end of the holidays my Grandmother could write on 30 April *He comes back from school so mute and quiet but returns (to) his own cheery – even cheeky – self and he does look grand.*

I seem to have settled in reasonably for my third summer term, writing to my parents on 3 May, *Dear Mummy and Dady, I have been at school for 2 and a half days so far. I am in a dorm called Pheonix wich is a big dorm and I am having jolly good fun.* My next comment on my state of mind comes two terms later when on 2 February 1954 I wrote, *Dear Mummy and Daddy, we have had freezing weather. And I have not played any games (except ice hockey). We have had a wizard time except for the cold as I have lost my gloves.*

My mother returned after a two-and- a-half year absence in June 1954 and came to see me at school. My reaction seems to have been much more positive than her experience in 1950. On 29 June she wrote about her trip to my father: *It was most exhausting and expensive but of course lovely to see Alan again, just the same, he doesn't appear to have grown much but was looking very well and was full of chat.*

When I returned home for that summer, my mother gives a description of my general state on 25 July.

> *Quite an eventful week and the house is bulging at the seams with Robert and Alan back, its great fun to be held up by masked gunmen behind every door and the stutter of machine gun fire echoes down Corfe Lodge Road to the discomfort of the few of them who aren't stone deaf.*

Nevertheless, she is still worried about my development, commenting that, *Alan still doesn't seem to have reached the constructive stage, meccano or model aeroplanes – but is much more independent and its so nice that the three of them can at least meet on common ground.* Later in the holidays she writes on 9 August that *The kids are fine, Alan is full of cheer and the three of them get on very well when they're not fighting furiously.*

When I left for the start of my last year, my mother wrote on about 23 September 1954, *Alan went off very cheerfully, I haven't heard if he arrived, he was to spend the day with my godmother in London and catch the train to Oxford in the evening.* She then visited me for a performance of Iolanthe and wrote on 14 November:

I'm just back from a Sunday taking Alan out, and am sitting in my cheerless hotel room feeling very tired and a bit sad as I always do after leaving him, wish you were here to take me out and give me a brandy! But I was very pleased with Alan who looks very well and was most cheerful and full of chat.

I returned from the Dragon a few days early as there was an influenza epidemic and on 15 December my mother wrote, *Alan came back on Saturday, as I think I told you, in good form and very chatty, but yesterday morning (Tuesday) he started feeling low, and to-day has been in bed with 'flu – so I'm relieved I got him back in time to nurse him here.*

At the end of these holidays, on 11ᵗʰ January 1955, my mother wrote, *Alan and Fiona are both looking forward to going back, but Annie is very undecided.* In a slightly pained note the following week, she wrote *I shan't go down to Oxford this term, Alan doesn't seem to mind whether I do or not!* Yet she seemed to think I was quite content, writing on 22 January that, *Fiona has asked if she can bring a friend to stay next holidays, they haven't wasted much time, so different from Alan, though in his quiet way he seems to be quite satisfied.*

The final comment, when I returned from my last Easter Term, is positive. On 27 March my mother wrote *Alan arrived on Friday evening a friend of his travels all the way with him and they seem to enjoy the journey. His sickness turned out to be nothing, thank heavens. He looks tired as usual after the term but very cheerful and is very absorbed with his electric trains and is really taking pains and concentrating on them which is a change.* This illness, was noted in my mother's diary: March 19 Alan sick 22 – Alan better.

Both my parents visited me in my last summer term, my mother noting in her diary for June:

10   To Oxford. To Woodstock for night.
11   Alan's fathers match 12 p.m. He made 6.
12   On river with Robert. Cold & wet. To film "Laughter in Paradise"

I remember this occasion well, not the cricket match, but because of its finale. We missed the last bus back from the river and decided to split into two groups to try to hitch a lift back to Oxford. My father and I got a lift almost straight away from another Dragon boy's parents. My mother and Robert stood in the rain for several hours and arrived bedraggled and very irritated at the Randolph Hotel. I was somewhat embarrassed by it all.

If this were all the evidence, it would suggest that while I found the terms a strain and needed the holidays to relax, be wild, eat and play, I was, on the whole fairly happy and content at school. It also shows that the rhythm of discipline at school and relaxed support, and my grandmother's good cooking at home, was quite a satisfactory one. The remarks certainly dispel the rather negative memories of my purgatorial childhood at a boarding school. I seem to have been happy to return to it, and reported that I was having a whizzo time, even in the depths of winter.

*

In 'Dragon Days' I describe the very special ideology and culture of the school, the fairly harsh material life, and my progress through the various classes and forms. We learnt Latin, French, English and history, geography, science and divinity in formal lessons. But more important were the worlds we explored in our minds, through comics and books, films and the start of television, plays and musicals. There we went to numerous lectures, sermons and speeches and participated in debates on topical issues. I learnt to paint, to make things, and to sing and appreciate music.

Perhaps most importantly we learnt through socializing with other little boys. Formal team games taught us how to be brave and how to work together and I ended up, to my parents' delight, with my school colours for rugger, football, hockey and cricket. Numerous playground games, particularly marbles, conkers and various ball games taught us life skills like risk assessment, the ability to win and to lose without worrying too much and the laws of the market, and we indulged in numerous hobbies and crazes which complemented the playground games. Here the school and home worlds overlapped, as they did in so many ways in our imagination.

I shall end the account of my early schooling by describing the results of my final term at the Dragon. My last school report, in the summer of 1955, noted that I had missed one day in the term, and was a few months older than the average in most classes, but was now doing well. In Classics in Upper 2B [the third class from the top of the school] I was placed thirteenth in term marks and eleventh in a class of 17. 'He has made v.good progress with v.good exams to finish up. Best wishes.' In English and History, in a class of 17 I was equal eighth and in the exams equal ninth in English and equal sixth in History. 'A very good term's work. Don't stop using your imagination in English. Well done.' In Mathematics, which was my best subject, in the second to top set I was equal first in the term's marks out of 18 and fourth in exams, 'A thoroughly good term's work: well done!' Even Geography, which had long been my weakest subject, was satisfactory. I was equal tenth out of 34 in term's marks and twelfth in exams and this was 'Very good'. Divinity was 'v.g. and Science 'Very satisfactory'. Joc my housemaster and the Junior Headmaster significantly wrote, 'Alan has done very well all round, and the smile has nearly ousted the frown! Best of luck to him at Sedbergh'. Hum the Senior Headmaster wrote 'Highly satisfactory – We all wish him a happy and useful career'.

Let me end on a positive note after the difficult start. This is also revealing about my mother's anxieties about me. After almost despairing of the little boy she had so adored, she discovered that I was less of a worry than she and my father had long feared. In November 1954 my mother felt she had to talk to the headmaster, Joc, about my progress and in particular whether I would pass my entrance into the next stage of my education, Sedbergh School. She wrote to my father about the interview.

> *I went to chapel service this morning and afterwards had my interview with Joc. He was very charming, gave me a sherry, and said Alan would definitely get through his Common Entrance but didn't think there was much hope of a scholarship but he would discuss this with his masters at more length. He said Alan was very popular with the other boys and with the staff which pleased me as Alan never introduces me to his friends or in fact mentions them! He also praised his rugger, especially his tackling which was marvellous he said, poor Alan, he told me he never enjoyed a game of rugger till it was over! Joc said there was terrific excitement over his Colours, much more than over the average boys, all of which pleased me a lot and will you too I'm sure, apparently he isn't the problem we have always imagined him to be!*

I stayed at the Dragon until the end of the summer term 1955.

*

Education at school was interwoven with that at home, which in turn is related to character. Obviously my mother's observations, mainly to my father, need to be set in context. My mother was relatively young by western standards as we grew up – by the start of these letters she was only twenty-five and had three children aged six, four and two. She was trying to cope with them while living with her parents in a shared house, with little money, with my father away in India and with all the austerity of the immediate post-war period. She was missing my father enormously and uncertain about how to bring us up.

My mother nearly always worried about me, and occasionally despaired. The reasons for this had much to do with her own high hopes and expectations, which I usually failed to meet, and her desperate desire to love and protect me, which she often could not do when she left me at home. It also has much to do with her own character, as I shall explore elsewhere, but which is revealed fleetingly in the poem below.

My mother wished me to be all that she had missed in her own childhood. She expressed her hopes and her sense of what she and my father had sacrificed for me in a poem on my first birthday in India. It is worth quoting this to see her high expectations and dreams which the confusing little boy seemed no longer to fulfil as he grew up.

First birthday (December 1942)

Fat hands, pink cheeks, blue eyes,
Filled with surprise
At the strange ways of the world.
Fair tendrils of hair that lie curled
On a damp brow.
You are so terribly, touchingly, innocent, now
Will it all turn to dust
This lovely trust?
Can we build a land of dreams come true
Out of this chaos, my son, for you?

All is for you. All that we did in the war
And more.
Fears in parting. Fears of being afraid.
Long loneliness. The wireless that played
His tunes and mine. Letters that didn't come
No home –
No hope. Telegrams that we didn't dare
To open. No-one with whom to share
The gift of youth and the high song we should have sung
Together while we were young.

This was our gift to you, our sacrifice
To keep that light in your eyes.
That you might live freely, that you might ride and run
And sit with your knees in the sun.
That you should have time
To discover the earth and the mountains therein to
    climb

That you and your wife
Would gaze into your fire and plan your life.

If we can give you that which we have lost,
It has been worth the cost
And worth the weary sameness of our days.
If we can raise
An ultimate, unchallenged faith for you
Something to make you of the chosen few
And lead you, conqueror of every breath
Unwearying to death.
If we can frame the clouds for your delight
And make each night
A wider conquest for your urgent soul
Then we have reached our goal
And know that all our suffering was meant
And know ourselves Content.

*

My mother's comments on her attempts to discipline me personally occur at three periods, which I shall look at sequentially. The first set of observations are in the three-quarters of a year in 1948, when I was aged six to six and three quarters. They are particularly revealing about our relationship and my character. I shall not excuse myself, but just note her observation that towards the end of this time I was already aware that she would be leaving me for a long period and dreading this. Also, as she mentions, my first six years had been one of constant uprooting, both in Assam and India, and then in England. It is clear that I was at my most unstable, and that my mother had almost equal problems with my sister who was just three in June.

On 14 July 1948 she wrote, *Before I forget, the Dragon School has definitely accepted Alan for September 1950, when he'll be 8 and three quarters. I'm glad about this ... I think he will enjoy boarding school, he is a sociable child really, and as*

118

you say when he doesn't have me around he will become more independent.

My mother was particularly worried by two features of my character at this time and confused as to how to deal with them.

> *What is bothering me is that he has again taken money (from Daddy's pocket) and spent it on himself – 6/9 to buy a toy on his way to school. He hid it all day and when he finally showed it me said it cost ½! I finally got the truth out of him and by that time he was trembling all over and I felt I couldn't beat him. In fact I feel it is my fault for not teaching him the value of money, but don't quite know how to cope with this. I have said I will cut his pocket money for 10 weeks but I don't know if that really conveys much. Do you think its serious ... or do you think its just childish thoughtlessness? I can't make out. It seems to me this is for psychology and not a stick!* Later she adds, *Alan is my chief head-ache, noisy rude and disobedient, bullying Fiona incessantly and yet the fear of parting from him is haunting me. He is so frightfully sensitive and is going to suffer so at school.*

A week later on 29 July my mother's resolution not to beat me gave way when I again stole.

> *I eventually got back to Broadstone at 7, more dead than alive. While I was away Alan had pinched more money and the first thing I did was to thrash him with his belt. I hated it, but felt I must try that as everything else had failed. The awful part was that he had spent some of the money buying me a shilling stamp to send a letter to you! Don't know what I shall do if it happens again. He is a problem in many ways, I suppose its due to his unsettled early life.*

This may be the incident I remember, though I think that was later, when I stole some money left lying on the sideboard and spent it on seeds and was chased round the garden by my grandfather. I don't remember being beaten, however.

It is clear that that I was becoming aware of my mother's imminent departure at some point around then for five weeks later, on 3 September, my mother wrote to my father about her departure and that *Poor Alan is fretting terribly about it.*

There is also a further reference to something which has already been alluded to, and which will recur throughout this period, both in my mother's letters and in the observations of others, especially on the comments on my courage and tenacity in rugger, namely my bravery in the face of pain.

As for my mother's assessment of our characters, it appears that she found me and Anne really difficult, and Fiona, the middle one, placid. *Anne is a handful with tempestuous rages, but so amusing that one can't help adoring her. She and Alan are more alike in temperament, Fiona is the placid affectionate one.*

*

Then my mother disappeared for two years in the middle of October 1948 and there are no more comments from her based on her personal observations of me until she returned in November 1950. Her next comments relate mainly to the three school holidays when I was at home.

When my mother came to take me out from the Dragon, after being away for over two years, she again noted my competitiveness. After lunch I taught her knock-out whist, but, *I had to be careful not to win too much and after we had evened the score satisfactorily we set off for the shops, where he was to choose himself a present.*

My competitiveness and aggression, the flip side to my courage and determination, are shown in a letter of 16 April 1951. The character traits which I had exhibited when I was-six-and-ahalf were still there three years later, despite two terms at the Dragon. And my mother's difficulty, in the absence of my father, in dealing with my assertiveness is evident.

Actually Alan is becoming his usual non-prep school self again and is almost too much for me on occasions. His nagging of Fiona is absolutely incessant. This morning I lost my temper with him. So he went under the bedclothes and refused to come out, saying he was going to suffocate himself. I left him to it, and at about ten o'clock he emerged and announced grimly that he didn't want any lunch or tea as he was planning to kill himself. I said that would make less cooking and he went off in a very dignified way, but when I bumped into him a bit later he said "Good-bye, I wish you'd Go" which was very cheeky and I only just restrained myself from slapping him! His nagging of Fiona is accompanied by punching and kicking in the shins, poor little thing she does nothing to deserve it and is so quick to forgive – and yet he is sweet with Ann and with me too a lot of time. I know you'll say I'm "analysing" him again but I can't see your putting up with the screams and scuffles for long darling. I love him so much and I can't bear to see the really nasty expression on his face when he addresses Fiona. Its obviously an inferiority complex of some sort. Anyway you'll be able to cope I'm sure.

On 6 May 1951 my mother wrote another long account, this time of my last day before going back to the Dragon for my first summer term, aged nine-and-a-half. It contains many of the elements of other accounts, my overwhelming desire to win, my desperation when I did not succeed, my aggression, but also my generosity and thoughtfulness. What a mixed up kid I was – but again the context needs to be taken into account.

Monday, his last day, was not a great success. It was a miserable day so suggested we spent it quietly at home and after I'd washed up lunch we took "Dominoes" and "Snakes and Ladders" by the drawing room fire and he and Anne and I settled down to what I hoped would be a cosy afternoon. However after a couple of games it ended in a shambles, Alan stalking out with much door-slamming and threats never to come back. Anne and I left feeling rather flat and cross. Alan simply cannot lose at any game and

*cheats at once if he is. I can quite sympathise (as you know!)
when his eyes fill with tears because he can't throw a six –
but feel he mustn't be allowed to get away with it all the
time. Don't you agree? I felt miserable that his last
afternoon should be spoilt and to round it off he climbed
on the kitchen table and knocked down (and smashed) a
bowl of batter which I had prepared to make pancakes for
tea and I was very cross about that too!* Yet she also noted
the other side later in the letter. *Daddy gave him a 5/- tip
and just before he left he pressed it into my hand and said
"This is a parting present 1/8 each". I was truly touched,
particularly as he just loves money, but of course couldn't
take it – but those sort of little gestures of his melt me
absolutely.*

My mother's last letter on this theme before my father
returned to join her was written on 17 June 1951 and again
describes her confusion and exhaustion in a year which had
also been awful for weather, disease and many other things and
where she was trying to cope on her own in a separate house
from my grandparents. She wrote that,

*The kids are sweet but I don't seem to have much
control over them in spite of the fact that they complain of
my "always being cross", probably it will be better all round
if I can show them they are not the only pebbles on my
beach – and get away from them occasionally! I do seem to
snap and shout a good deal but they simply don't listen
otherwise. The trouble is I get so deadly tired and mixed-
up, being a novice at cooking and housekeeping and now
this dressmaking – still it is hard on the poor little brats
though I must say they aren't particularly cowed. I'm too
much in a rut, like you, and we shall both be refreshed by
talking out our little grievances – and kissing out all this
loneliness that is weight on me so.*

*

My mother left again in January 1952. I saw her for three weeks when I flew out for Christmas of that year, but otherwise we were apart until she returned in the summer of 1954 when I was aged twelve-and-a-half. Now her comments are less anxious and on the whole I seem to be less of a problem, though a certain amount of bullying of my sisters continues and she is still worrying about my lack of concentration.

When I returned for the summer holidays, my mother wrote on 25 July,

> *Alan looks very fit but is slightly husky, he was very pleased as he got his cricket tie before leaving ("by some fluke") and has brought back a picture of himself in his team which I'll send onto you – he looks terribly tough but rather sweet! He and the girls get on very well at the moment. Anne follows him round like a puppy and they have made a wonderful town with their farms, zoos, trains etc. and we've had a series of devastating battles with his soldiers. Alan still doesn't seem to have reached the constructive stage, meccano or model aeroplanes – but is much more independent and its so nice that the three of them can at least meet on common ground.*

On 31 July she wrote,

> *The girls are longing to be socially inclined but Alan not at all and never seems to want to break away from the family circle. I enclose his report which is very good I think, but in view of his being older than the average age of the form I must find out if he is fit to take Common Entrance this year.* A week later on 9 August she wrote *The kids are fine, Alan is full of cheer and the three of them get on very well when they're not fighting furiously.*

It is clear that she was not really aware of how fast I was growing up, at least sexually. Thus on 16 August after I had been to the dentist she describes how:

we gave ourselves a treat and went to the matinee of "South Pacific" after the dentist and the usual grime café lunch – not very expensive as we stood in a queue and went to the cheapest seats, unfortunately I hadn't taken my glasses so saw it in a mist but it was very pretty and gay. I said to Alan "What is the principal girl like, is she pretty" and he said "Yes she is, but not as pretty as some of the girls in the chorus" which surprised me a little as I didn't think he would have noticed, must read the Kinsey Report!

On 30 August she wrote,

Sunday was better, Mummy and Daddy arrived back just as we were starting lunch and in the afternoon the kids and I went out onto the heath and they sailed boats while I sat in the sun and made clay animals, a peaceful occupation in spite of their quarrels which are almost non-stop, but not so wearing in the open. Alan teases Anne unmercifully and gets a rise out of her every time so life is a series of screams and scuffles, they appear to enjoy it, but I think these holidays are really too long and they get bored and hence the endless bickering.

Clearly we were still insubordinate. On 6 September my mother described how:

I was going to shop for the girls in the morning and then pack them off to the News Cinema while I got my coat but everything became unstuck because on the way in in the bus we saw there was to be a horse show near Bournemouth and of course it couldn't be missed so we were only left with an hour for shopping, this was spent chasing Alan round Marks and Spencers, every time we saw him and waved he dashed off in the opposite direction, I was nearly demented and finally walked out but of course had to wait for him, then we went into a shop to see if we could get Anne some jodhpurs and while we were trying them on Alan and Fiona disappeared, the whole shop was searched and I rushed up and down the pavement outside, when I was just about to call in the police they emerged with joyful smiles saying ha ha they had been hiding behind the coats. I soon wiped the smiles off their faces, but that was the end of our shopping!

A week or so before my term ended, in an moment of uncharacteristic openness, my mother wrote on 10 December *I'm longing to have Alan back.* I was back sooner than she expected, for the school went down with flu and she decided to bring me back early in the hope that I would miss it. I came back and my mother wrote on 15 December:

After 4 nights of it I went to the doctor and got a sleeping draught this morning – can't bear to be so tired all day with the kids around. They are so good and helpful (at present!) and its heaven to have them – Fiona and Alan are very pally and Annie is a bit left out but she's been making yards and yards of paper chains and so far no fights!

Towards the end of the holidays, there are two final small hints of how she regarded me and my behaviour in a letter on 11th January 1955. She described how my sister Fiona:

is getting enormously fat and bursting out of the new skirts I've made her. Alan knocks her over and sits on her frequently though, just to show he is far the beefier type. He had his friend to spend the night last week. An awfully nice boy and Alan was a different person with him around, obviously what he needs. They shot airguns and played trains and went fishing and were no trouble. We should have had another son you know, but its too late now...

She was again both pleased and confused by me, for in the same letter she wrote that, *I shall miss all horribly. They are really rather fun, the girls no trouble at all, Alan a frequent headache and quite beyond me sometimes!* What was beyond her, I shall probably never know.

Finally, my mother wrote on 7 April 1955, *the children are wildly excited at the thought of seeing you. I think you will find them fun, though they squabble incessantly and Alan spends his time "lambing up" anyone in sight - the hamsters are very sweet but the children's manners are even more revolting since their advent as they now "pouch" their food in imitation of the hamsters!*

*

If I were to summarize my mother's attitude, it would be in the phrase that I was a 'hopeful monster'. That I could be sweet, sensitive, often brave, with some natural intellectual abilities. But also that I could be a little monster, a slow learner, lacked concentration, a bad loser. In fact, as she admitted to my father, I was probably just a typical little boy who knew how to wind up his over-anxious and perhaps over-loving mother. Possibly I blamed her in some way for constantly abandoning me for several years at a time. I may have sensed her disappointment in me. I certainly missed the presence of my father, who was never with me for more than a few months at a time and hence could not really relax into a loving and disciplining fatherly role. Nevertheless, that I have not turned out worse is largely the result of my mother's and my grandparents' huge efforts, as well as the excellent boarding school to which they sent me.

All this account needs to be set against that of others. As will be seen in 'Dragon Days', my teachers and contemporaries seem to have had a reasonable opinion of me during these years. There are also hints in the letters from my grandmother quoted elsewhere that she had some admiration for my grit and determination. Nor are there ever signs that she found me particularly difficult. With the experience of bringing up her sons and my mother in India she was experienced - and very formidable. My Scottish aunts also seem to write about me with affection. So it seems that outside the fraught relationship of my mother and myself, I was just a normal little boy.

7. GAMES

Playing games were seen as a form of education. It was football I enjoyed most. It combined the excitement of rushing around, was much less boring than cricket, but without the pain and roughness of rugger. It was on a par with hockey in terms of satisfaction, requiring both skill and thought.

It was particularly important to me because it was a game I could and did play a great deal, not only at school but also at our Broadstone house, and my enthusiasm for it started well before I went to the Dragon. My uncle Robert was a fanatical football player and we organized numerous games, rising to a crescendo of tournaments involving all members of the family who happened to be around. There are photographs of the period showing me kicking, heading, shooting and being a proud member of a winning team holding up my trophy.

Football could be played anywhere there was a small flat piece of land – in the garden, on the beach or elsewhere. It just required a ball and a couple of stones for goal posts. One could practice it on one's own for hours against a wall, as with cricket. And above all it depended on the combination of individual skill and team co-operation which would train one for life in the adult institutions where being a good 'team player' was so essential. It also taught me early on, with my uncle's patient coaching, the delicate art of throwing oneself wholeheartedly into something, desperately trying to win. But at the end, if one lost, not being too involved – being a good sport mattered as much.

The first reference to this important game at home was in a letter of 23 April 1948 when my mother wrote to my father, *He and Robert play a lot of football together on the lawn.* Three weeks later she wrote on 16 May *He has a passion for football and I am forced to play one game a day.* A few weeks before she left that Autumn to be with my father, my mother wrote described my passion and difficulty in accepting defeat, a desperation which may be related to her impending departure. On 3 September she wrote:

> *I shall be seeing you in about 6 weeks time. Poor Alan is fretting terribly about it, but I think he will be quite happy in time, with his school and Robert in the holidays. The football season has started again and Alan takes it frantically seriously, he usually plays with the tears pouring down his face and ends by swearing he'll never play again, he'll never be able to play, he's bad at everything, he always will be. Remind you of anything?! Actually I think he'll be quite good if not very, he's so keen.*

My first school report at the Dragon eighteen months later showed the effects of these early efforts: I was reported to be 'Keen and skilful'.

When my mother returned two years later, the enthusiasm for football was continuing. On 29 April 1951 she wrote:

> *the apple trees in the garden are suddenly covered with buds, the cuckoo is calling, butterflies and bees are out and even some of my seeds, but mostly they've been trampled on by hordes of "cowboys" and Red Indians and football players! ... Alan has been up to play in various football matches, including the Cup tie in which he and Robert beat Richard and Paul Burny 7-1!*

This is noted in my grandfather's diary as 'footer on lawn'.

The games on the lawn continued until the end of our time at Broadstone, and I remember them dimly with great pleasure: the skills of dribbling, passing and weaving past an opposition player which my uncle taught me. It was not just a spring game, for in July 1954 I wrote, *Robert and I have been playing football on the lawn.* [illustrated with a painting of two football players]. This was echoed by my mother on July 25 who wrote, *Robert is very good value with the kids and the football season is in full swing again, Anne was completely winded in goal yesterday.*

My progress in football at the Dragon is described elsewhere, but it is worth noting that the effect of football was not limited to just playing the game with my family and friends at home. It impinged in a myriad other ways. I supported Wolverhampton Wanderers, whose centre left Billy Wright was my hero (and one reason I played as a Centre). It is implied that I went to Wembley with my grandmother when she took me out in my second term at the school, for I wrote at the end of February, *I will be going with grany after the skool service I am going to show... a picture of a Football match* [picture of a football match with the crowd with the word 'Wembelly']' On 6 April 1953 in my grandfather's diary it is noted that I was taken to see Bournemouth against Bristol City.

We also listened to matches. On 16 April 1951 my mother wrote to my father, *On Saturday Alan and I listened to the Football International (Scotland won!).* It seems that two weeks later on 29 she wrote that she sent all of us children off to do things at the park in Poole and, *went off to listen to the Cup Final which was being broadcast ... I was backing Newcastle* [Newcastle won 2-0]. Two years later on 24 April 1953, my mother wrote *We listened to the Football International between Scotland and England on Saturday, terrific excitement when Scotland scored that last goal!* I was firmly identified with Scotland, as was my father, with my mother somewhat ambivalent.

Apart from miniaturized football (Subuteo) described elsewhere, the other way in which football affected us through these years was my grandfather's passion for the football pools – his equivalent to my grandmother's betting on horses. I remember the masses of coupons, the occasional small win, and the hours he spent mulling over the choice, reflected as one of the major sets of entries in his diaries. There is only one reference to this in a letter when my mother wrote to my father about my grandfather on 26 November 1954 *He is sadly in need of something to do, as he has no hobby, except football pools and can't seem to even read a book.*

*

My uncle Robert was a fanatical cricket player. His obsession is captured in a letter of my mother, on 13 April 1948, when he was about fifteen. *He is a strange child, he was given a boat, a wireless set (the kind you can make yourself) and a FROG aeroplane for his birthday but is quite uninterested in any of them and goes on throwing his balls about and cheering his own efforts, all day.* I remember his imagined world of roaring crowds and the ball endlessly thrown against the house wall.

His obsession drew me into an early interest in home cricket. When I was at kindergarten, my mother wrote on 6 May 1948, *he told me we'd be starting cricket to-morrow which will be less energetic I hope.* We then moved on to athletics. On 14 July *He is now All Olympic and instead of playing cricket we have to run marathons round and round the house and putt weights across the lawn – even more exhausting if anything!* Two weeks later, however, on 19 July my mother wrote, *Robert got back yesterday and we had a terrific cricket match this evening, boys versus girls. I can't remember who won now, it was very funny anyway. Alan is mad keen, I wonder if it'll last?*

Seeing a real cricket match being played on the grounds of my future preparatory school at the Dragon may have increased my interest. On a trip to Oxford my mother wrote in August: *On the way back we found they were playing Real Cricket at the Dragon School, so we watched that for a bit.'* By 'Real' my mother seems to have meant proper cricket as opposed to the kind we played in our garden.

When she left me and returned to India my mother tried to get me to write to her by asking me about my enthusiasm for games. On 15 April 1949 she asked, *Are you playing football or cricket at the moment?* and a month later on 22 May, *Have you started cricket yet or aren't any of your friends at school interested?* On 16 August she again wrote, *Our wireless has gone funny so we don't know what sort of weather you are having but I hope its nice and you're getting some cricket.* A shared interest in cricket, like other sports, held us together across the globe.

The practice I had at home was supplemented by playing on the beach. On 16 April 1951 my mother wrote about a seaside visit: *in the end we had a lot of fun digging and playing cricket.* Two weeks later on the 29 she wrote: *The day before we had all gone for a picnic in the park and the girls and I churned our way across the lake in a paddle boat while they sailed and afterwards we played French cricket.* French cricket was an ideal game for such occasions, being played with one person with a bat, and the others trying to bowl him or her out by hitting the legs which acted as stumps. Three years later on 11th September 1954 my mother wrote again, *We had a day on the beach with the Mermagens before we left, a really warm day and I bathed and we all got very burnt and played rounders and cricket and touch rugger and every other game all day.*

We could also play another game which is described on 30 August by my mother. *My trips with the children in cars recently have convinced me that it will be just you and I touring the continent, it is either free fights in the back seat or Car Cricket which is the most dizzy-making game I know so I think we will fit in our tour when they are all at school.* This is the game where one scores by adding up the number of legs on pub signs and one is 'out' if the sign mentions legs.

*

As in the affected 'Anyone for tennis', it is clear that tennis can be an important class marker. It was played constantly by my parents and grandparents in India, and was an important part of the entertainment of the Raj. It was the central game one played at the Club with other Europeans and in my mother's pre-marriage days in India it was a place where young people could begin their courtships.

When they were in India during my Dragon days, there were a number of tennis courts. My parents seem to have had one on their tea garden, my mother writing to my father on 19 April 1948 to ask, *Did you get our tennis net back by the way?* But it was at the Nazira Club, and at the General Manager's bungalow (the Burra Bungalow or BB) that the social hub of tennis was found. In May 1950 my mother wrote to me that: *Anne and I have been leading a very quiet life, the only excitement for her was last Saturday when we took her to Nazira and she and all the other children swam while we played tennis.* Two years later on 29 March 1952 my mother wrote, *Yesterday we drove to Nazira in the afternoon for Daddy to play tennis, the girls swam for a short time but as I have lost my costume and couldn't be on hand to rescue them, they couldn't do very much.*

My father was keen on tennis and it was also good to be seen at the special Christmas tennis match at the Burra Bungalow. On 26 November 1954 my mother asked: *Have you arranged to go away for Christmas or are you going to brave B.B. tennis?* After Christmas my mother wrote on 3 January, *I got a letter from you, written just before Christmas, and I hope you managed to get some fun out of B.B. tennis.* They clearly regarded it with some ambivalence.

In England, however, we were not part of the upper-middle-class tennis set. We could not afford a full-sized tennis court and though there were tennis clubs at Poole and elsewhere, it was not felt worth the effort to join them. We did occasionally go to watch the game. For example, my grandfather noted in his diary for 28 April 1952, 'Richard takes Robert and Alan to Bournemouth tennis tournament', but I do not remember these tournaments.

I might have been expected to learn to play in order to continue the tradition at the Dragon School, which clearly had courts and boys who could get their colours for the game. Yet I do not ever remember playing at the Dragon or even owning a tennis racket, which was, of course, an expensive item. The only reference in any of my letters is ambiguous. On 23 May 1951 my mother wrote of me, *His letters have been a couple of scrawls saying when is half term and the end of term and could I send him a tennis ball and some lemonade powder!* But tennis balls were coveted for many games, including 'bad eggs' and various games of catch, so this is no evidence that I played. Nor do I remember playing tennis at the Christian boys camp at Swanage to which I was sent in two of my summers, even though its prospectus mentioned, 'other outdoor games, like tennis, padder-tennis...' What I may have played, however, was padder tennis, a game that substituted in our family for tennis.

This 'poor man's tennis', played on a half-sized court with wooden rackets was about our social level and there are several descriptions of the game. We got our first set of 'Padda' or 'Padder' on 23 August 1953 and it was specifically a present for me. My grandmother wrote to my mother after yet another bout of dentistry that I had been given a Padder set to console me, and the same day I wrote to my parents explaining the consolation prize. *I am probably not going up to scotland as I have to have four teeth out soon. I have got a padder set and we have played one or two games so far.* On 10 September 1953 my grandfather notes in his diary 'Mermagens for padder', a visit from my cousins.

The following year on 16 August 1954 my mother wrote to my father *dozed till tea time and then we played Padder,* and the following year my grandfather noted on 18 April 1955, 'Iris and Alan play padder.' A large lawn not being necessary we continued to play when we went to our Lake District house.

*

As well as the formal, outdoor, sporty games, we also played numerous other games, both formal and informal. One favourite was 'Murder in the Dark', which we played at my thirteenth birthday party a couple of days before Christmas 1954, as described by my mother, *We played the usual games including Murder which consisted of everybody including the murderer rushing screaming downstairs every two minutes saying it was much too frightening but they insisted on going on playing!*

Obviously another form of amusement was dressing up – the world of charades, enacted plays, of games of cowboys and Indians etc. The conductor's uniform, which my grandmother notes as the present my mother left with me to wake up to at the age of eight when they left for India and which included a real little ticket-punching machine, as well as the games played with dustbin lids, with various uniforms are also very evident in the photographs of me. I can't remember that dressing up games continued much beyond the Dragon years, or that we dressed up much at the Dragon (except in plays).

Much of our playing was centred on war games played with toy guns, bows and arrows, spears and other weapons. The first reference I have to six guns is in a photograph of 1948 when I was seven. There are two further photos when I was about ten where I am armed with a rifle, six guns slung round my waist, and in one of them also waving a sword. I pretended to be Billy the Kid or Wyatt Earp, massacring unsuspecting Indians. My mother wrote on 24 April 1951, for example, of games of Cowboys and Indians which damaged the flower beds. We rushed around robbing banks, killing here and there in our imaginations and with loud reports from the caps which we bought on little pink-coloured rolls.

One of the themes of our early games were King Arthur and the Knights of the Round Table. This was based on books we read and films and I remember that I always wanted to be the mysterious Sir Lancelot of the Lake. My grandmother in a letter to my father describes one such game shortly after my mother had left for India and left us for the first time. On 24 October 1948 my grandmother wrote that my sister and I had been playing in the garden dressed up as King Arthur, with my sister as a 'fair maid'. There are photos of me, aged about eleven, posed with a Naga spear in one hand, and another with both a spear and a rather battered silver shield which I remember with fondness. This spear was the one I had brought back from my first return trip to India. In a letter on 18 January 1953 to my parents I described the flight back. *We arrived two hours late but I enjoyed the flight very much. Me and Granny saw the naga spear and the porter said "I am afraid it will not get into this bus" so he was going to put it into the second one but when it arrived they could not find it. Granny thinks it went down the back of the luggage thing and nowone looked there. It might have turned up by now but it soon will if it hasn't.* It obviously did; the family still has a miniature version for a child, but with all the blood-curdling associations of stories of the dipping in blood and use in head-hunting.

At the same time we were also playing in the world of Robin Hood, again derived from films and books. My mother wrote on 30 November 1948 from India, obviously enclosing a long and brilliant jungle cock feather, and saying, The *big tail-feather is for Alan and is from the jungli cock that Daddy shot the other day, I thought you might like to show it to your friends at school and it would look lovely if you made a cardboard hat and stuck it in the front, for a prince or Robin Hood.* The Robin Hood games took on a new dimension when I acquired my first bow, which I describe under 'Sport'. They were complemented by games of Pirates stimulated above all by my favourite childhood film 'The Crimson Pirate'.

*

We clearly played card games. My mother in a letter to my father at the end of November 1950 wrote of the time at the hotel. *We had lunch here and he thawed a lot, and afterwards he taught me "knock-out Whist" a whizzo game that is the rage at school now.* Around the same time, during the holidays after this, she mentions that, *Alan seemed tired with a slight party hangover so he stayed in bed for breakfast which meant that they all stayed in bed, in fact till nearly lunch time and we all gambolled furiously at "Happy Families" and "Knock Out Whist".* I don't remember any card games which involved putting down stakes, or gambling with marbles or other objects of value, but I suspect there must have been some. We played 'Snap' and 'Vingt-et-Un'; for example my grandfather noting in his diary on 29 March 1952 'Played Vingt et Un'. Another game which was clearly important at some point was 'Racing Demon' which I played with my grandmother and others.

A slightly unusual game linked to my imperial background, which I played at home, was 'Mah Jong'. Mah Jong was much played in Burma and India by my grandparents and then my parents, and my grand-mother had a lovely set of Mah Jong tiles which were set out in red lacquer holders, which also contained a number of thin ivory tokens. The whole gear was very exotic and exciting and I still remember the joy of watching the combinations grow on one's red stand, the piling up of the crisp white tiles into walls at the start, and the joy of declaring.

We obviously started young at this game. My great-grandmother Annie's diary for 1950 records that on Tuesday 3 January, when we were visiting her in Exeter, 'In doors all day. Ma Jong with M and children'. On Friday 6 it is noted, 'Walk in town. Mah Jong after tea with Alan and Fiona', and a week later on Friday 13 'Violet arrived mid-day played mah jong with Alan and Fiona'. I was just eight and Fiona still five at the time.

On 20 March 1951, when my sister Fiona was still six and Anne was four, my mother writes, *She* [Fiona] *and Anne have been very good and been playing Mah Jong steadily for days. Anne can play on her own now and you would be amused to hear her say "Oh good, a hidden pong" or "I'm doing duty pairs" and she wins nearly every time!* A month later on 16 April, my mother wrote to Mac. *On Tuesday we went up to tea at 'By the Way' as it was Roberts birthday, and played Mah Jong...* The first reference to my playing at 'By the Way' was in my grandfather's diary which notes on 2 August 1952 when I was ten-and-a-half 'Mahjong with Mrs Mac. Robert Alan and Violet'.

On 25 July 1954 my mother notes in a letter to my father, *Yesterday was one of those days we don't often get when it poured and blew a gale all day and we didn't put our noses out of doors all day – but the kids brought me breakfast in bed and we amused ourselves with large meals and games of Mah Jong.* On another rainy day later in the year, on 26 November before I returned from school, my mother also notes that with my two sisters, *as it was raining so hard and we sat by the fire and played Mah Jong instead.* There are a number of other references to playing the game in my grandfather's diary.

There were two games which involved manipulating small models, overlapping with games with toy soldiers and dinky cars, but more specialized and commercially marketed. One was 'Subbuteo', a form of miniaturized football which I particularly played with my uncle Robert. My mother mentions on 16 April 1951 in a letter that my sisters and Robert played, *a football game that you play with little men on a table.* Thus emerged 'Subbuteo' into our lives. I still remember the tiny figures on their plastic pedestals – I think mine were in the colours of the team I avidly supported: Wolverhampton Wanderers in their black and gold. It was a delightful game of real skill and excitement, and a good substitute on wet days in winter for the real thing – and I still have one or two battered players in my 'Museum'.

The second was a game which I adored where a long green strip – the course – was attached to a device which, when you turned the handle, made the horses race along. I still have some of the horses, mainly with broken legs. There is a photo of us playing the game taken in about 1947/8, when I was seven, so it was there from an early period in England. We played this often at home, placing some kind of bet on the winner.

Finally there were two games which came later in the period. One was the highly capitalistic game of 'Monopoly', to which I referred on 25 March 1953, when I wrote to my mother, *I am enjoying the game of Monopoly you gave to me very much and I have played it 4 times already this holls.* The other was the crossword-like game 'Scrabble', where one built up words with differently valued letters. We were given this for a Christmas present in 1954 and my mother describes in a letter two days after Christmas to my father how, *we played Scrabble, a new game which they had been given.*

8. OUTDOORS

In Dorset we lived in a relatively isolated setting, down an un-surfaced lane. We were half a mile from the nearest bus route or shop and more than a mile from our kindergartens and proper shops or railway station to Bournemouth. My mother and grandparents had no car, and only when my uncle Richard or friends visited could we easily travel to the sea or elsewhere. So we really needed bicycles.

Bicycles would also open up the many tracks and paths across to Corfe Mullen and out onto the heaths behind our house, or to more distant places to play and explore. It was an ideal place for cycling, apart from a few pine roots and rabbit holes. Even the road itself was relatively safe since cars were few and slow. In those days was a relaxed attitude to allowing young children to go off on their own. A combination of much less traffic and a world before the obsession with threats to children from adults, made cycling one of the central parts of my growing up, my first real adult skill and a key to independence.

Soon after we arrived, my mother obtained a bicycle. On 2 March1948 she wrote, *On Sunday we went next door to try a bicycle that the owners said they would lend me.* Two weeks later on the 18 she noted that, *I've been wildly extravagant latterly and have bought, (or am about to buy) a bicycle for Alan...*

For a while I rode on the back (or front) of my mother's bicycle, for example on 29 March my mother wrote, *The weather has been groggy and yesterday it deluged all day, the first real rain we've had ... Alan and I went down the town on my bicycle and had to squeeze each other out when we got back.* But this was only a temporary arrangement and my bike finally was bought with further apologies for the expense as described in a letter of 7 June.

I don't know when it arrived, but I seem immediately to have started to learn how to ride it and by 22 June my mother writes: *Alan can almost ride his bicycle, he can get off but not on, so I launch him and he goes off in a rather drunken way, clings on like a limpet to the handlebars. He never loses his nerve and falls off though.*

Only two days later on 24 she wrote:

> *Great event to-day, Alan rode to Broadstone* [about a mile-and-a-half away] *on his bicycle, with me riding beside him. He tried to be frightfully nonchalant when he met other boys and whistle a tune, clinging rigidly to the handlebars at the same time, it was really very funny. He fell off once coming back but was pretty pleased with himself. I can't remember how long I took to learn but I think he has done quite well.*

Three weeks later the same grim determination is described, as well as the panics it caused my mother. On 14 July she wrote,

> *A small boy came over to play yesterday afternoon and they hurtled around on bicycles. Alan's face ashy grey and drawn with terror but he is very plucky and refuses to give in. He has inherited my nerves, alas, but has plenty of grit.* In the same letter she described how, *Both* [Alan and a friend] *having bicycled down an almost vertical sandy path within a couple of feet of a sheer drop of several hundred feet – you can imagine how I felt following their tracks and expecting them to go over the edge any minute – I was trembling all over by the time I found the little brutes!*

One strong memory was cycling up the small road from Broadstone. I still remember the spot, the shrubs on the left, the rising bank with pines on the right, the steepness of the climb and my determination to cycle as far as I could before I gave up. I recall forcing myself to thrust down and down again with my legs until I could bear it no longer, and then the glory and release as the road levelled out through the pine woods on both sides. Recently I returned and found the very spot, with the gatehouse I remembered still there. But the hill which I remember as enormous is just a fairly gentle slope of only fifty yards.

My sister obviously learnt to ride a couple of years later and when I was just nine and she was still six, on the first of January 1951 my mother wrote:

> *I forgot to tell you that a couple of children from near here came to collect Alan and Fiona for a bike ride the other day, I let them go rather unwillingly as I don't think them old enough to be on the roads on their own, but within half an hour they were back having had a furious argument as to whether tea grows on trees or bushes, mine holding out for bushes you'll be glad to hear.*

We clearly all had bikes, but they were as much weapons of sibling warfare as riding machines. The same first of January my mother wrote,

> *After the endless washing up of Sunday lunch we went out for a walk. Alan grumbling like mad, but we all felt much better for it though we didn't get far as they all took their bicycles, swopped, fell off, argued, chased, blocked each other and generally skirmished up and down the road until the neighbours must have been deafened.*

Three months later, when I was nine-and-a-quarter, I made my first independent ride described on 24 April by my mother.

> *Yesterday he [Alan] asked for a picnic lunch and went off on his bicycle to "explore". I was a little apprehensive but felt it was a good thing to let him be independent – but I was relieved when I heard that he had eventually turned up*

at "By the Way". I'd been visualizing him alternatively drowned, squashed or dying of exposure in some deserted woods. [From 'Pinecot' to 'By the Way' is about one and a half miles.]

My mother was apologetic and defensive about the cost of buying proper bikes for my sisters. On 21 June 1954 she wrote

> *We had the usual gasping rush across the heath for the bus, it is too agonising and I'm afraid I've invested in bikes for the girls, £2 down and the rest in instalments – I hope you don't mind darling but we are utterly cut off otherwise. Fiona's is green and Anne's blue and they will hardly be seen out with me on my battered black wreck, of course I've been dragged out for endless bike rides, nice but the traffic frightens me to death and we spend most of the time walking.*

The full cost was noted when the bank account arrived half a year later as described in a letter of 21 November. *The Bank Acct. shattered me as usual ... £29.0 for bicycles but getting near the end.*

There were benefits, however. My mother describes on 11th July 1954 how my younger sisters went off on their own to church, a distance of a mile-and-a-half, aged ten and eight.

> *My darling, Its Sunday afternoon and I've packed the kids off to church and am sitting in the sun in the garden ... I wish we had a car and could go to the sea but moving about by bus on a Sunday is murder and I bicycled all yesterday and am on strike as far as that's concerned! I feel a little anxious as it's the first time the girls have been to Broadstone on their own and I keep having visions of their mangled corpses but they're pretty careful, specially Fiona, Anne is the harum-scarum one now.*

The presence of bikes allowed us to roam round parts of Dorset and later when we went north round Windermere. I dimly remember those rides and I suspect that this encouraged part of my love for the English countryside. Two early expeditions, with me and Fiona on our bikes and my mother with my youngest sister on hers, are described on 15 May 1951.

We woke at 4 p.m. very refreshed, and went out on my bike into a golden afternoon and found a lovely wood full of bluebells, primroses, violets and every other wild flower you can imagine. A heavenly place and we picked a bunch of flowers and went back very content. The next day I made plans to take a picnic tea there, but it was cold and cloudy and I felt terribly tired and dispirited for some reason and wished I hadn't. However we set out with two other children and biked and biked and eventually had a nice afternoon and picked huge bunches of bluebells so that this room smells like a spring wood. As usual I felt sad that I couldn't somehow preserve the smells and the birdsong and the green fields of buttercups for when I got back to Assam.

Three years later, on 3 July 1954, my mother writes: *In the afternoons we've been for nature rambles on our bikes, they are both quite fearless now but we keep to side-roads and lanes as traffic makes me feel ill.*

Almost a month later on the 31 she wrote:

The kids are over in the woods opposite building a house and getting gloriously wet I should think, the idea started when we took a picnic tea to those lovely woods by the side of the main Wimborne road. We had a lovely time exploring and finally chose a site for a camp but by that time it was time to go home and we planned to go again to-day but the weather is not conducive to carrying tents and axes on long bicycle rides so the kids have compromised.

*

If we had been a good deal richer, or in Assam, we would have supplemented or even replaced cycling by horse riding. I may have been able to ride early in my life – there are photos of me on a donkey in Assam when I was about four and my parents refer to buying a pony for me around that time. It was necessary that a young Sahib or future country gentleman learn to ride, as Siegfried Sassoon describes in *Memoirs of a Foxhunting Man*. If I was to join my ancestors (including to a certain extent my father) in the tradition of polo, pig sticking and riding to hounds, I needed to learn to ride – and preferably early in my life.

Whatever skill I had in India I lost when I returned to England, and I had to start again. Appropriately, along with my sisters, I started with a very large rocking horse. On 25 March 1948 my mother notes *To-day the rocking-horse arrived and caused great excitement of course and was ridden hard all afternoon – until it broke! Sad but I hope we'll be able to mend it.* Mended it was and incorporated into a number of our games and I was photographed astride it around this time.

The attempt to train me to ride occurred when I was nine. On 3 March my mother wrote to me at the Dragon, *I hope you'll like your riding lessons, you'll get some riding here so mind you learn quickly!* On 7 April my Grandfather wrote to my mother about the preparations. *Your mother was able to get an inexpensive pair of riding breeches for Alan and he is to have his first lesson tomorrow at Camford.* This was in fact Canford where, my grandfather notes in his diary on 5, 8, 10, 12 April - 'Took Alan to riding school at Canford for riding lesson'.

I remember it was an indoor ring with something like sawdust on the floor. I was led round an enclosure, wearing a rather uncomfortable riding hat and the aforesaid breeches. I think I was taught to trot and perhaps even to canter, but not to gallop. I did not progress to jumping. I found the jolting momentum and the confined spaces uninteresting and the horses somewhat intimidating. I may have shown unwilling, since there is no more reference to my riding, though a photograph in India when I was about sixteen on a horse suggests that on my trips to India I did ride.

The real problem was that whereas in India riding was within my parents reach, and indeed almost essential in order to be a member of the Planters Club, in England it was different. In India horses were quite cheap, stables available, 'sayces' and other servants abounded, and games of polo or lovely rides through the tea estate made it worthwhile. In England at our social level it was really beyond our means and our competence. We had nowhere to keep a horse in a rented house, even if we could have afforded one. Even the riding gear and the lessons were very expensive.

*

Yet the world we inhabited in Dorset abounded with horses and horsy events, and my grandmother, particularly with her Indian background and love of gambling on horses, was very keen. It also seems, as it still is, to be a gendered activity. My sisters, especially Anne, were obsessed with horses for much of their childhood. Anne's equivalent to my imagined games of football before huge crowds was to set up 'Horse Shows'. I still remember her horse shows in our garden, with prizes, with her firm assertion that she was Pat Smyth on 'Jump for Joy', and our neighing and galloping. When we moved to the Lakes my sister continued to be obsessed with horses but because we could not afford our own horse she had to wait for periods in India, or riding on horses belonging to friends.

There were many kinds of show which were a pivotal part of our social world. I still remember the smell of hay and animal flesh, the long hours sitting beside roped enclosures watching the animals pass by, the ice creams and the occasional diversions.

These shows were graded from the county or even regional level down to the village. My mother describes a regional show on 6 June 1951.

*On Friday I took the kids to the Bath and West Show ...
There was masses of machinery being exhibited, judging of
cattle etc. but we went straight to the main ring where the
jumping, trotting horses etc were being judged. We had to
fight our way through a solid mass of humanity and pay a lot
to get a seat in the grandstand but it was worth it as there
were some beautiful horses being shown, and some
wonderful jumping, followed by hansom cabs which were
priceless with their high-stepping ponies...*

The next level down were the county shows, of which the
most influential for us was the Ringwood Show, about fifteen
miles from where we lived. On 11th July 1954 my mother
describes this:

*On Saturday was Anne's big day, the day of Ringwood
show which she had been looking forward to for weeks, and
thank heavens it was fine ... We got there just as the pony
jumping was about to start and got a ringside seat and
proceeded to roast, we had sundresses on but were grilling,
the first time I've been really hot since leaving Calcutta. The
jumping was very feeble but Anne was entranced... Anne's
best remark was when she looked at her programme and
announced "Now we have the cows jumping" and Fiona
surprised the people round by saying loudly "That cows
udders aren't nearly as big as Mrs Warrens", poor Mrs
Warren, I hope they were none of them friends of hers! ...
The show was held in the grounds of the most beautiful
manor house and was really very enjoyable. Now of course
Anne has tied bits of rope all round the lawn and decorated
it with bits of flowers and we are to have a show of our own
to-morrow.*

My mother described a similar horse show on 6 September
1954 near Bournemouth.

*The horse show was the same as all the others we have
been to, same horses same leathery females riding them and*

same enchantment for Anne, the others went off and bought themselves toffee apples and rode on the merry go round but Anne sat and watched the horses for about three hours, I finally dragged her away and she was so angry that she took off the ring she was wearing and flung it dramatically over the hedge as if she was breaking off an engagement, it looked so funny.

There were also mixed shows, with some horses but also farm animals, and I begin to remember some of these from our first summer in the Lake District. For example, my grandfather mentions our visit to the Cartmel Show on 24 August 1955 and to the Hawkshead Show two weeks later on 6 September. The events conjure up memories of huge bulls being led round and our boxer being proudly entered for dog competitions. But these memories may be from later years as we tended to go regularly to these shows.

At the bottom of the hierarchy were the gymkhanas, an imported Indian word linking this world of horses to the central imperial role of horses and horse shows. On 11 July 1954 my mother described one at the small village only half a mile from our home.

Yesterday I took them to a gymkhana at Corfe Mullen, it was cold and cloudy and we sat on the grass for three and a half hours watching cocky little girls on ponies which I found boring after a bit, I got cold and was dying to get home and we stayed till 7.30 p.m - she [Anne] was very quiet and I felt rather sad to think how much better she could have ridden than most of them - but when one looked at the women it made one wonder if it wouldn't be better to keep daughters away from horses completely - they were the most dreadful collection of bony, chinless horrors I've ever clapped eyes on, exactly like their mounts even to the hair!

My mother's mixture of regret that she could not afford to enable Anne to join this world of horses with all its class associations, softened by her comments on what it might have done to her, captures a world where sport was one of the main social markers.

Apart from the shows, the main way horses impinged on us was through horse racing – watching them and betting. Both of these are combined in the point to points we used to go to quite often, both with my grandparents and uncles. My grandmother, for example, is noted frequently by my grandfather as going to the point to point at Wincanton and I am noted as going to point to point meetings in 1952 and 1954. One at Bradbury Rings on 25 April 1953 I feel I dimly remember, though we visited Bradbury Rings, an important ancient monument, quite frequently.

One proper racing event, the Salisbury Races, I missed because I was going to the dentist. My mother described it in a letter on 16 August 1954.

> *Richard took the girls and Mummy to the Races at Salisbury ... The girls loved the races as it was a reasonable sort of day and lovely setting, but they drove Mummy mad by picking all the winners and saying triumphantly afterwards "You should have backed my horse Granny, mine won", the racing craze lasted a couple of days while they buried themselves in Granny's racing papers and wandered round talking about Hotspurs Nap and listened to the results with fearful excitement as if they had hundreds of pounds at stake ... but it passed over like everything does, very rapidly.*

The allusion to my grandmother's betting is the tip of an iceberg. My grandmother from the time she returned to England up into her eighties spent much of her day planning out a strategy to make money from racing. An early success in the Grand National in 1948 may have been a contributory cause, for my mother noted on 1 April 1948, *Did I tell you Mummy put 2/6 on "Sheila's Cottage" in the Grand National and won £8!* I still remember the excitement at the win – a rank outsider. In fact, thanks to Google I discover the context. No mare had won since 1902 and this horse started at 50-1 and only won because the leader ran out before the last jump. My grandmother backed the horse because we had an Aunt Sheila, and such a whimsical reason often guided her choice.

My grandmother's obsession with horse racing affected our lives not only in sweeping us to horsy events, but because it meant that she was deep in concentration for several hours a day and lunch was often late. It also caused tension between her and other members of the family. My grandfather did the football pools, but on a much lower level and he felt the strain of the constant minor losses on the handful of betting firms which my grandmother's efforts subsidized.

The atmosphere and some of the reasons for her lack of success in making money, but her feelings of triumph nevertheless, are shown in two letters from my mother in 1954. On 16 June she wrote: *Mummy spends all her time betting, she backs with 3 different bookies every day and spends hours with lurid newspapers called "Racing News" or "Form for 1954" picking horses, as she picks 8 out of 10 horses for every race she always comes out about even and it seems a frightful waste of effort.*

Even when we were trying to pack to leave for the Lake District, my grandmother could not be diverted. On 18 October, a few days before the move, my mother wrote *Mummy got 1 and 3 in the Caesarwitch, but as usual had also backed 6 other horses! She still spends hours poring over her racing books, in spite of the pressure of events!*

To what extent the involvement of my grandparents in the football pools and horse racing was related to insecurity and a desire to somehow escape the relative poverty of their last years, I leave others to decide. It certainly added excitement to their lives. It was probably not something entirely new, being a continuation of competition, betting and gaming in which my grandparents had indulged in India.

*

Country life for the gentry, upon whose fringe we lived, revolved around the triumvirate of hunting, shooting, and fishing. As regards hunting and shooting I normally inhabited a lower and cheaper world. I had catapults from at least 1952. I drew a picture of one in a letter of 12th May 1952, and promised to *bring out a catapult* to India on 5 October, a couple of months before my trip to see my parents. What I fired at or whether I was skilful or not I do not remember, though I seem to remember graduating from a wooden to a metal one.

Much more to my taste was archery. There were the strong associations with Robin Hood and his Merry Men who featured in several of the films which I most enjoyed and whom I impersonated with gusto. There was also a cross-association with Assam as I may even have had a bow as a little boy before I came to England. The first bows, such as those mentioned in July 1948 when I wrote to my parents from Scotland that *We play Red Indians with bows and arrows*, were probably home-made.

A notable event was when, as my grandfather noted in his Diary for 3 April 1952 'Alan gets bow'. Four days later, on the 7, I wrote, *I have a lovely bow and some arrows which go a terrific way and which I love.* My grandfather added a letter in which he commented, *We bought a bow (of plastic material) for Alan for 13/6 and he uses Aunt Nell's arrows with it.* I seem to remember that it was green and made of steel rather than plastic. I still remember the professional, sturdy and beautifully feathered arrows of aunt from whom we were also renting our house. On 30 I wrote to my parents, *I have been having fun with my bow and Arrows.* I remember the deep satisfaction of hitting a target, the mystery of the flight, the tug of the bow, the smoothness of the bamboo arrow with their sharp tips and bright red feathers.

This was something I played with between ten and thirteen, though I am pretty certain we were not allowed such dangerous weapons at the Dragon.

The bow was used in games and there is a photograph of me with it. But it was mainly used for shooting at inanimate targets. I do not remember ever using the bow to hunt with, just as I do not remember hunting with my catapult.

*

Shooting with guns was a very central feature of my father's life and the life of the planters in India in general. There is a photograph of me at about three with my foot on a dead tiger with a large rifle and throughout my mother's letters when she was in India I was given news of my father's shooting.

A year later on 24 November 1949 my mother wrote to me: *Daddy is going shooting to-morrow and spending the night camping, I wish I could go too but I will next time I can find somebody to take Anne. I hope it doesn't pour with rain the whole time as it quite likely might. Last night a tiger killed fairly close to the bungalow but then it deluged so Daddy couldn't sit up for it – he's been hoping for a kill for so long too.* In fact, as I recall, my father shot about four tigers, one or two teeth are all that are left to me of this tragic destruction. It was clearly something I was proud of at the time, as recounted in a reported conversation in a letter my mother wrote to my father on 30 April 1948 about my first kindergarten. *He said he told the small boy next to him that his daddy had shot a tiger, to which the boy replied that so had his Daddy. 'Ah" said Alan after a moment's thought "but my Daddy's tiger was a mad tiger."*

At the end of February 1951 I wrote to my father, *The term is flying by I think and I hope that there know Tiggers eating the cows.* This suggests I was aware of one of the reasons why my father shot tigers. I urged my father on. For example on 1 March 1953 I wrote from the Dragon, *I hope that the tiger will be shot soon.* Furthermore, the fact that two of my earliest pictures in my letters featured shooting also shows how this had gripped my imagination. On 28 July 1949 I wrote from Scotland and included a painting of a fisherman and of shooting birds on Loch Morar. On 16 April 1951 my mother noted, *Picture on the reverse is you shooting I presume, either a butterfly or a fox or perhaps a left and a right.* The picture on the back looks to me like a primitive attempt to portray my father shooting a tiger, though it certainly looks more like a fox.

There was also a good deal of less dramatic shooting of wildfowl which abounded in Assam. On 16 February 1949 my mother wrote, *Daddy is going out duck shooting again this week-end, I don't know if I shall go but I hope I'll be able to. There are about ten other men shooting too and we hope there will be enough duck to go round.* The following June she noted, *We have been out with Daddy shooting green pigeons once or twice, he always hits them but often loses them in the jungle.* He also shot the beautiful jungle cock which supplied me with fly-tying equipment for fishing.

My father was clearly a strong role model and also urged me on in this manly pursuit. The one example of his views in these early days is in a letter appended to that of 16 February 1949. He wrote, *We are going duck shooting this weekend and I wish you were here to come with us. I am sure that you would both love it. When Alan grows a bit bigger and can manage to hold a gun I shall probably give him mine.* To his and my mother's credit, they became disillusioned with slaughtering birds and animals well before they retired from India, so I never inherited his gun.

I went out with other boys who obviously had guns. On 30 April 1953 I wrote to my parents, *And in the afternoon we went into some woods with two boys and they shot 4 adders, one of which I nearly trod on, and a grey squirrel.* It was, however, more than a year later that I got my own gun, an air-gun, and this became one of my most beloved and well-remembered sports. On 16 August 1954, when I was twelve-and-a-half, my mother wrote:

He [Alan] went off this afternoon with Richard and spent all his savings from Christmas on an Air gun, I hope you approve, all his friends have them apparently and he is very careful and quite a good shot, we set up targets and he knocked down tin after tin while I spattered the Crappers garden with gunshot. I don't think he will do anything silly and it will give him a lot of amusement going after rabbits and pigeons though I doubt if he will get anything with it as he is far too afraid of hurting things. I was a little apprehensive but I suppose boys must live dangerously.

The reference to being 'too afraid of hurting things' is echoed at the end of the summer when my mother notes on 11 September, *He's also been out after rabbits, with no luck. I think actually he's too tender hearted to even fire!*

My mother noted the target shooting aspect again on 23 August, *did I tell you that Alan had bought himself an Air gun? We've had a lot of fun with target practise and he is horrified to find I can usually beat him. I'm rather a natty shot in fact as long as I can see the target.* My mother was aware of the dangers. A week later on the 31 we organized a 'show' in our back garden for our friends. *Alan was in charge of various competitions and guessing games. I thought one of the most interesting guessing games should have been how many people were going to get killed with his air gun, but fortunately there were no corpses to my surprise.*

We clearly took our air-guns with us when we went off on holiday to Scotland that year as my mother described on 11th September the confusion of travelling with: a *mass of trunks, suitcases, fishing rods, guns and packets of sandwiches which had to be manoeuvred in and out of trains and taxis, augmented as we went along by comics and chewing gum ...*

I also continued to play avidly with the air-gun for a period in the Lakes, for example, when a friend visited us my mother wrote on 11th January 1954, *They shot airguns and played trains and went fishing and were no trouble.* From this period, in particular, I remember buying, alongside the usual lead pellets which could only be used once, some re-usable darts with different coloured wool or feathers to make them visible on a target. The advantages of the new house which we purchased in Summer 1955 were described to my father on 18 February of that year by noting that, *there is free fishing in the becks and lakes and I should think shooting though I haven't looked into that.*

In fact, as with horse riding, the cost of serious shooting in England was beyond my parents' budget and I do not remember that my father ever had a gun in this country. He may also have begun, along with my mother, to have been on the point of becoming disillusioned with the sport, though other planters had larger houses with their own shooting, for example on 31 July 1954 my mother noted that, *We spent the day wandering round feeding things and Tim [Edye] took Alan off to see if they could shoot some pigeons in the afternoon, but they didn't but saw a deer.*

As for organized shooting at school, there is only one mention of this in my letters, when, on 27 September 1953, I note, *I am doing shooting this term.* I remember nothing about this. The Dragon was quite a keen shooting school, as I recall, as was Sedbergh, and boys won competitions and prizes at Bisley.

*

My first memories of fishing are recorded in 'Confessions of a Schoolboy' quoted above. These were at Oxford when I was six or seven. Although I put this event in the summer of 1947 when we were first in Oxford, it may in fact be the event referred to by my mother when we revisited Oxford for a few days the following summer. She wrote to my father on 24 August 1948, *I bought Alan a fishing line for 2/- and he caught 3 fish, two in the canal which he ate, and one in the park! Great excitement of course.* I was an enthusiast from then on.

The earliest fishing was in canals, rivers, ponds and the sea. My mother wrote on 18 September that she had, *Taken the children out to tea and had a party here and this afternoon took them into Poole to fish in the park.* And throughout the following years we fished whenever we could, either on the Dorset coast or at school. Fishing was a relatively serious sport at the Dragon and my enthusiasm is shown in a letter written on 12ᵗʰ July 1954 to my father. *Dear Daddy, I hope that you are not feeling very lonely. I have just started fishing seriously. I caught two small perch yesterday one was used for live bait by a boy and it was eatan by a pike which was later caught by the same boy with another perch as bait. It was a pretty small pike about 1½. It has been rainy and bright periods. I am going after big perch today which is about 2 lbs.* My most searing memory of fishing, however is of a terrible occasion when I left a baited hook by the river and discovered a dead bird on the end of the line the next morning.

My enthusiasm was reinforced by that of my parents. On 6 May 1948 my mother wrote to my father: *Daddy's uncle has offered us his fishing tackle, he is very wealthy and says its very valuable stuff and complete, so I might bring it out if it comes in time. In any case we must have that fishing holiday when you next come on leave.* In August she wrote again *Another thing – that fishing tackle I told you of is off, but I saw a second-hand small fly-fishing rod in a shop to-day – is that what you want? Let me know and I will get it. It is for trout-fishing the man says.*

On 15 April 1949 my father wrote encouragingly to me.

> *Another thing I am sure you could do, is help me catch some fish. In the small lake below our bungalow, some time ago I put some wee, wee, fish and now they have grown very big and should be caught. I am sure that they would be very nice to eat. Do you know anything about fishing? It really is good fun and maybe when we come home I shall try and teach you. It is quite difficult really, because in the lake there is a lot weed and the fish when caught rush down in the water and this tangles the line round and round the weeds and you simply cannot pull it out without breaking the line. When you come out I will show you what I mean.*

The promise of fishing on my first trip out was fired by several descriptions of my parents' expeditions up the great mahseer-filled rivers flowing down from Himalayas near their tea garden. Mahseer are sporting fish, caught with a fly or spoon in rushing water, and it was this kind of fast-water fishing that I became deeply enthused by, especially as it was this fishing that my parents tried to arrange when they came on leave, and which could be found when we moved to the Lake District. Basically this was trout fishing and one of my first letters to my parents written on 14 July 1949 from my grandparents house in Glencoe where we were on holiday notes, *We are in Scotland and I have a boy friend. His name is John. I have a fishing rod. We went fishing and I nearly caught one, but the slug came off. Lots of love Alan xxxooo*

A week or so later I wrote again and expanded on this, *John caught a trout in the burrn. I can put worrrms on hooks but I can't put on slugs. I like best fishing and the next best the island the coachman's house... We have a minnow in the small burn that divides the island from the mainland. Much love, Alan.*

The following year on 28 July 1950, aged eight-and-a-half, I wrote again from Glencoe that, *We had a nice Journey up from England. I have cort a little trout and two big ones. I am looking forward to when all of you come back. What fun we will have! I hope we will go to Loch Morar fishing. We are writing because it is wet and we can not go out to play... Lots of love and kisses for Ann, Alan. P.S. Sorry I spelled caught wrong.*

This great event, my first trout, is captured in a photograph. Perhaps helped by this image, this is one of those flashes of memory – the heavy rain turning the burn peat coloured and frothing; dropping a worm in a whirlpool and the tug of the fish and the joy of landing it.

I set about increasing my stock and moving from worms to flies. So my mother wrote on 1 January 1951 to my father, *Alan went into Bournemouth to-day to buy flys for his fishing with you and has been collecting match-boxes to store them in.*

Towards the end of the next month I wrote to my father *Please if you* [shoot] *duks or wild mourgy* [jungle cock] *Keep the Fethers if you can because then we can make Fishing Flys For when you come back.*

My father was returning that summer and a central feature of those precious few months when we would all be together for the first time for a number of years was a planned holiday in Scotland, including fishing, specially for my father and I.

This took much planning and again shows my parents were seriously hampered by a lack of money.

On 20 March 1951 my mother wrote:

Our Scottish tour hasn't been fixed properly yet, I've had various hectic letters from Pat and one from a hotel I wrote to in Lairg, none of them is ideal as the hotel (with good fishing) is particularly expensive, while the cheaper places haven't much fishing. As it stands now we're trying to book in a farmhouse in Argyle for 3 weeks and I plan to book you and Alan for 5 days "real fishing" in the hotel during that time – now don't start making objections darling, I want you to go and the girls and I will be quite happy dangling worms into rock-pools and much more in our element.

In 1952 I went up for a Scottish holiday, this time to East Lothian, on the North Sea coast. My grandfather noted in his diary on 15 August, 'Alan goes north', and on the 23, 'Alan goes to Patty' (my godmother). My mother wrote on the 26:

Darling Alan,
You'll be with the Cowans by now, but I don't know their address so I hope this will catch up with you. I'm longing to hear how you're getting on and what that part of Scotland is like, do you like it as much as the West Coast? I suppose you will find a big change in the Cowan children, especially Richard. Have you caught any fish?

I seem to have gone for holiday with the Cowans at the Old Mill Cottage, Oldhamstocks. I wrote: *I have been having a lovely time up in Scotland I had a lovely journey in a night train to Wishaw. They had a small burn but it did not have any fish in it. ... Sometimes we go to the beach and sometimes to cocklor and other old Places. Yesterday we went to the beach where I swam and I caught 3 big shrimps and about 9 small flat fish Lots of Love Alan.*

There was clearly no trout fishing there, though on 19 September when I returned to Dorset I wrote that, *I had some fishing with uncle Alan.* Alan Cowan, my godmother's husband, was as keen as my father and rich enough to fish for trout and salmon on the Tweed.

On 17 December 1952 my grandfather noted 'Alan flies to India'. This was a three-week holiday, my first return to India since I'd left in early 1947. I remember that I fished in the small pond near the bungalow and also, I think, that we went on fishing expeditions on the bigger rivers, though I don't have any indication that I caught anything. So it was perhaps an anticlimax, but still fishing when I wrote the following 30 April 1953: *I went to the Burys farm about a week ago. In the morning we fished for minows.* There is no further mention of fishing in that year.

In 1954 my mother returned. Towards the end of the summer we went up to Scotland again and she wrote from my father's brother's house near Wishaw on 11th September. A couple of weeks later on 23 she noted, *On Monday he* [Alan Cowan] *took my Alan fishing on the Tweed but it was another wild day and the river very muddy so they didn't get a bite.*

*

Why was fishing so important to me? It was my one really absorbing, passionate sport until the age when I went to university and even beyond. Fishing was a justified escape. It was a licence to be alone and in control of one's own thoughts and destiny. It was a calming, Zen-like, pursuit, especially canal fishing, and I early discovered that it took me away into my own world. Fishing encouraged escape and much of my childhood revolved round this, especially when we moved to the Lake District around my thirteenth birthday.

I think that fishing must have meant so much because it brings several things together. There is the escape to solitude, something akin to what Yeats describes in his poem on 'An Irish Airman Foresees his Death' or St Exupery memorably captures in *Flight to Arras.* It provides a time to think and sort out in a quiet way the pressures of growing up. There is clearly the excitement. Everything is still and in waiting, then the sudden tug, splash, flash of gold beneath the water and the battle is on. Then there was the fact that it took me to so many beautiful places. I would never have spent hours at dawn, in the heat of the day, at sunset and even at night in glorious countryside, watching the changing seasons, noting the minutiae of insect and other life, and entranced by swiftly flowing water which soothes the eyes, if I had not fished.

Other factors were the praise and esteem of others – a special treat to cook the catch and perhaps share it. Then the sociability, the discussions, the stories told, and especially the sharing with my father with whom I found it more difficult to relate to as I grew older. He was passionate about fishing, and later we would go on a special fishing holidays together. We could write to each other about the expeditions, and plan and exchange notes. Even my mother, for a while, was very enthusiastic. And finally it was an outlet for my dreams and plans. Later in my teens I would spend the barren winters drawing maps, making flies, repairing rods, and working out stratagems. Then through the summer in numerous different becks and burns, tarns and lochs, I would pit myself against the prey.

That fishing was probably the only real sport which our family could afford – we could not keep horses or have an estate large enough to shoot over – was something I never considered, though I was aware that every piece of tackle was precious and each new acquisition of a rod, reel or fly was part of the pleasure.

*

There were other sports one could indulge in, either on or in the water. India was a perfect place to learn to swim. The water was warm, there was a pool in our tea-estate bungalow grounds, and there were servants around to encourage and watch over us. I think I remember becoming a good swimmer, learning to spend time under the water, and revelling in the feeling of weightlessness. Perhaps breaking my arm towards the end of my time in India put a temporary stop to this.

My parents continued to write about the wonderful swimming in the rivers up which they made expeditions. When I went for my holiday to Assam in 1952 I again savoured these delights and this may have made me keener on swimming.

The problem with swimming in England was the water. I don't recall any public baths in Dorset. The only one I note in my letters was in Edinburgh, the famous Portobello Baths that we visited in September 1954, and which gave me a particular pleasure because there was a family legend that my father had helped to design and install the artificial wave-making machine there. All we had in the way of bathing apart from the sea and rivers was the small rubber dinghy filled with water which we put out in the garden, too small to swim in but the water would at least be warm.

*

In the period before the Dragon we occasionally went to the sea, but that was bitterly cold and often uninviting, even on the south coast. I was ambivalent about the experience and later really disliked the feeling of sand inside my swimming costume and the sting of the salt. My mother captures the spirit of these expeditions in a number of vignettes, and tiny fragments from them remain in my memory.

On 15 June 1948 when I was seven my mother wrote:

> *On Sunday we hired a taxi and went to Sandbanks – it was a boiling afternoon and we were most agreeably surprised to find that we could actually move on the beach. It was a lovely beach too, all sand, much nicer than Charmouth. We all bathed, the children ecstatically, me in a spirit of dumb resignation, the water was achingly cold. Anne was a little tentative about it and wouldn't do more than paddle. Altogether it was lovely.*

Two years later, on 16 April 1951, my mother wrote:

*Wednesday looked like being a fairly nice day so I threw
together a picnic lunch and took the kids to the sea. We
went to Bournemouth which I always forget is on the sea.
Actually its awfully nice. You follow a stream down through
some gardens to a lovely sandy beach. Of course in the
summer I imagine its frightful but we had it almost to
ourselves. It started off badly as Alan had taken his fishing
rod and then of course there was nowhere to fish so he
wanted to go on a boat and I said I couldn't allow him so he
scuffed the sand and scowled and said well what could he
do then and I told him he could go home at which he
wandered off with tears in his eyes ... All quite unimportant
and in the end we had a lot of fun digging and playing
cricket. I did understand his feelings as I remember the
awful flat feeling when something you wanted very much
didn't happen, but found it most irritating to be told there
was nothing to do when I had presented them with the sea
and the sands on a sunny day.*

A month later on 15 May she wrote, *Yesterday we went with
the same two children and their grand-parents to the sea (their
parents are in Malaya) it wasn't very warm, a freezing wind, but
we found a sheltered spot. My two were not at their best,
squabbling incessantly, but enjoyed it I think and we are all
quite brown to-day.*

Three years later in 1954, when my mother was back in
England again, she gives various accounts of swimming in the
sea. On 19 July she describes in a letter how:

*We made another sorty to the beach last Wednesday,
the sun came out brightly in the morning and we had heard
of a "quiet" beach near Bournemouth so set out after lunch
full of hope – but it was not a success. In the first place we
couldn't find the beach and after wandering for ages we
finally went to the usual beach. By this time the sun had
gone and a strong, cold, wind was blowing but this hadn't
deterred the crowds and we spent a miserable hour*

160

guarding our small patch of sand from the usual squalling children and scuffling dogs, Fiona actually swam for about half a minute and turned bright blue and it was altogether loathsome.

Three awful fat women with false teeth and pink plastic slides in their dyed hair came and sat beside us. They all got into their bathing suits and took photos of each other, huge busts and short blotchy legs, really they were too awful and pathetic, afterwards they put on their dresses again and paddled with girlish squeaks and sideways glances, I was fascinated but I must say the human species, though amusing, are too much in such masses and I'm never going near the place again. The girls agreed with me, though they enjoyed the "Punch and Judy" show which we stood and watched for hours with sand blowing into our faces.'

This letter is one of several instances of an obvious class disdain. My parents, and no doubt myself and my other close relatives certainly including my grandparents, had their eyes fixed on those above them. The 'lower classes' hardly figure, and, when they do, are usually described in a derogatory way.

On 9 August she wrote that:

Unfortunately the weather is still unsettled to say the least of it, but we did get a lovely afternoon on Friday and he [uncle Richard] took us to Corfe castle and on to Studland for tea and a swim – actually I was organising the tea so didn't have time to swim to my great regret but the rest of them did and turned bright blue – I put my feet in and was practically frost bitten, I can't see myself swimming ever again.

On the 16:

Friday was fine ... We went to Studland but decided to try a different beach and sent the three girls down a path to reconnoitre, as they didn't return we followed after an

> *interval but when we got to the beach couldn't see them anywhere and Richard and I spent about three quarters of an hour looking for them, finally discovered them when my temper and feet were in ribbons. Not a very good beginning, and the afternoon wore on in the same way, Fiona and Janet giggling and groaning alternately and refusing to co-operate with the others and Alan making sarcastic remarks in the background while Anne shrieked that crabs were biting her and she wanted an ice cream. I would have drowned the lot of them if the sea had been warm enough for me to get into, actually Fiona Richard and Janet bathed and said it was nice and it didn't look quite as grim as usual.*

In the same letter she wrote that:

> *We had a day on the beach with the Mermagens before we left, a really warm day and I bathed and we all got very burnt and played rounders and cricket and touch rugger and every other game all day.*

And on 23 we were collected by friends and:

> *We took them to Studland and had no sooner got ourselves and lunch things established than it started to rain in earnest, my three were in the sea by then but we dragged them out and made them eat their lunch, cold and sandy as they were, and then we packed ourselves all back into the car again and went to see a film in Poole.*

I also remember that swimming was strongly associated with Christianity. I went to a kind of kindergarten Christian camp at Milford on Sea on 15 April 1952 when I was ten and wrote to my parents on the 30: *I had a nice week at Milford on sea.* My grandfather adds, *Alan is very fit and looking grand. He seems to have enjoyed his time at Milford. He was there for 10 days. We think he should go there in the Summer hols but for not too long as beach morning and afternoon is apt to get monotonous after a bit.*

The next stage up in the religious camps was again on the coast, at Swanage, where I went twice. The first was noted in my grandfather's diary on 10 August, *Richard took Alan to Swanage camp.* Two days later I wrote to may parents, *The other day Richard drove me in his car to Swanage and we had two bathes wich I enjoyed.*

I have the brochure for Swanage. There are photographs of the house and the sea, of the sea and bathing, of Corfe Castle, of cricket. 'The house is within a few minutes walk of the sea, and, standing on a hill, commands a fine view of Swanage Bay. The bathing, boating and sailing in Swanage Bay are excellent and safe; and these activities are very carefully supervised. Swanage is in the neighbourhood of very beautiful country, and we shall visit some of the places of particular interest. In recent years these have included Corfe Castle, Dancing Ledge...' I remember changing in the beach huts and clinging on to rafts and boats. I also vividly remember leaping into the sea off some rocks, perhaps at Dancing Ledge or Durdle Door in Dorset and realizing I was drowning in the huge waves until I was saved by a master or bigger boy. A horrific experience.

*

As far as boats are concerned, I think my interest probably started in my infancy in Assam. I seem to recall having a special little bamboo raft made for me, which floated on empty petrol cans. We also went fishing up the wonderful rivers in long canoes, though this may have been later on my return trips. Then there was the long sea voyage home when I was five – but I was seasick a lot and don't remember much.

In the first summer in Oxford there are a number of photos of me and the family in rubber dinghies with fragile sails, probably near the Dragon on the Cherwell. On a return trip in August 1948 I showed my first signs of boating skill, my mother writing, *We took the children in a punt yesterday. Alan rowed violently all the way and we shot from one bank to the other in an alarming way. Actually he has quite a good idea of handling a boat.*

My uncle Robert was keen on boats too and my mother describes our plans to repair an ancient mud-clogged boat we discovered on a nearby river. She also describes at some length the various bits of rowing and sailing I did at Poole on the indoor pool. On 25 March 1948, *We all went into Poole yesterday to do bits of shopping and look at the park which has a bit of the harbour in it and boats some of which are for children. They weren't working unfortunately, but should be fun later.*

On the next leave, my mother describes in a letter of 29 April 1951:

> *Yesterday which was Saturday I promised Alan I would take him sailing (his latest craze) and duly did. So, also the two Burry boys. It was a cold bleak afternoon with a strong wind blowing and I was perished with cold (and a bit nervous) as I had vision of us all being tipped into the icy water, the Burry boys sat looking grey with fright but Alan very gamely took the tiller and mainsail and tacked backwards and forwards 5 or 6 times most professionally though he told me after that he didn't "exactly enjoy it". We only stayed out about half an hour and then I sent Alan and Paul out in a canoe to get warm...'*

I also did some boating, canoes, and punts in all probability, at the Dragon, noting on 3 of June 1955 that *the boat club is starting.*

These were small boats. As for the real thing, our family was again just on the edge of those who had proper boats and, as with horses or shooting, could only watch with envy the richer boat owners among our friends. On 9 March 1948 my mother described how, *We walked along the beach collecting shells (sack-fulls of the damn things) and then went and investigated the Boat Club where all the lovely motor-yachts were being painted and varnished and how I'd love to have one, just a tiny one. George (Heathers husband) has a motor-boat which he has promised to take us in to Alan's joy and my inner dismay!*

Three months later, on 7 June, she wrote: *Yesterday we went down to Poole harbour its rather fascinating with lots of boats and tar smells and funny little shops full of compasses and* [tiny ships] *in bottles.* This was a constant source of frustrated hope, a great sailing harbour which we could see from the heath behind our house, but we had no boat. On 11 July, *we went down to the harbour and looked longingly at the boats.*

On 21 September my grandfather notes that my father went out sailing on a friend's yacht, and Robert my uncle also went sailing with a friend and to the Broads. But we could not afford a boat ourselves.

Our enthusiasm for a world of boating just beyond our reach continued when we moved to the Lake District with the plentiful yachts and motor cruisers. My mother wrote hopefully on her first visit on 26 September 1954, *this is the place to live and the house is heaven and we shan't need to go anywhere else for our amusements as it has everything – coarse and trout fishing, boating, sailing, golf and heavenly walks and rides.* A month later on 25 October I repeated in a letter to my father this news: *I hope that we stay at Ambleside as there is nice, fishing, riding, sailing, swimming, walking.*

We did not get the sailing until I bought a little clinker dinghy at the age of eighteen and, apart from an occasional trip on a richer friends boat, or a hired rowing boat, boating remained elusively beyond our reach. This was particularly frustrating since my favourite books of the time were Arthur Ransome's 'Swallows and Amazons' series. I could only live in my imagination on those fascinating waters.

9. IMAGINATION

My grandparents were keen readers. My grandfather listed the books he read, many of them being detective fiction, but also poetry and other genres. They would have encouraged my reading. My mother was an even keener reader and had a highly developed critical sense. She wanted to be a writer and devoured literature as one step in this direction. Hence I was under considerable pressure to read and as widely as possible.

My mother's high expectation and disappointment are shown in a letter she wrote on 15 April 1949 when I was a little over seven. *What can we do to make you want to learn to read Alan? What about ten shillings the first time you open a book (any book) and read a sentence straight off without stopping? I wish you knew what a lot of lovely books there were waiting for you to read, I'm sure you'd learn in a week if you did.*

My mother's view seems to be echoed by my kindergarten reports. I started off well until I was about eight, and then declined to that well-known euphemism for average mediocrity: 'fairly good'. The change more or less coincides with my mother's leaving for India.

My school reports suggested that my reading at kindergarten was slow. My grandparents, however, started to coax me into reading for myself. My grandmother reveals one way in which she did this, through a combination of reading aloud to us and encouraging me to read to her, in the first letter that she wrote to my mother after she had left for India. On 18 October she wrote, *as he had a reading book for home work – he read me a page and I read a page of his Comic and so in turns we got through quite a lot.* My grandmother seems to have encouraged me not only to read but also to tell stories, noting in the same letter, *Alan gave us one of his gentle flowing stories at lunch.*

I must have come under increased pressure to read sufficiently fast to enjoy the process at the Dragon, though I only mention reading a few books. Quite early on in the Summer term 1951, I write that, *I am reading a book called the sign of the wolfes head* [a book I cannot trace]. Nine months later, however, it still appears as if it is worth my grandfather writing to my mother on 30 March 1952 that *He reads quite a lot to himself and has been playing chess with me.* My interest was probably stimulated by listening to stories on the radio, noting on 30 May 1953 that, *Tonight I will be listening to Treasure Island on the Wireless.* And by this time, aged eleven, people were giving me books as presents. On 18 February 1953: *I got a book from aunt Jean and uncle Alan and a letter from the other granny.* And on 18 May of the same year I wrote to my parents, *Thank you very much for the lovely book.*

As for what we read, either through being read to by others or reading ourselves, there is very little explicit record. My mother mentions on 8 December 1951, when she is preparing to go back to India with my sisters and will be teaching my sister Anne, that she went to London, *and enjoyed browsing round among all the children's books, they are going to be taught from all sorts of fascinating things like Arthur Ransome and Winnie-the-Pooh!* These were clearly two of the texts. Kipling in various forms, especially 'Mowgli' and 'Puck of Pook's Hill' were favourites, as were Beatrix Potter, 'The Meeting Pool' and other imagined worlds. Other childhood favourites, certainly included Arthur and His Knights, Biggles, Worrals and Ginger also figured there. 'Treasure Island' and I think 'Robinson Crusoe' were favourites. Also A.A. Milne and 'Wind in the Willows'. I also read, or listened to the reading by others, of 'The Railway Children', 'Five Children and It' and 'The Secret Garden'.

Other books emerge from my letters. For example, I had forgotten that around my thirteenth birthday I became obsessed by murder and detective stories, especially 'The

Saint'. Also I wrote on 11 January 1954, *I have taken up reading Agatha Cristie in the last three days I have read three different books 1 "Mr Hercule Poirrot's Christmas" 2 "The Murder of Roger Ackroyd" and "Murder on the Orient Express.* When I returned to school a popular theme of boarding schools emerged when I wrote on 17 January 1954, *I have read an extremely funny book wich I advise you to get. It is called down with school or you might get "The Honor of St Trinians".* They are verry good and I think the girls would love them.*

My interest in detective fiction, shared particularly at this time with my grandfather, is noted further at the end of the year. On 15 December 1954 my mother wrote of me, *he is running a temp. of 100.8 which is nothing much and has read two detective novels to-day and listened to the wireless without a pause and is no trouble...After lunch we left Alan to his 3rd murder and went out on our bikes exploring...* In fact I had become such an avid reader that my mother a few months earlier, on 6 September 1954, complained that when we went out to see some other children, *My kids weren't particularly sociable, sat about reading books most of the afternoon but of course hers are a good deal younger.*

Probably comics were as important as books. I remember that 'The Eagle', 'Beano' and 'Dandy' were our staple fare, and can still remember some of the main characters, Dan Dare and his arch enemy the Mekon; Dennis the Menace, Beryl the Peril, Corky the Cat and others. A particular episode I remember vividly. For some reason all high tech devices normally used by Dan Dare and the Mekon were disabled, but Dan reverted to using swords, bows and arrows and the like. As I was going through my bow and arrow phase, I was delighted.

When my mother first left me to go to India, my grandmother wrote on 18 October 1948 that she read to me from my comic, but did not say what it was. On 6 May 1951 my mother wrote, *On Wednesday Fiona stayed in bed and I read tripe to her all day out of "Beano" and "Chatterbox" to her great pleasure.* Clearly my mother disapproved of this level of comic, though what she thought of 'The Eagle', which was my special comic at the Dragon, I have not discovered. The only other mention is much later in a letter of 7 April 1955 when the house, my mother wrote, was, *so cluttered with straw, plaster, comics and hamster droppings that I can hardly bear to look round.*

*

Watching films were rather special, one off, events. Consequently I have a rather detailed account of the films I watched throughout my childhood, and there is no doubt that they had a tremendous effect. At home, my mother describes some of our outings to the cinema at Poole and Bournemouth in her characteristically caustic way, along with some of our reactions and comments. Some of the films, like the 'Crimson Pirate', which I first saw in Calcutta and scenes from which (like scuttling along the bottom of the sea in an upturned rowing boat) have remained with me since (later fortified by 'Pirates of the Caribbean'*).*

The films we watched in the holidays were just as important to me as those at school. Indeed the reason I wrote so much about films was because, much more than books, they were something I could share with my parents. In India, films were a link with Britain and we could compare notes. It was an important part of our imagined unity.

Furthermore, the expeditions to the cinema, usually accompanied by other treats such as a meal or ice creams, were special family events and we would re-live them in our imaginations for weeks afterwards. My mother's accounts of some of the films we saw and our reactions gives an unusual insight into the world of family viewing in the 1950s.

I still very dimly remember the Walt Disney animals in all their cuteness, especially 'Bambi' which I saw in 1948. Later, when my mother described (and I encountered on my visit to India) her little deer Miranda, I could relate that to this early film.

We then move to when I was ten. In 1952, on 8 August, my mother wrote to me from Assam, *We had a film at the club yesterday called "The Half Breed" which was all about Red Indians and the wild west and villains were rolled over the edges of precipices and horses tore about in clouds of dust (in Technicolour) – it was rather fun. I wished I'd kept the girls up for it. We have one or two good ones coming which they'll enjoy including "Where No Vultures Fly" again.*

On the return from my first trip to see my parents in Assam over Christmas 1952, I saw my favourite film, 'The Crimson Pirate'. I saw it in Calcutta with my father as he escorted me on the way home and I described its effect obliquely at the end of my journey home when I wrote on 18 January 1953 from the Dragon. *I saw some saber jet fighters at rome. I nearly went to the CRIMZON PIRATE again but there was not time so I went to a news theatre.* During the summer of 1953 I saw the 'Crimson Pirate' again and on holiday in Scotland I wrote on 11th January 1954, *On Thursday I went to "Shane!" Wich is a very good Cowboy Classic but I think I liked "The Crimson Pirate" as much.*

*

My mother returned to England in the spring of 1954 and started to take us to films again. The first two were during term and so I was not present. On 21 June my mother wrote of my sisters

They have nearly thrown off their colds, we rather rashly took them into Bournemouth to see a film on Anne's second day up, it was "The flight of the White Heron" and we saw it on "Cinemascope" which is a great improvement and makes it look exactly as if it were on the stage. It was the complete tour (the Queens) and very good, much better than the one we saw in Nazira. At one point it went quite silent (on purpose) and Anne said "Oh, its broken down" in a loud, matter-of-fact voice, shades of Sonari club but our neighbours were rather startled!

Three weeks later on 11ᵗʰ July she wrote, *On Wednesday I took the girls to see "My Friend Flicka" in Poole... The film was lovely, all about a horse and I was in tears most of the time, but the film shown with it was all about gangsters and half-naked women and most unsuitable.*

My first film with my mother was partly to compensate for the effect of a very painful visit to an ear specialist. My mother wrote on 9 August:

> *I decided I'd give them a treat and take them on to see a film in Bournemouth... we squelched round looking at the various cinemas and landed up at a promising film called "Prince Valiant" but decided to get a snack first ... We started the programme at 12.30 and believe it or not darling they made me sit through the whole lot twice, we finally staggered out at 5.30 absolutely dizzy and got home at 7 with nothing but the memory of the soggy fish and splitting headaches, but the film was ideal for the kids, knights in armour and King Arthur and boiling oil and endless sword fights, all in 3D and broad American, it was really terribly funny and appallingly bad but they lapped it up and were clattering round with the lids of all the dustbins as soon as we got home. We saw some of the Empire Games on the News.*

This is a good instance of the way in which films fed into our games.

My mother's attitude to the Raj films we were seeing is shown in her account two weeks later on 23 August of another film outing.

> *We had missed the last bus home before lunch so I was persuaded to buy some sausage rolls and take the kids to the "King of the F[K]yber Rifles" which was a frightfully lurid Technicolor film on the Frontier, Tyrone Power run to fat and (Ghastly thought!) a half-caste, galloping about the desert in the hot weather in thick serge up to his ears. It was terrible tripe but went down well needless to say though*

Fiona and Anne spent a lot of their time with their backs to the screen demanding to be told when that particular bit was over.

In the same letter she describes how, *we went to see a film in Poole, luckily it was a very good one, "The Rainbow Jacket", all about horse racing and most amusing. We also saw the Bannister race which was exciting.* The frequent references to the newsreels is reminiscent of the days before television news gave much in the way of outside reporting.

When we moved to a temporary home in Windermere we were only ten minutes walk from a small, cheap and cheerful cinema, and my mother obviously enjoyed taking us there. Just after Christmas on 27 December 1954 she wrote, *We got back for tea and then out into the rain once more to the local cinema to see a funny film called "Up to his neck" which was extremely funny in bits, the cinema is very one horse but matey.*

There was also a bigger cinema in the neighbouring market town of Kendal which we could reach by bus. On 11th January 1955 she described how:

We went into Kendal instead and did a bit of shopping and were going to the matinee of "The Living Desert" but found there wasn't one, so had to tramp round in the teeth of a North-Easterly gale for 4 hours till the evening performance. I was so cold that even in the cinema, which was packed, I couldn't get warm and thought I would be struck down with pneumonia at once – but apparently I'm pretty tough after all. The film was wonderful, you would love it, all about snakes and tarantulas, most thrilling and we saw the Test Match on the News.

This is another film which I remember slightly, and which came back to me when, over fifty years later, I visited a desert zoo in the southern States of America and saw similar creatures.

At the end of the holidays we saw one last film. On 17 January 1955 she wrote: *In the evening we turned out again to see a last film "The Charge of the Lancers" which was a fearful hash-up of the Crimea but much approved of by the children. The local Cinema is a great success, the most expensive seats being 2/- and all very chummy.*

It is worth mentioning that television was only just starting to creep into our lives. At the Dragon I occasionally watched television, either at the school or at the homes of friends. We did not have a set until 1957, but our fascination with the new medium is shown in a letter written at the end of our time in Dorset. On her birthday on 22 July 1954 my mother wrote to my father:

> *On Tuesday we went to a friend of Mummy's to see the International Horse Show on T.V. – it was a longish bus ride but we were most intrigued, we didn't have very much of the horses but what there was very good. Children's hour followed which was a historical drama and quite fascinating and we only just tore ourselves away in time for the bus – now the children have seen it they sigh deeply and say "Lucky beggars" every time they pass a house with T.V.*

*

The role of pantomimes in family entertainment and in fostering the imagination of children is difficult to recover in the age of television. It is captured a little, however, by my mother's descriptions of a couple of these events that I still remember in flashes.

The first is described on 11 January 1951, soon after my mother had returned after her first long absence. She wrote:

> *We had two days recovering from the Christmas orgy and on the 28 went to the Pantomime in Bournemouth, it was "Alladin" and really excellent, you would have loved it, most amusing with lots of nice dancing girls, and the funniest Widow Twankey I can remember seeing, the*

children of course took most of it in dead earnest and looked askance at our paroxysms of mirth. Anne couldn't take much of it in and got restless in parts and was very frightened of the wicked uncle but cheered up a lot when he was put through the mangle. There was a sweet performing dog which was the chief attraction for all the children. We got home eventually over-tired, over-excited and stuffed with chocolate in the time-honoured fashion.

The second was during the only other Christmas I spent with my mother in England, my last in the Dragon years, when we had moved to the Lake District. Here the centre was Morecambe rather than Bournemouth. On 27 December 1954 my mother wrote, *To-morrow the children are going to a party and the next day is the pantomime...* Then on 3 January she wrote again:

On Wednesday Richard drove us in to Morecambe to the pantomime, we did it in record time and all arrived feeling rather sick as it was a switchback sort of road but restored ourselves with bars of chocolate and ice-creams and the pantomime was terribly good, not too sophisticated or frightening and we all enjoyed it. Afterwards we had tea in the restaurant and ate cakes full of very mock cream and were feeling sick again by the time we got in but altogether enjoyed the afternoon.

I remember that drive past the lower hills of the south Cumbria fells along the curvy roads and the pleasures of the pantomime itself. A third reference to going to the pantomime is in my grandfather's diary on 22 December 1951, but since we were all together there is no reference to it in a letter.

One other performance which lies on the boundaries of musical and pantomime is mentioned in a letter of 1 February 1955 from the Dragon, *Then on Thursday afternoon we went to 'Listen to the wind' wich is a very funny Musical Pantomime and I think it was the best I had seen.*

I distinctly remember going to 'Peter Pan' – I think as a pantomime, and the terror of Captain Hook and the crocodile, and delight of flying, and the urgent calls of Tinkerbell for us to cry out that we believed in fairies. The only reference to this is to 'peter pan' in a list of films and plays I went to in the summer of 1953 in my letter of 27 September of that year.

*

The 1950s, as I remember them, were the great days of American musicals, particularly Rogers and Hammerstein. Most of my relatives, including my father and especially Robert and my Mermagen cousins, were particularly keen on this art form. So 'Oklahoma', 'Annie Get your Gun', 'Call me Madam' and other musicals haunted my life. We would sing songs from them on car journeys, while doing the interminable washing up ('A you're Adorable, B you're so Beautiful...'). I can still sing quite a lot of Oklahoma and hearing a song from these American classics still brings back the excitement and energy of those days. They brought light and warmth into a tired and rationed post-war Britain, a touch of exotic romance in a bleak world.

We also heard a good deal of 'popular' music of the 1950s on the 'wireless', as we called it, though, as yet, I can't remember much beyond the theme tune of 'Much Binding in the Marsh' and 'Dick Barton Special Agent'. Especially with the Mermagens, but also with my musical grandmother, mother and uncles, there was a certain amount of music-making in the evenings.

There must also have been quite a bit of singing at the Christian boy's camps I went to – not just rather jolly hymns, but 'sing-songs' of various kinds. My uncle Richard, in particular, was very keen on classical music and there are mentions of concerts he went to. For example, my grandfather mentioned on 19 September 1952, *Richard and Robert have been to several concerts at the Winter Gardens Bournemouth.* Richard may also have started to learn the clarinet and I vaguely remember even at 'By the Way' the plaintive notes of the slow movement of Mozart's clarinet concerto being endlessly repeated. I have also discovered a note on 29 January 1951 in my grandfather's diary about my uncle Billy: 'Billy plays recorder'.

*

Another form of spectacular entertainment which we occasionally enjoyed was the circus. One of the main delights was the exotic wild animals. For me they had a special association since I had seen animals such as elephants in India, and in the letters there are several references to these animals.

This other world, the world whence the animals came, is described a little in a letter of 26 August 1952 from my mother in Assam.

> *The girls enjoyed their week-end as on both afternoons they were taken to see a troop of performing elephants which are being trained near here for a circus. I think I told you. Apparently this circus has toured all the way from Hong Kong, via the Philippines and Burma and is next going to Australia, then America and finally England. There are 12 elephants and Fiona and Anne have been demonstrating on all available stools and sofas, the sort of tricks they were teaching them, they've even tried getting Candy [a dog] to stand on her hands on a cushion, but without the slightest success! There was one elephant called Sonny who did everything wrong, apparently, stood on his hind legs when the others were on their front, and overbalanced into the bargain but the girls thought he was "too sweet"! I'm hoping to see them myself soon and can tell you more about them and then I hope we'll see the circus itself.*

To this I replied on 19 September 1952 that, *I liked to hear about the Performing elephants. I wonder if daddy saw any more wild ones.*

In England, I could only see wild animals in cages or performing. On 15 June 1948 my mother wrote to my father:

Oh I forgot, I took the children to Bertram Mills Circus in Bournemouth last week. I felt I couldn't resist it as it would never come so near again. It was a bit of an effort, we left the house at quarter to 1 and got to the circus at 3.30 and then started to queue. It was lovely though, Alan was enthralled and Fiona liked the clowns, but the excitement and heat were too much for her and she soon got tired. There were all the usual things, including lions and a most sickening trapeze act, but the clowns went down best, especially the part where they threw interminable buckets of water at each other. Do you remember that dreadful thing I dragged you to last year and how cross you were?!

Fragmentary images of painted clown faces and lions on their stands being flicked at by the tamer seem to be lodged in my mind.

We went to the circus again, this time in Edinburgh, some six years later. My mother wrote on 11th September 1954. *On Saturday* [uncle] *Alan took us all to the circus, a very good one which my three loved but John and Alison found too noisy, the usual elephants, lions and ghastly trapeze artists, also some most amusing chimpanzees and of course lots of ponies to Anne's joy.* I was clearly impressed and on the 23 my mother wrote, *Nicky and Fiona got on well too, so Alan was a bit left out, but amused himself with a couple of white mice which he was teaching circus tricks, the poor things were worn out by the time he left...*

*

My mother gives a graphic account of our family visit to the zoo during my penultimate summer term at the Dragon. The legend of how the lamas chewed the daisies off my mother's hat was long recited in our family. My mother's awareness of the melancholy of such places, which I felt when I recently visited the London zoo with my grand-children is clear.

On 29 June 1954 she wrote to my father:

> *On Monday, yesterday, I took them all up to London to the zoo – not as crazy or extravagant as it sounds – the trains from Oxford here are so bad I would have to stay another night there and fed and amused them all day so it wouldn't have worked out any cheaper and I didn't know what to do with them in Oxford anyway. I got some free zoo tickets from Celia and we had an exhausting day in Undergrounds and buses, sustained by smiths crisps and Ice lollies – you would have hated it – the girls went up and down the moving staircase till they were turned off forcibly! We tramped the zoo for 4 hours until I could hardly put my burning feet to the ground, it was packed but I think the kids enjoyed it, especially the children's zoo where goats and llamas were loose – I opened my small bag to get a handkerchief and two goats and a llama put their faces in and I was horrified to see the llama striding off with one of the daisies from my new hat in his mouth – I was carrying it in my bag. Fiona rescued it, rather mangled! We "did" most things, though it all seemed rather shrunk and shabby to me, the animals all looked so fed up. The birds were best, especially the peacocks which all displayed for us.*

*

A form of educational entertainment which again had great impact in the pre-television age was that of museums and exhibitions. My interest in collecting things may have partly been linked to the growing realization that there were people who had 'Cabinets of Curiosities'. This is exactly how I remember the little museum at the top of the stairs in the centre of the playground at the Dragon.

The fact that I received strange stamps, animal's teeth, coins, spears and arrows and so many other things was both an education in itself, and also an encouragement to keep this other – to collect and categorize. Certainly the objects impressed my friends and gave me some status, and it preserved links, and gave me something to share with my parents, just as fishing with my father, or poetry and literature with my mother, was a form of sharing in a shared imaginary world.

It is also worth noting here that I lived in a sort of museum throughout my childhood. My grandmother was a great hoarder of things and she had brought back, or inherited, a number of Burmese and Indian objects. Lacquered boxes and the little golden statue from the Palace at Mandalay, surrounded me, along with woven cloths and many small ornaments from the last days of the Raj. I half took these for granted, but also they made me curious about other worlds.

My parents I think (and the school) took me to one or two of the big London museum. I don't really remember anything of these visits and any memories are probably augmented from later visits.

The only exhibition that is noted in my letters is the Festival of Britain in 1951. I cannot remember attending, though a letter quoted below suggests that we all went to it. My parents also talked about going, but did not do so in the end as far as I can see. They did, however, have views on it as shown in several letters. This started on 1 March 1951 when my mother wrote, *Mummy went round the Festival of Britain site when she was in London and said it was pitiful, a sea of mud with a few hideous eruptions like fungus erupting from it, not a sign of the wonderful gardens stretching to the river etc.* Three weeks later, on the 20, she wrote, *I suppose we ought to see something of the Festival of Britain too as its costing such millions of our money.*

Finally on 24 April she wrote to my father about plans for his leave. *Then on Monday what about seeing something of the Festival. The Dragon School are taking all the boys that day and parents are invited to join the fun, but as I know your views on "conducted tours" I think we'll keep clear of that! Still, it would be quite fun to wander round on our own if you wouldn't be too exhausted.* The school arrangements are noted

179

in the 'Centenary History' of the Dragon School, which states that 'Then it was Festival of Britain Summer, with Bursar E.L.F. organising a huge expedition to the South Bank for Dragons, Staff and Parents by special train.'[1]

*

The joys of making collections began early and has influenced me throughout my life. Indeed this very account flows out of the passion for collecting since I have also collected as much of my life as possible, and later this took the form of paper, films, photographs and other traces of the past.

My collections early on followed the usual patterns, including seashells and chocolate wrappers, which became a serious collecting interest at the Dragon and which I still have. The chocolate wrapper collection is particularly important when one remembers that these were the post-war years with sweet rationing at the start and chocolates were rare and precious. I especially remember managing to collect (presumably from swapping) some exotic chocolate wrappers from Switzerland which were my pride and joy.

Somewhat more exotic was a small collections of animal teeth and tusks – I still have a couple from tigers, two from leopards, and a wild boar tusk. A letter quoted later from my mother illuminates the history of the leopard teeth and shows that she was well aware of the cachet of such things.

I might have been in a good position to collect stamps because my parents wrote from India, and I did collect a few dutifully, but it never became an obsession. I do not remember being a member of the Stamp Club, which it was said 'still flourishes' according to the Easter 1954 'Draconian', and which had started its own Dragon School Stamp Album. Stamp collecting was very much a product of British imperialism, the king or queen's head arriving from far-flung corners of the Empire, but I seem not to have been gripped.

---

[1] C.H. Jacques, *A Dragon Centenary 1877-1977* (1977), 191.

My mother tried to encourage me to collect butterflies. On 24 October 1948 she wrote to me, *I'm also going to start butterfly hunting, and I want to get a book about them because we get some wonderful ones here as big a birds. I want to find out how to stuff them or whatever you do to keep butterflies.*

A few months later on 16 February she wrote again.

> *We have quite a lot of flowers out now and they are bringing us butterflies and bees which is rather nice. I'm going to make myself a butterfly net and see if I can catch some and dry them, we get some wonderful ones here, perhaps you remember them. What about you doing the same and we'll see who can get the most different kinds, except there are two of you and you can run faster than me. I haven't discovered how you dry them yet but I'll let you know as soon as I do. Of course your butterflies in England don't start for a bit yet and you don't get as many kinds.*

She did not give up and as late as 7 April 1952 I wrote to her, *Dear Mummy and Daddy, Thank you for your letters. And thank you for the butterflies.*

I don't remember more than the odd desultory chase in fulfilment of my mother's dream. As she has pointed out elsewhere, I hated killing things (except fish) and may not have enjoyed the slaughter. The same may be the reason I did not collect bird's eggs, but preferred to feed birds. On 25 March 1948 my mother wrote to my father, as noted above, that, *Alan has hung a saucepan full of crumbs in a tree and a whole crowd of birds come and eat from it, to his delight.* This was in the back of her mind when she returned to India and on 30 November wrote to me and my sister, *Are you feeding the birds yet? You wont forget them in the winter will you, because they can get so little food then. Tell me how many kinds you see and if the same ones come every day.*

As for other collections, I cannot remember anything specific, though I suspect we kept and swapped cigarette cards and such like.

*

As children, we lived much of our life in invented or imagined worlds, spinning out stories and adventures and scenes which blend together what we read and watched around us, with further elaborations of our own making. This is, in many ways, the most important part of childhood as I remember it. While I have forgotten almost everything about how I was formally educated day after day in class, I can remember quite vividly aspects of the world of serious play with my sisters, my uncle Robert, and my friends at home and at the Dragon.

All this took place in a more or less pre-TV, pre-computer, pre-internet age. That is one reason it is worth reconstructing. We did have access to gramophones and also wireless, whose history and effects and importance can be reconstructed from my letter collection. But mostly we had to amuse ourselves and play with our friends.

The models, the dressing up with guns, hats, shields and other 'serious play' enabled the childhood imagination to take off. It does not require much external help. The hours of imaginative play are as 'real' in a different way as the 'real' world. What is most interesting is not the actual toys but the imagined world which we learn to make as children and which we continue to construct through our lives, though later we give it more grown up names like 'art' or 'drama' or 'academic writing', or 'parliament'. This draws me into the heart of this endeavour, trying to penetrate the growth of the imagination of the child.

It seems to me that while Wordsworth was right to suggest that much of this imaginative growth came out of his encounter with nature – the world which I shall later describe for the Lakes – he was only dealing with a small part of the formative influence. He hardly deals with the much larger area of socialization through inter-action with friends and others in games and discussion. Nor does he write about the imagination woven around objects which we have made or been given –

toys, models, and so on. This is just as important as rocks and stones and trees.

Though it may not lead us into the kind of ecstatic mysticism which Wordsworth described, and later became important for me too, it is perhaps more important than anything else in shaping us, though soon given great support through art and literature. Again this subject does not separate off conveniently into play at home or in school – the games and models and crazes overlapped.

*

The scene is set for my recollection of model toys by a somewhat illiterate letter I wrote to Father Christmas from my pre-boarding school on 25 of November 1949, when I was a month off my eighth birthday. I specified a broad range of desirable presents as follows:

> *Dear Father Xmas, I hope you are very well and you have lots of Presents for me. Can I have a salinge ship. And a trn* [train] *plees and a meccano set and a woch* [watch] *and sum sweets and sum soldiers and farem anamals with love from Alan*

Gradually either Father Christmas or others provided me with most of these and my uncle Robert enormously enriched my world with his collections. The four main types of model are mentioned six years later in a description on 25 July 1954 when I was twelve, in a letter from my mother to my father. *He* [Alan] *and the girls get on very well at the moment. Anne follows him round like a puppy and they have made a wonderful town with their farms, zoos, trains etc. and we've had a series of devastating battles with his soldiers.*

All this collection of toys, my uncles and our own, had to be moved from 'By the Way' when we went to the Lakes. My mother's irritated account of the packing gives another hint of the extent of our collection. On 10 October 1954 she wrote to my father:

Not an eventful week, though fairly hectic - Collecting all the kids and Roberts bits and pieces and packing them was quite a job – specially Robert's endless aeroplanes. I spent a whole morning unscrewing Meccano things that Robert had made to pack them away. His only reaction to the move was to send instructions that everything of his was to be packed with great care or there would be trouble – if I'd not already done so I'd have thrown the lot onto a bonfire!

I found that toys really excited me because of the overlap between collecting 'sets' of things and those things being models, miniatures of reality, with which we could begin to explore and manipulate the adult world within our own scale. The central preoccupations here are still to be found in my toy collection.

I wrote in a letter to my mother on 25 March 1953 from home that, *I have got an enormous army of toy soldiers including 3 camels with riders waving rifels.* The soldiers with their attendant guns and other equipment reflected in microcosm the British Empire and beyond – camel riders referred to above from Arabia, natives with spears from Africa, Scotsmen in kilts, Red Indians and Cowboys. My collection of toy soldiers overlapped with Robert's great collection, part of which he later told me I destroyed as an infant in India when I pulled down a cupboard.

The battles we fought with these soldiers still live with me. We had forts, for example, the wooden fort made for me by Mr Crapper the retired dentist who lived next door at Broadstone, real spotlights with batteries, guns that fired matchsticks and a mass of soldiers. I spent hours playing with all these with my sisters and young uncle, learning the arts of war which might have come in useful if, a generation earlier like my father, uncles and before that my grandfather, I had gone into the army.

The martial atmosphere was not just felt at home, where all my older male relatives had recently served in the war. The same was true of a number of Dragon masters and war veteran

Old Draconians. This gave the period 1950–5 a sombre, post-war, tone: we were still fighting the battles of the Second World War.

*

Another training was with the world of animals. There was an obvious classification in the animals I collected with such fervour – the domesticated farm animals such as pigs, cows, sheep, horses, and 'wild animals' such as tigers, lions, giraffes and wolves. The farm animals were a bit too tame for me, I seem to remember, and were largely played with by my sisters, but I loved the wild animals. Some of them I still have, especially the ones which were metal and had a kind of fur on the outside – an elephant, tiger and polar bear, which made them seem even more real. Of course it was our imaginations which placed them in forests, and watched them fighting, and which stalked and killed them in preparation for a life as a big game hunter in the future years of adult life in Empire, which were never realized.

There were also the dinky toys – cars of all kinds, vans, buses, and so on. These were multitudinous and I think they were something I took to the Dragon, especially the racing cars which I remember being predominantly Italian. I still have some sleek and brightly coloured red, blue and green Masaratis, Ferraris and Alfa Romeos which we used to race down constructed race tracks. For example, on 25 July 1954 my mother describes in a letter how, *about 4 p.m the sun came out and Robert rigged up Silverstone in the garage and they had wildly exciting car-racing with Alan's set of Dinky Racing Cars – Stirling Moss eventually won the Grandpa Grand Prix!* The comparison between these exciting cars and the rather small, modest and slow early Morris and other cars that began to feature in my life was quite dramatic.

Bridging the gap somewhat were small cars in which we could actually sit and drive. In my 'Confessions of a Schoolboy' I mention that at Charmouth in the winter of 1947, when I was nearly six, 'The hill was very steep and was a superb track for my little jeep'. This was the jeep in the first group photograph of the family when we returned from India. A year later my grandmother writes to my parents on 18 October that *The Crappers (our neighbours) have mended the jeep and we have bought some sand paper and paint so as to scrape it down and re-paint it as Jack says it will rust away otherwise.* Later in the letter she notes that, *Alan painted his jeep extremely well.* On the back of the airmail, in pencil, between ruled lines in large letters is the following letter from me. *Darling Mummy and Daddy, I have painted my Jeep green. I Love my Present. You are very well. Lots of love from Alan.*

*

The fourth obsession was miniature trains. No doubt I had wooden and then plastic trains earlier on, but, probably influenced by Robert's enormous enthusiasm for model railways which stayed with him into adulthood, I developed a passion for double OO gauge electric trains from at least the age of ten. The first reference to this is in a letter from my mother in India to me on 29 March 1952 where she writes, *I wonder if you manage your electric train on your own and if you will add anything to it this hols.* But as I recall, and it seems evident from the letters, it was around the time of my thirteenth birthday and our move to the Lakes that it became a real obsession. I remember the longing for new rolling stock, platforms and lines as I gazed intently on the items on display in a small toy shop near our house in Windermere.

I obviously received model train presents at Christmas 1954, for a couple of weeks later on, 11 January 1955, my mother writes, *Alan has been wrapped up in his electric trains and has spent all his Christmas money on a new engine, coaches and a few rails and has quite a nice lay-out now all over the drawing room floor so we can barely move.* I remember I had an express train engine, perhaps a 'Flying Scotsman', and also a goods train, solid and workmanlike.

I also shared this enthusiasm with boys at the Dragon, though not at school but when they took me out. On 1

February 1955 I wrote to my father, *Then on Sunday I went out with a friend and we played with his trains.* More detail is given later in the letter when I go out again, *and had duck and roast potatoes and peaches. We mucked about with his air rifle and his Trix trains. As you probably know I am very keen on Hornby Trains.* There was clearly a distinction between makes of trains I don't know how Trix and Hornby were then ranked.

We may not have had train layouts at the Dragon, but the Science Club enabled us to pursue our passion – into which we tried to drag our busy parents. So a month later in March 1955 I wrote to my mother, with an attempt at ironic humour, *I know it you have nothing to do I expect you like to make stations and tunnels for Hornby. I have a terrific craze for electric trains and I am going to make some electric signals they cost about 8/- in the shops and about 4d in the science club. I hope you will make some things that I can look forward to.* I do remember painting pieces of the train layout which were bought in an unfinished state, but whether my parents helped with this I am not sure. But they clearly approved of the fact that I was, as my mother seemed to think, at last really passionate and consistent and dedicated to something.

The passion, however, faded out during my early years at Sedbergh and I remember that when I moved on to another hobby, the idea of buying a motorbike around the age of sixteen, my grandmother, with my agreement, sold my electric trains to help raise the capital for this.

*

One particular obsession of my uncle Robert was toy aeroplanes, and this may have infected me as well. Robert had been about ten during the Battle of Britain and so the models of spitfires and tornadoes and German Fokkers and other planes which he made and hung up around his room, including bi-planes and amazing brightly coloured tri-planes from an earlier period, and with which we fought battles, had a personal resonance for him which I never felt.

My interest was in the new jet planes – I had been on a Comet from India and mention watching modern planes when I visited a friend. On 30 April 1953 I wrote to my parents that: *I saw the commet twice today once very low. There are two very big Airports one a Civil Airport wich has big B.O.A.C Airliners landing there. And on the other one there are lots of Meteors and Vampires.* I also drew in some of my Dragon letters pictures of modern planes.

I do remember the excitement at the Dragon at the radio-controlled planes. I remember the smell of petrol in their tiny engines and the way they spluttered into life and dived and soared round the playing fields. This was part of the new wave of radio-controlled toys which was significantly developed at the Dragon. I wrote on 15 March 1953: *Girt our science master who is a very clever scientist has built a radio controlled jeep about two ft long and about ¾ of a ft wide. It can peep a horn revers in 2 speeds and go forward in three.* This was Gerd Sommerhoff, whose photo showing him displaying a radio controlled boat to the Duke of Edinburgh in the early 1950s, filled us all with pride. However, I am pretty sure that I did not, unlike my uncle and more scientific boys, construct planes myself – which I found fussy and boring.

I think I was playing with model boats as a child in India, and certainly my mother referred to plans to make and send such boats from India in a letter in late November 1948, when she wrote about getting some made for us in Assam.

Years later, on 9 August 1954 my mother wrote to my father, *In the afternoon the kids and I took a walk across the heath in the teeth of a gale and found a small pond by the quarry to sail their boats in, quite bracing but too much wind for the poor little boats, three sailing boats were sunk at Cowes that day so it wasn't surprising.* I still remember the blue-green depths of the clay quarry, the tiny boats skimming across and then lying flat as the wind whipped across.

A more successful description occurs three weeks later on 30 August when, *Sunday was better, Mummy and Daddy arrived back just as we were starting lunch and in the afternoon the kids and I went out onto the heath and they sailed boats while I sat in the sun and made clay animals, a peaceful occupation in spite of their quarrels which are almost non-stop, but not so wearing in the open.* The other boat memories I have were of sailing toy boats at Poole marina, and the wonderful model ships that my uncle Robert made at this time though these were not for sailing.

*

There must have been a whole set of locations for our toys. I remember the two main forts, one of which I still have, but can't clearly recall the garages, castles, doll's houses and railway stations which went along with the toys themselves.

As late as 25 July 1954, when I was twelve-and-a-half, my mother wrote to my father. *Alan still doesn't seem to have reached the constructive stage, meccano or model aeroplanes – but is much more independent...*

This somewhat runs against my memory, which was that I was quite keen on using various construction toys, in particular mini-bricks and Meccano from about the age of ten – and had indeed asked Father Christmas for the latter when I was eight. The assembling of bricks, straws, metal parts and later plastic parts, figures large in my life. I still have parts of my mini-brick set, the brown rubber bricks, the white bases, the odd window and door, out of which we used to make zoos, forts, towers and anything that furthered our current obsession. I suspect from their cracked and dried shapes that some had come from India and may have belonged to my uncle Robert who was again very keen on construction toys.

Meccano was definitely important. I remember the frustration of looking at the amazing things one could construct if one had a set 6A or whatever, and remembering that I only had the first two sets. As with Hornby trains, these kits with their basic starter, and then supplemental additions, quickly attuned me to the ideas of accumulation, of starting with very little like some infant Robinson Crusoe, and then adding. But while I found it fascinating, I think my mother was right that I found Meccano required too much fiddly effort screwing up things and I never really took off into the higher realms, unlike Robert.

As for other constructing games, plasticine may have been important and indeed is alluded to in one of my mother's letters. On 25 July 1954, aged twelve-and-a-half, my mother writes, *I took the kids to church on Sunday morning – or rather Richard took us all – armed them with bits of plasticine to keep their fingers quiet in the sermon but wasn't a great success. Alan made his into a jet bomber and zoomed it round the prayer books. I don't think Richard was amused!* This is further evidence of my interest in jets – which were much easier to mould quickly out of plasticine than make out of kits. The diversion was sufficiently successful to make my mother regret in a letter a month later on 23 August that: *Yesterday we went to church in the morning but forgot our plasticine so there was an endless clatter of pennies being dropped...*

As for other plastic arts, I expect we made mud pies, we certainly had a sandpit both at home and at the Dragon, though I only half remember these. I don't remember modelling with clay, though there is a photograph which appears to show me aged six beside a tray on which are laid out various clay objects, and another is beside me.

*

Alongside the toys and models, we kept small pets, incorporating them into our adventures. My mother, especially in the enforced absence of her children for long periods, found in animals a partial outlet for her frustrated love and a healing for loneliness. This continued almost until her death in a succession of cats and dogs which she adored. My mother's love of animals formed an important part of our world also, both when we were with her, and also in our imagination from her letters and the children's stories she wrote for us and read to us. Many of our favourite stories, of course, were filled with anthropomorphic animals.

For us the human and animal kingdoms were not greatly separated and we learnt an enormous amount about how humans and human societies worked from reading about and living with animals. We lived semi-rurally, both in Dorset and later in the Lakes, and much of my life has been surrounded, it would seem, not only with pets but with domesticated animals, not just the chickens, but also with sheep, cows and goats.

Here I will deal with the pets, a particular obsession of the English. There were a number in my infancy. For example, my grandmother bred dogs in India, especially dalmatians. So, along with ponies, dogs surrounded me, and my father used to keep labradors, partly as retrievers for shooting. So I grew up with dogs and no doubt cats as well, as recorded in my mother's letters.

The pets which received most attention in my mother's letters were rabbits. My mother describes in a letter of 18 March 1948 to my father soon after we arrived at 'By the Way' that:

> *We are also (we think) embarking on Rabbits and we plan to give the children a couple of babies for Easter, with ribbons round their necks! We spent do-day making a hutch and painting it a sickly green – the children painting themselves and surrounding as well.* A week later on 25 she wrote, *We have found a pair of rabbits, which are arriving on Saturday, and we plan to have them dressed up for Easter morning. We have been given a "run" for them, complete, by the people next door, so the only worry left is what to feed them on.*

The real Easter bunnies were a great success at first, as my mother recounts in a letter of about 1 April (my sister Fiona's birthday).

> *Easter was lovely though and the children spent it lying on their tummies in the grass watching their rabbits. We smuggled two in on Saturday night and they discovered them on Easter morning. They are perfectly sweet and very tame. They stand up on their hind legs and nibble Alan's ears and nose (he is the only person who can get in to feed*

them!). All will be well until they start their usual rabbity fun and produce babies every second day. Fiona said she asked one of them if it was pregnant and it shook its head violently to say it was!

Soon, however, they started to escape, for a week after, on 7 April my mother wrote:

To-day while we were away Fiona let the rabbits out, and we have only got one of them back – I fear we shall never get the other. They are so tame and guileless that a fox is bound to get it. I feel terrible about the little thing, it was so sweet and so trusting. I do so hate it when wild things die, I wish I'd never got them now.

This last sentiment was a recurrent cry of my mother, who fell deeply for the animals she nurtured as surrogates for her children in Assam, and then felt their loss painfully. On this occasion, however, the threat disappeared for in the same letter she reported, *We found the other rabbit this morning, or rather our next door neighbour did! I can't think how it survived the night, but we are all relieved and are petting and pampering them and over-feeding them generally. Its fatal to get too fond of animals though and its too easy to get fond of rabbits.*

The rabbits very quickly faded away, however. At the end of this very month, on 30 April 1948 my mother noted that, *We have been given a kitten which is as sweet as kittens always are but gets no peace from the children. The rabbit is completely forgotten.* Six weeks later on 15 June there is a terse reference to the fact that *Our rabbit has escaped finally.*

This was not the end of rabbits as far as my mother was concerned, however, for when she returned to India she kept them there. In a drawing she did of the tea garden house and surrounds at Deopani in 1950, she showed, among other things the Ayah's house, cook house, rabbits, chicks, ducks and sandpit.

In the same month in an undated letter she also wrote to me that:

> *I think I told you our rabbit had produced a family, two of the three died but the one that is left is very sweet. The mother has made a nest for it in the corner of her wire netting and we can watch it, it sleeps most of the time but when its hungry it starts leaping and twitching like a shrimp, it's the size of a largish mouse at present and still a bit pink.*

*

Kittens and cats were important in our lives. My mother wrote to me about their role in the life in Assam after she had left me for the first time. On 15 April 1949 she described how, *The kitten is very funny but always at the wrong time, it loves Anne in spite of the fact that she holds it round the neck until it makes gurgling noises but it stalks our pigeons, so far it is too small to do much harm but I'm afraid will catch them later.*

In an undated letter in the following month she describes how:

> *Yesterday I took Anne for a walk after tea and we looked into the next-door bungalow where Daddy's assistant lives, to see his menagerie, he has a puppy of a few weeks and a kitten of a few days. Anne wasn't interested in the puppy but fell for the kitten which was a minute ginger thing the size of a frog. Unfortunately the mother cat got a bit worried and grabbed the kitten by the scruff of the neck to carry it away and Anne thought she was killing it and tried to pull it out of her mouth and I thought they had killed it between them. An awful scrum.*

When my mother returned and rented a small house in Broadstone, she decided that the home would not be complete without a cat. The cat's arrival three weeks later, however, was not the success she had imagined. On 19 February she wrote:

> *The big event of the week has been the acquisition of a cat – a short-lived glory alas as he disappeared again to-day! We tracked him down to a farm nearby (Betty Deane told us about him) and it took 3 afternoon walks to find him and bring him back, in fact he arrived the day before yesterday. We had prepared boxes, ash-cans and endless saucers of food for him and kept him shut up for 2 nights and a day, but this morning decided to let him out in the garden – foolishly but he hadn't used his ash-can and I was getting worried. Of course he bolted and we have been yodelling for him all day without success, I hope he's gone home. He was a lovely silky black creature but too old to be moved really and I think a kitten is the only solution. He was amenable with me but dead scared of the children and they were very disappointed that their advances were spurned.*

Whether it was this same cat, or a kitten, which settled in I am not sure, but on 6 May 1951 my mother wrote, *You'll have to be patient about a lot of things, having the children under your feet all day particularly, not to mention the cat! He's lying on my lap now, hence the writing being worse than usual. He's like black satin but not properly house-trained yet.* In a revealing note a month later, just after my sister Anne's fifth birthday, my mother wrote on 6 June: *I can't believe my baby is five, I wish we could afford another but I shall have to find a different outlet for my maternal instincts I fear. Cats perhaps?*

This cat was probably the one which we unimaginatively called 'Pudy' and which settled down with my grandparents after my mother left for India again at the end of 1951. In a letter on 3 February 1952 I wrote from the Dragon to my grandparents, ending by stating that, *I hope pudy is getting on well.*

The danger of cats to our other pets and livestock was brought home starkly the next month when my mother wrote on 3 March from Assam about the death of two baby rabbits, killed by the cat. And it was not just their attack on other pets that was a problem. As my grandfather wrote on 30 April in the following month to my mother, *The cat has a voracious appetite for fish and is quite expensive.*

The same consideration struck my mother about some cats adopted by my sister two years later. On 30 August my mother wrote that, *The wild cats Fiona has been feeding are quite tame now and come tearing up to us every time we go out, rather sweet but beginning to be quite an expense.* This suggests that for a struggling family like ours, even keeping cats was a real financial effort. How the world has changed.

Dogs, of course, were potentially even more expensive. They were a symbol of status in the Raj – the hunting dogs such as retrievers which my father kept, and the display dogs such as the Dalmatians which were so important to my grandmother. But in the straitened circumstances after the war my parents seem to have scaled back on larger animals in England. Dogs became important when we moved to the Lake District in 1955, so they belong to the next stage of my life.

*

Finally, my imaginary life was fed by exploration to other parts of Britain, memories of my infancy in India, and the one trip to Assam. The southern English landscapes, Dorset and Oxford, were in stark contrast to two other British landscapes which I experienced in my early years. One was the northern fells and moors. We went on a number of Scottish holidays. The first two were with my father's parents at Glencoe, where I caught my first trout and encountered the great mountains around the Devil's Elbow. I still remember the brown burn in spate with a small island which we crossed to on a bridge.

Then there were several Scottish holidays, partly in Edinburgh with its tall bleak houses, cold winds, the Edinburgh Tattoo with my father, and the great swimming baths. I also remember Wishaw, where we stayed at the coach house on the Belhaven Estate with uncle and aunt, where the crumbling Belhaven House and weedy tennis courts haunted my imagination. The colour purple was everywhere – foxgloves and flowers that grow on railway embankments.

Also we went once with both my parents, and once with my god-mother and family and uncles, to the west coast of Scotland around Appin and Morar and I encountered the heather and lochs of my imagined Scottish ancestors. I felt a deep sentimental attachment and loved the feeling of the air and the sea winds, as well as the trout fishing and living on a farm. I think I remember the smell of cows, the butter, scones, and walking over springy heather with my father as he told me stories of his childhood.

Then at the end of 1954, during my last year at the Dragon, the family moved north to the Lake District and I began to explore the tarns, becks, lakes and fells which would become the background to my next twelve years of life. The soft gorse heaths and beaches of Dorset receded and the land of trout and Wordsworth became my home. That will be the background for my next account.

10. ASSAM

One central theme of this account is the interplay between the Empire and Britain. My own experience at the end of this process was of the contrast between the world where I had been born and spent my first five years, and revisited at eleven and sixteen, namely India and particularly Assam, and my experiences in England. It seems clear to me that while I soon forgot particular details of my early childhood in India, I was constantly reminded of that alternative world.

My mother's letters from Assam when she was away from me kept the memories alive and they were given a boost when I re-visited Assam for my eleventh birthday. Living at home surrounded by the artefacts and memories of my grandparents of their years in India and Burma, also meant this other world did not die. They stirred my imagination and I felt a sufficient longing to return to it, when I finished my university history degrees I retrained as an anthropologist and tried to head back to my roots in Assam.

What sort of alternative world did I carry in my mind over these years? I can only see this through my mother's writings. She wrote to me almost every week when she was in Assam, and I still have many of these letters. I shall quote just a small selection.

*

During her first absence I was too young to read them myself, yet the letters were long and chatty. They assumed that I was capable of understanding and appreciating a good deal, including quite adult humour. The stream of letters I received over the next fifteen years, until my parents retired from India, no doubt had a considerable effect on my imagination and also my writing style. During the first absence, the letters were often accompanied by lengthy children's stories, based around animals, which she especially wrote for my sister Fiona and myself.

Here I have merely extracted some sections from a few of the letters which show the level at which she thought I could understand and some vignettes which became lodged in my memory and kept our two worlds in some sort of synchronization, even though she was so many thousands of miles away.

The first which has survived was written about six weeks after she first left us, myself aged six-and-three-quarters, my sister four-and-a-half. I shall quote it in full because it shows the trouble she took to entertain us. In it she was already anticipating the first Christmas that we would spend apart and it was written on approximately 30 November 1948 from the Tea Estate at Deopani to 'Master and Miss Macfarlane'. I have added paragraph breaks to separate topics, though the original was all in one stream.

> *My darlings,*
>
> *Its getting quite near to Christmas now, aren't you getting excited? I expect old Father Christmas is sitting up late every night trying to get everyone's presents ready, I cant think how he manages. Mind you be extra good or he might forget "By the Way"! Anne wont know what its all about this year which is lucky because we wont be able to have a nice tree or even many presents for her as there aren't any shops near us, but we shall have to give her a little stocking to hang up.*
>
> *Yesterday she and I went to watch Daddy playing polo, or rather practising, and she rode right across the field and back on the front of his horse. He made the horse run quite fast and she bounced up and down like a jack-in-the-box, laughing like anything. She is much braver than her*

Mummy I'm afraid. I wonder if she would ride on an elephant like you both did?

Next Christmas we hope to have you both put into an aeroplane and flown out to see us. We will find a nice pony by then, and I will see if I can get Daddy to make a boat with an engine so we can go camping and fishing on the river, and it will be lovely fun. If Daddy flies home to see you it means Anne and I have to stay behind so we thought it would be more fun for you both to come out here, don't you think so?

Anne is very lonely with nobody to play with too and by that time she will be old enough to play properly. We have been given an old gramophone, and we got out all those dusty old records you used to like "The monkey and the masher" and some others, and Anne wants to play it all day. As she only likes one record, Billy Boy, it gets rather dull!

The other night Daddy and I were asked over to see a poojah on another tea-garden (a poojah is the same sort of thing to the Indians as Christmas is to us). We had to take Anne too but put her to sleeping in our friends house as soon as we arrived as it was quite late. I wonder if Alan remembers the Poojah he went to, with all the coloured lights and funny people dancing. It was rather like that, there was a huge tent all lighted up, and in the middle Indians all dressed up came on and danced and sang and an Indian band played loudly on and on. Then they acted a play, we couldn't understand a word they were saying of course so had to guess what it was all about, and I'm afraid we laughed a lot though I think it was supposed to be very sad as there were lots of fights and dead bodies all over the place. It went on till twelve at night, at least that is when we left though it wasn't even finished then.

Are you doing a play at school Alan, and if so what is it called and what part are you taking?

The lady who lives quite close to us here is going home to England next week and she is taking a very small parcel for you – nothing very much because she hasn't any room in her trunk. I'm sending three little bracelets for Fiona which she might like to wear when she is pretending to be a princess or when she goes to a party, Anne wears two all the time and looks very sweet in her sunsuits with bracelets round her fat arms but I don't think yours would look quite right to wear all the time until you are in your summer frocks. The big tail-feather is for Alan and is from the jungli cock that Daddy shot the other day, I thought you might like to show it to your friends at school and it would look lovely if you made a cardboard hat and stuck it in the front, for a prince or Robin Hood. I'm going to see if the mistri has time to make two tiny boats which you can paint and make little sails for and sail in puddles.

I've also sent off a parcel with two tins of condensed milk and two tins of peanuts, it is addressed to you but I hope you wont sit down and eat the whole lot by yourselves! I thought you might give one tin of the nuts to Granny and share the other, you could take a few to school each day. I will get some more in a little while. Anne simply loves them and we cant get the tin away from her once she starts!

Are you feeding the birds yet? You wont forget them in the winter will you, because they can get so little food then. Tell me how many kinds you see and if the same ones come every day. Our china duck is very funny, he hangs round the door of the cookhouse nearly all day now and when I get the chickens food ready he and Bruce rush for the pieces that fall on the floor and the duck usually wins. We don't have many kinds of birds round the house, but when we go out we see some lovely ones, parrots fly over in hundreds sometimes.

Yesterday evening Daddy heard there was a leopard on the road so he got his gun and went out in the jeep and there it was sitting by the side of the road. It was quite high up but it just sat and looked at him, so he rushed back to get a better light to shoot it by, but when he got there again it had gone. As soon as he shoots one I will send you its teeth, I don't suppose any of the other boys at school have leopards teeth! ...

I have just been reading all about worms, did you know that there were 2,000 different kinds of worms and that they moved 11 and a half tons of mud in one field in a year?!

Well darlings, Anne has woken up so I must say good-bye for now, but I will be writing again in a day or two and sending that Story I promised. All our love, Mummy. xxxxx

[note in pen at top '*Daddy has shot the leopard!*']

*

There are equally detailed letters after my mother left me for the second time in January 1952. I had just gone back to the Dragon School for the Spring Term and was going to be left on my own – because they had taken Fiona as well as Anne this time – until July 1954, some two-and-a-half years later. This was punctuated, however, by a three-week visit I made over the Christmas of 1952, which brought back many infant memories of Assam.

The first surviving letter from her second absence is dated 3 March 1952, written from the new tea garden (Tingalibam, near Nazira) where they had moved and which I would visit in 1952. I shall quote the whole of this as an example of how my mother was communicating with me now that I was on my own at the Dragon, where I had been for a couple of years, aged a little over ten.

Darling Alan, Thank you for your letter this week, but we were sorry to hear you'd been in bed a week, was it your cold or something else? I hope you're quite alright now and getting some hockey, jolly good being in the seventh game. I wonder if you've been out at all this term, it is sad that Granny is so far away but you'll have to make friends with a day boy and get out that way! Did you do anything special at half term or were you in bed for that too? We have had our troubles here, as Fiona had one of her really good bilious attacks the other day and felt very miserable and fed on salt and water for a couple of days. She got up still feeling washed out, but is alright again now touch wood. The result is that our lessons have got a bit behind but they couldn't care less of course. The first enthusiasm for school has rather worn off I fear and I'm wondering how things will go when it really gets hot, the trouble is that Anne likes one kind of lesson and Fiona another so one of them is always bored. Still we shall plod on and hope they don't get too far behind. I am learning an awful lot anyway.

We had an awful tragedy to-day, the children were given two tiny rabbits a couple of days ago and were playing with them on the lawn this morning when the cat crept up and pounced on one of them. It was Fiona's, the smallest of the two, the sweetest little white bundle of fur with pink eyes, and that was that. Fiona was frightfully upset of course and I was nearly sick on the spot, because Daddy and I were upstairs and could see what was going to happen but couldn't get down quick enough. We are going to get another to replace it, but even so it was a horrible thing to happen and Fiona will never forget it I'm sure. We're hoping to be lent a pony any day now, so are gradually collecting a menagerie as I thought we would. Are you going to get your white mice next holidays? I hope you'll like your riding lessons, you'll get some riding here so mind you learn quickly! We've just bought a new wireless and can get programmes direct from England, it makes us very homesick to hear "Rays a Laugh" and "Take it from here" but its nice to feel we can be in touch with home, though how it crosses all those seas and hills and comes to us at the turn of a switch beats me. The dear old Humber hasn't arrived yet, and we don't expect it for another two months as it comes out on a cargo boat and then has to get here by river steamer, but we're lucky to have a Land Rover on the garden and can go into the club in that. We are having a drought here, or rather we were until yesterday when the skies opened and it poured from morning till night, and to-day we've had another good soak. But before that there had been nothing for ages and all the water tanks have dried up so we get nothing running out of taps and have to drag it miles from various streams and ponds – we often find tadpoles in the water we're washing our hands in which makes life quite exciting, Anne was wondering if we couldn't manage a salmon for you but I hope the water crisis will be over by then I must admit. Daddy has been writing about your air passage, friends of ours on a nearby garden are flying their son out for Christmas too so it might be fun if you came together. We're hoping to make a small swimming pool during the summer, Fiona was beginning to swim on the boat and could do half a dozen strokes or so before she finally drank so much water that she sank – and if you get a decent summer you should be flashing around in no time.

I'm enclosing what is supposed to be a painting of the bungalow done from one end, I'm afraid you wont be able to make out much from it but I'll try to do a better one next time. We go up some stairs on the right of the car and they land us on the verandah above with the rails running all round it. This verandah is about 6 foot wide and runs the whole length of the bungalow and all the rooms lead off it. Daddy could have done a much better painting but was too lazy. We take rugs out on Sunday afternoons and read and paint in the shade of the bamboos, and watch the comings and goings of two owls that live in a tree nearby.

Well darling its late and I still have Fiona's and Anne's lessons to prepare for to-morrow so I'll end this. Fiona wrote the enclosed on my typewriter, Anne wrote one too but it said bat, hat, pin? Fgmlnvojkorvum – j so I didn't bother to send it!

Lots of love from us all, Mummy x x x x

A second letter I shall quote is in the middle of the monsoon and dated 13th August 1953. Although I was only eleven-and-a-half, it seems to me that my mother described life as if she were addressing me as more or less grown up, both in content and language. I shall quote two passages to show this. It also had added meaning and embedded the memories of my visit to Assam for Christmas 1952.

Here we are struggling along, beginning to count the days till the cold weather, August is about the worst month I think, very hot and one is getting tired of it. We went to Borpatra last week-end to stay with the Edyes and collect Elizabeth, poor Mrs Edye had to leave after lunch on Sunday to have her tonsils out, as she is nearly fifty it must have been perfectly beastly especially in this heat. We've since heard that is alright, but also that there was a minor hurricane at Panitola where the hospital is, rooves blown off and railway lines ripped up which must have been just the last straw. We saw their baby whistlers, only two survived out of the ten that hatched but they were terribly sweet. The mongoose has gone wild and lives outside and we didn't catch sight of him though Celia said he often came out to pass the time of day. We collected Elizabeth at tea time and since they had a rowdy re-union which has gone on ever since, she is the noisiest creature I've ever met and I spend my time trying to get out of the sound of her voice which is like a fog horn and never stops. She and Anne are great buddies but Fiona is inclined to be superior, she has built herself a wigwam down the other end of the pokrie where she sits a good deal of the time talking to herself and catching minute fish in the butterfly net which she sells to the other two.

To-day is Independence Day and a holiday, at 7.30 this morning there was a ceremony of pulling up the Indian Flag and saluting it, Daddy had to do the pulling but there were only two men and a boy there to do the saluting! After breakfast there were sports which were a bit better patronised, we went to watch the first few events but by half past nine it was too hot to stay out any longer and it made me feel a lot hotter to see them all panting round in it... After tea we had to go and present the prizes for the sports, there was a bit of speech making first and some band-playing, rather like Christmas day, and then I had to give out cakes of soap and dirty looking mirrors to a lot of even dirtier looking kids, who were thrilled with them of course.

Then to round off the day the flag was supposed be ceremoniously pulled down, but this was a bit of a flop as it stuck and refused to budge, even when all the bits of string were broken. Altogether a rather exhausting day in this weather.

In March 1954 my parents moved to their last Tea Estate, Cherideo, the one I remember most vividly as I visited it in 1958 for my seventeenth birthday. It is the setting for my mother's book *The Children of Bird God Hill* (Cherideo means 'Bird God'), a book for children based on the life of my sisters Fiona and Anne. This is the one and only surviving letter I have from this tea garden while I was living in Dorset and I shall include it all as a portrait of their new world.

Darling Alan, Sorry for the gap, but you will have gathered I've been very busy moving and to-day seems to be the first time I've sat down for a week, my legs are so tired I can hardly carry my shoes around! However its been fun, and we are all intact, including the animals which are in heaven here, with paddocks to graze in all over the place, we have a couple of acres of lovely grass at the bottom of the garden where the cows spend most of the time and it looks like an English country scene to see them grazing from our verandah. The goats joined them this afternoon, but spent their time pounding up and down the fence to get at the shrubs which are the pride of this garden. Silly things, typical of them. Vicky [a monkey] has been the menace all along, a perfect pest while we were packing and even more when we got here as she felt so strange she clung even more ferociously to my neck and screamed madly if we tried to shut her up anywhere. She is settling slowly, but this bungalow has lovely shrubs and creepers all round it which she is tearing to shreds so we have decided we shall have to keep her caged most of the time, sad but she is incredibly destructive for anything so small!

Daddy moved on Friday in awful weather, and we and all our possessions followed on Saturday morning in sunshine. The girls went off on the first lorry with their livestock, all bleating and scuffling and quacking, and I was a little anxious about whether one or two of them (Fiona particularly) would be dropped off en route but I found them all safe and sound when I arrived. On Sunday morning we did some unpacking and then went for a drive round the garden, it is so attractive, all up and down with a couple of enormous water tanks where we plan to do some fishing, the girls took a picnic down to the bigger tank yesterday and counted 52 people fishing it so I fear there isn't a lot of chance for us amateurs! Cherideo has large hills all round, one of which used to be used by the old kings of Assam as a "holy" hill and a temple was built on it to which they made a pilgrimage every year with all their elephants and gods and what-nots – we climbed it on Tuesday and found only a few pillars in a tangle of the jungle but a wonderful view of the Assam valley all round. Can't think how they ever got elephants up, it was all we could do to drag ourselves up and coming down was worse – we wish we could find some buried treasure, we are sure there must be plenty, perhaps we'll dig one day. There are several huge mounds where they used to bury their dead which I'm sure must be full of gold – or pottery at least.

I will describe the house and garden in my next letter – I must get this off or you will be writing me letters beginning "Still no letters"! My love to everyone – and lots and lots to you darling – X Mummy xxx

My mother returned to England in June and there are no more letters before then. She remained in England for fifteen months, leaving again shortly after I went to Sedbergh. So this is the end of the flow, only a tiny part of which is captured here. It is worth noting that along with the letters and occasional photographs and paintings, my parallel world in India was reinforced a little by home movies (which sadly have been lost) taken by my parents on their erratic and often broken small film camera. Thus on 23 August 1954 my mother wrote to my father,

I also went in to collect the films which they have joined for me onto one reel, they ran them together and thank heavens they are alright although they haven't joined them very well, just a hotch potch but perhaps you can have a go sometime. Alan enjoyed seeing them.

These constant reminders of a more exotic, animal-filled, world in Assam have affected me throughout my life. They knit together my infancy in India with my later visit to Assam, and then a number of visits to India and Nepal as an anthropologist many years later. My mother clearly made a huge effort to keep this parallel world alive in my imagination, for these are only selected extracts from a few of the letters she wrote. Nor have I included the two short children's books she sent to us in instalments. There is enough, however, to show one way in which invisible ties were constructed and maintained across the huge Empire which the British had created and was just at this point vanishing.

*

In an earlier age, when family ancestors were in Jamaica, Calcutta, Burma, and elsewhere, the distances they had to travel were not only immense, but there was only one practicable way of doing the major part of the journey, namely by boat. The period of my life saw the large change from steam ship to aeroplane, reflected in my own accounts in the contrast between the first and second trip made by my mother.

The psychological distance between England and Assam was shortened by the aeroplane, but it was still immense. The detailed accounts my mother gave of several of these journeys are a record of the effort of getting from the homeland to the Empire and back again. The early planes took much longer than modern jets and beyond the journey to Calcutta there was the further trip up to Assam. My feeling of being unable to appeal to my parents from school, for example, is related to the sense I had of the physical distance between us. There was also a considerable added expense. It is thus worth examining these trips in some detail.

We all came home by boat in March-April 1946. I do not know how my father returned to India at the end of 1947, but suspect it was by boat. Yet the account which my mother gives of her plans for returning to Assam in the autumn of 1948 show precisely that transition from ship to air which was the great change of the period.

My mother had intended to go by boat but found it very difficult to get a passage, as described below. The cost of the air flight was crippling, but she could not wait too long. So she went by plane. I shall just give her account of an early journey by plane to give an idea of the fairly lengthy effort even this required.

My mother flew on the 18 October 1948 from London. In an undated letter in late October she described her first journey by air, along with my sister Anne who was aged two. Since detailed accounts of these early flights, where one had to stop every few hours to re-fuel, are not that common, and since I experienced the same kind of flight four years later when I visited my parents. I shall include the complete letter.

> *Darling Mummy,*
>
> *To go back to the beginning, Barbara met us at Waterloo after a very easy journey, and we arrived at the Troups [relatives] in good time. All went well till the next day when I had to start ringing up to confirm the time of the plane, and from there on it was a muddle and we finally arrived at Calcutta completely sleepless. The plane started eighteen hours late as I think I told you, and most of that time Anne and I seemed to be hanging about at Airways house waiting to be told what to do next. The morning we left we had more hanging about, this time at the airport from 7 to 9 when we finally took off, and very cold it was and tiresome for Anne. We had nothing to eat or drink till we got to Brussels at eleven but there they produced wonderful omelettes and bacon and strong coffee which made us feel a lot better. Most of the passengers were taken*

on a sight-seeing tour but the two other mothers and I decided a quiet spell in a hotel would be better for the children, and were dropped there – the bus drive from the airport into Brussels was the most dangerous part of the journey I think, we went at least a hundred miles an hour on what (I was firmly convinced) was the wrong side of the road with a driver who was much more interested in us than the steering wheel! I thought the countryside very dull and bare, but apparently the other side was prettier. Anne and I slept from 12.30 till three and then ate a vast lunch which I wont describe in detail, it must have been all black market. Anne had banana with every course which amused the waiters very much. The shops had quite a lot of unrationed stuff, chocolate and so on, but I thought the people looked shabbier and less well fed than in England – everything in the shops, make-up, sweets, medecines, seemed to be English too which struck me as queer. We flew off again at 5.30 and by that time it was raining with thick cloud, but we went up through it into bright blue sky and the sunset on the darkness underneath us was very beautiful. Once you get up really high the plane gets very steady and you don't appear to be moving at all, but going up and down through the different air pressures is sickening, its amazing how such a vast machine can bob about like a cork, the first few times I was simply petrified but got used to it. There were no sleepers which meant that I had Anne spread across the two seats and myself hanging over the edge, not conducive to restful sleep.

We got to Istanbul at midnight and had to go through the whole tedious business of standing in line to show passports etc. and then waited two and a half hours while they searched the plane for arms (so the rumour was). From there we flew to Damascus which we reached at about 6 a.m. and the same process over again. It got very hot while we were there and another long wait – we were all (the mothers and children anyway) sleepless and browned off by now – I imagine if the start hadn't been delayed we would have reached all these places at a civilised hour. From

Damascus to Karachi took about 7 hours, and it was queer arriving at 2 p.m. and finding the sun just setting. Karachi was stifling and here we had medical inspections as well as the usual. They asked me if I had yellow fever certificates and I said no, well had I got cholera certificates, but I had not got vaccination certificates, at which they all laughed heartily and said that didn't matter a bit. It amused me that when we landed, before we were allowed to get off, a little man with an enormous flit gun came and sprayed us like mad, as if we were bringing germs to India! We stayed about an hour and a half there and on to New Delhi which we reached at about 11. Out again, children and all, and eventually Calcutta at 4.15 a.m. The last straw was a cow on the runway, and we had to circle round the aerodrome for twenty minutes before anyone thought of shooing it off. I don't think I had more than half an hours sleep in the last two nights and Anne only got a few hours undisturbed, but still all things considered it was a good deal better than a sea voyage. We had the final last customs inspections to cope with (and here they opened every box) and then a long drive to the hotel. Mac had brought a taxi so we did it as quickly as was humanly possible. Anne slept from 9.30 to 2.30, when we roused her for lunch, took her for a drive round, and by 5.30 she was drooping again and asleep by six. She looked absolutely blue with tiredness, and had caught a streaming cold on the way (from Chloe I think) so looked just about the bottom as I knew she would. Actually to-day, over a week later, is the first day she hasn't drooped round looking as if she was ready to drop. Poor little thing, she was very good in the plane but re-acted violently afterwards. Calcutta seemed exactly the same, apparently there are a thousand more Europeans there than before the war and quite a lot of Americans. We looked up some friends and went with them to the Swimming Club for a drink, and I was amazed to see how much the same the life seems to be. As far as the European is concerned things are much pleasanter than previously, though I believe they (the Indians) are tying themselves into knots over government.

210

Sealdah station is full of refugees dying of cholera and starvation and nobody able to cope at all, rail travel is really out of the question now.

We stayed in Calcutta two days and flew up here on Saturday. *We came up in a Dakota piloted by a Yank, but even so I didn't care for it a bit, it was very bumpy and he seemed to be rather a wild-looking young man to me! I was horrified to see him and his co-pilot engrossed in newspapers with the plane leaping around any old how. We eventually fetched up here at 5 p.m. and a great relief it was. Mac has got the house looking so nice and it is all shining clean of course, with lots of enamel and chromium fitments in the bathrooms and with our curtains and lampshades, when they arrive, should look quite gay. It is perched on a little hill with views all round and we have started excavations which we hope will turn into flowerbeds. I feel disembodied and quite unreal suddenly finding myself so isolated but will enjoy it once Anne has settled down I think. She is still liverish and bemused most of the time, a surfeit of bananas I shouldn't be surprised, they hang around in hundreds and she has one every time she passes.*

The only other note, which indicates the airline and also a characteristic forgetfulness on my mother's part, is later in the letter. *Oh one thing, I lost my glasses in the aeroplane, my bag upset and I thought I'd retrieved them but found them missing. I wonder if you could write to Pan-American headquarters and ask if they found them – dark glasses with pink rims – and if so to send them to you? I think that might be better than them sending them direct to me.*

*

My mother returned to England with my sister Anne by boat towards the end of 1950, after two years away in India. Two surviving letters to my father describe in detail the stages of the journey and give a good picture of the huge distances and the difficulties of travelling with a little girl, now aged four, by boat and plane.

The first letter was undated and written to my father in late October from the 'Great Eastern' hotel in Calcutta.

My darling,

I'm writing this in bed, and feeling rather guilty I haven't managed to send it off sooner – but we were so tired last night we couldn't cope and this afternoon I'm afraid I passed out again (so unusual?) after being up since 5.30. But Peggy got off a note this afternoon so you will gather that our bones are not whitening on the Naga Hills or anything! Actually we had a good flight and I wasn't as frightened as last time, the first hour was pretty grim but after that I began to feel perhaps the engine would be able to keep us up after all and after Silchar Anne began to go green so I was busy persuading her not to be sick. The first bit was the pleasantest flying as it was cool and pretty smooth, except for one big bump which caught Peggy in the bathroom. The door flew open but luckily everyone was clinging to their seats too hard to notice her predicament! Silchar was very hot and from then on we flew low and it was warm and joggly – no bad drops but a continual switchback effect that was rather sick making. The whole family behind us was prostrated and Anne threatened to be but luckily fell asleep instead and slept until within half an hour of Calcutta. She didn't care for the noise of starting up, but otherwise wasn't worried – her only comment on looking out of the window on top of the clouds was "How funny – the sky's fallen down"!

We arrived about 4.15 and were duly met by several cars and kyas (and Cowan) and swept to the hotel in a Humber Hawk – a lovely car, darling, but too good for Tingalibam [Tea Estate] roads. After a cup of tea I took Anne for a stroll – it was pitch dark of course and she was thrilled with the crowds and lighted shops and buses and had got a pair of shoes out of me in five minutes, red glace and very common-looking but she would have nothing else. We had baths and an early dinner with her and were in bed by 9 and were all awake at 5.30 this morning – this wretched timing. We spent the morning shopping which was most exhausting as you can imagine, me leaving my passport on every counter and Anne demanding priceless jewellery and raging because she couldn't have it – my feet and temper were in ribbons by lunch-time. I sent your shirts V.P.P. as they were rather expensive, they were the best quality but I thought worth it in the long run. Whiteaways are selling out and had lovely stuff going very cheap (glass, china etc) but I resisted buying any. My money has been vanishing at an awful pace, though I don't seem to have bought much. I got you a paint box darling. Very insignificant looking but they're such a price – you could transfer the paints to my box. After a sleep and tea Anne and I went for another walk (or hobble as far as I was concerned) and then had long baths and a drink before dinner. The food is much improved and the service excellent. Peggy is sharing a room with us, which is a wee bit cramped but there's endless hot water and it's really very nice. The only thing is we look out onto the courtyard where they clean the deshies and most of the cleaning seems to be done by crows! Anne hasn't eaten a thing since we arrived and is inclined to be liverish, the pace is really too much for her and I can't slow it down as well as if we were on our own – but she was brighter this evening and loved watching the dancing at dinner, embarrassing the band by standing a few feet in front of them and staring into their faces. She does this to everyone actually and pals up with all the fattest and most repulsive Indians in the place, there are an awful lot of them, in fact the majority of the inmates are black to a greater or lesser degree. I haven't met anyone I know. We leave at 11 to-morrow and I'm not looking forward to the flight but it shouldn't be any worse than the other. We embark on Friday morning so I hope I have time for the bank, I'm sure I will... I hope I'll be able to drop you a line from Bombay. Always yours – Totty.

She then wrote again on 10 November from the Suez Canal, presumably about a fortnight later. The letter is damaged and I have indicated this with question marks.

Darlingest, We're due at Port Said to-morrow but are not going to be allowed to stop, or rather get off, as we're supposed to be full of cholera bugs – i.e. we've come from India. However I'm hoping they'll post letters and maybe I'll get one, your letter (?) to Aden didn't catch me. The last couple of days through the Red Sea have been very sticky but to-day is quite cool with a good breeze and from now on it should be pleasant. We've settled down into a routine and Anne is loving it all and is very loath to arrive, she keeps saying "England's a long way, isn't it?" and gets very annoyed if I say not its? quite close. She's being no trouble, sleeps????? and plays in the cabin while??? the nursery is rather a grim place, ??? iron bars all round and a couple of ???, stern Australian nurses in charge and the only use I have for it is as a threat if Anne won't do anything. It takes me a good half hour to clear the cabin after I get back from meals as she amuses herself by emptying all the drawers and cleaning everything in reach with white shoe polish! Life is very quiet and sometimes I feel most terribly lonely and depressed, specially when I see other people with their husbands to look after them, still on the whole its not too bad and I'm beginning to feel more like myself again... She [Peggy] is quite different now and we have great fun tearing strips off everyone, there are some amazing types on board. Most of them are very smart and common and spend their time changing from one exotic creation to another, I feel terribly drab as I slop round in my dhuizi??-made cottons – though I must say very few of the women are as exotic as what they have on. The Australians are awful ??? but oozing money. Nothing the least ????aboard that I've seen, although ???? a lot of time trying to ???? iques". I haven't been on the ??? Deck, even in broad daylight, such a disappointment!

We got off at Aden and stopped for about an hour, I spent £3 nearly, 3 prs nylons, a "Biro" pen for Alan, and a building set for Fiona. Apart from that I've only bought one or two little things in the shop here, and one or two drinks. Gins are 6d each and beers 10d and everything else on a similar scale! I wish I'd had more time and money at Aden as everything was so cheap. Anne saw a camel-cart which thrilled her to bits, but was quite restrained about asking for presents, in fact I fobbed her off with a dinky car. I've just cashed off my second £5 and hope it'll see me through, it should unless something unexpected happens. I've ???? hair done, and Anne's cut, that. ...(last page(s) missing)

*

There is a full account of the trip back to India of my mother, father and two sisters in January 1952. I went back to school about 16 of January and wrote to my grandmother:

Dear Granny,
Please could you tell me what the Adress is of mummy. I hope this letter gets to you in time. And will you tell mummy that I have got one of her yellow gloves lots of love to mummy the girls daddy. And lots of love to you and Grandpa Love Alan. And pleas when you right tell me wether Ordanary envelopes are allright.

A few days later I again wrote to my Grandmother,

Dear Granny,
I hope you and Grandpa are well I should think this letter will be After mommy has gone off. I am enjoying school Already and the days are much quicker now....

In fact, the family seem to have left on the 22, for my grandfather noted in his diary on that day 'V[iolet] sees Iris and Mac off in Billy's [uncle] Car'.

215

I had an airmail envelope addressed by my mother to 'Mrs Macfarlane Passenger S.S.Chusan, Aden', which is dated by me on 27 January. It started,

> *Dear mommy and Daddy, I hope you are enjoying the trip and it is not to rough. It has been snowing quite hard and on Saturday we had half a inch of snow and we had some nice slides and it has been nice. I am keeping my diary up so I can tell you what is happening when I come out. ... Thank you for your postcard of the ship it looks very pleasant. And thank you for the parcel with the glove and tie and photograph. I will do a picture of the photograph and I will show you where about I think you are on the boat.*

My mother wrote to me from the boat. Sadly the first part is missing, but what remains of this undated letter, presumably from the Suez Canal in early February, is as follows:

> *... come up on deck and they play around till 11.30 when they have their lunch! After lunch I give them an hours lessons in a quiet corner and at 1.30 we have our lunch. They don't have another meal until 5.30 in the evening so are ravenous by that time, and sit down to soup, meat and savoury or pudding. They go to bed early as they are rushing around all day long. There are simply masses of children on board and they've made friends with a little boy called Howard and chase each other up and downstairs indefinitely. They have quite a lot of things organised for the children and yesterday was their Fancy Dress Party, Fiona went as a fairy and Anne as an elf, Daddy and I had an awful time cutting stars out of silver paper and making wire wings but in the end I was helping someone else and Fiona didn't arrive in time for the judging. Still they enjoyed themselves and ended up with a large tea with crackers and balloons. The swimming pool is open now and they're in it at the moment with Daddy, we're in the Red Sea and its HOT – can you believe that? We reach Aden to-night, but too late for the children to get off I'm afraid, about midnight*

I think. We have stopped twice so far, once at Ceuta in Spanish Morocco (on the north Coast of Africa) where I got these stamps and once at Port Said where we weren't allowed to get off and lots of English soldiers came on board with guns. We also had to anchor in the Suez Canal for quite a long time and saw some jeeps and armoured cars but not much else. We were quite close to Ismailia where the fighting is and thought we might hear a shot or two but not a hope! We haven't seen any flying fish or sharks or anything else so really its been quite a dull voyage. We got off the boat at Ceuta and bought a couple of Spanish combs for the girls from some Spaniards who set up stalls on the quay-side, they were selling lovely shawls and bracelets too but far too expensive.

I think I had better finish this letter now as I don't know what time they get posted, and I don't want to miss it. The girls send their love, and Daddy and I send lots – it won't be long before we see you again we're planning it already

Lots of love, Mummy

*

I then went on my first solo trip by plane to India for the winter holidays in December 1952. At present I only have a slight written record of this, and no particular memories. On 3 March 1952, shortly after she had left for India, my mother wrote *Daddy has been writing about your air passage, friends of ours on a nearby garden are flying their son out for Christmas too so it might be fun if you came together.* There are then several references in my letters to my mother to say how much I was looking forward to seeing them.

Then at the end of the Christmas term my grandfather noted in his diary on 16 December 'Violet leaves for London' and on the following day 'Alan flies to India', and on the 18 'V. returns from London after seeing Alan off'. I sent a picture post card from Calcutta to my grandparents. On one side was the Argonaut airplane I had been on, on the other a short note: *Dear Granny this is the Argonaught I am flying in it is very comfortable and we get wonderful food. We are about 2 hours travelling and I have not been sick we got a shower bath at Karachi and I am feeling nice and cool lots of love Alan*

I stayed until the second week of January and there is another card, this time with a picture of the first jet airliner, the Comet, on which I travelled home. On the reverse was written: *Dear Mummy and Daddy, I am nearly at rome I have had a nice journey so far I am sending another Postcard when I get to school and I am sending two Broaches. I hope that everything is going well and Mopsy is getting on. Lots of love alan.*

I was clearly again met by my grandmother, as my grandfather's diary on 15 January notes 'V. leaves for London to meet Alan on comet'.

*

My mother's return journey to England in June 1954 with my sisters Fiona and Anne was by air and there is again a full account of this written by my mother to my father. However I shall omit this as the flavour of these journeys has already been well illustrated. Air voyages were becoming more customary. Yet when my mother and father went back to India in October 1955, leaving all of their children in England for the first time, it was by ship, the Strathaird. They embarked on 1 November and arrived at the Suez Canal on the 9 and landed on the 17 at Bombay and then flew to Calcutta and then up to Assam, arriving at their bungalow Cherideo at 5 p.m. on Sunday 20 November, a journey, with two flights, which still took almost three weeks. Meanwhile I had started at my new school at Sedbergh. What was the psychological cost of these separations?

11. SEPARATIONS

In her 'Daughters of the Empire', my mother describes the hidden burden of the Empire, especially for women, of their separation either from their husbands or their children. This is one of the themes of 'Dorset Days' and there is much on the costs in terms of my own loneliness and my mother's attempt to keep contact with me and my sisters. An even greater pain was the separation of husbands and wives.

The English kinship system with its emphasis on romantic love and companionate marriage places the husband-wife bond at the heart of the emotional and social system. My mother was a very romantic and idealistic person. Her courtship, marriage and early years with my father show that while they were often apart during the war, they were also enormously dependent on each other. This chapter is a continuation of that account of their relationship.

The letters are important for this story because they give insights into my parents' relationship. They describe my mother's anxieties that she was getting older and less attractive, especially when all her teeth were removed at the age of 32. They convey the fears when they met again after prolonged absences – love would have waned and they would be strangers. They convey the anxieties over faithfulness – a real worry when my father was alone for long periods in a culture that was pretty tolerant of planters having local mistresses or of romances with other European women. They give a vivid insight into the daily pain and loneliness which I, as a growing child, never seem to have paid much attention to - except that I did write to my father several times expressing my hope that he was not too lonely without my mother.

Unfortunately at this period all my father's letters to my mother seem to have been lost. We can only estimate what is missing when we look at the letters he wrote to my mother in their courtship and the first years of their marriage. These show that while he was not as gifted a writer, he was as infatuated as my mother.

In sum, the letters show the real depth of their relationship and how it was tested by the fact that during the nearly eight years covered in this volume, my parents were apart for over two-and-a-half-years. The communications were difficult, the distances very great, and the state of the post-war world added to my mother's distress.

*

Against this background, here are some extracts from the letters which need little editing of which but which give a moving account of a marriage in its early days. The separation made it necessary to put on paper those thoughts and emotions which are seldom revealed in the humdrum of married life.

When I suggested she read and indexed their letters to each other, my mother said it would be too painful to do so. Since she committed her letters to me in trust, I hope that she will approve of this revealing of the deep heart of their relationship. Without doing this, a good deal of the rest of my account will not be fully comprehensible.

The letters are extensive and really belong to my parents' story, so I shall leave the bulk of them on one side at the moment. Here I shall just give extracts relating to their first separation of about ten months when my father left England until the end of 1947 and my mother joined him in India in October 1948.

In her first surviving letter of this period, undated but around the middle of February 1948, my mother noted their forthcoming seventh wedding anniversary on 1 March.

Darling this letter was written originally as a celebration or rather in place of the celebration we should be having on our wedding anniversary, but my news seems to have got ahead of me. I expect you'll be celebrating in any case if you have your polo match that day – whether you win or lose! I hope you win though, I shall be thinking of you. Next year we'll be together for our anniversary and every year afterwards. That's a promise isn't it? The next seven years of our marriage have got to be yours and mine, the children have undoubtedly had the last seven. But that's not because they come first darling, only that they need so much attention now, or so it seems to me though maybe I overdo it.

On their wedding anniversary my father sent a telegram. A day later my mother wrote to him with reflections on their seven years together.

> *My darling sweet,*
>
> *Thank you for your anniversary wire and it was sweet of you to send it, and it cheered me up no end. We certainly haven't had much of a marriage up to now, but we must make up for it now. No more babies to separate us! I was re-living our wedding day, and thinking about the Rampur Palace. How glamorous it was, the whole thing quite unrealistic. Sitting here in my apron and darned stockings I can hardly believe that it was the same person who sipped champagne in a white velvet housecoat. I wouldn't live these seven years again, but of course I don't regret it darling! We've come a long way and I love you more for a hundred reasons than I did on our wedding day. The children have nothing to do with this – you do believe that don't you? I'm always wondering if you don't feel I've put the children first in everything – I haven't meant to but the very early years seem to be so important, after that they can be turned over to the tender mercies of schoolmasters and mistresses. I spent our anniversary in the usual way, except that I had Fiona in bed and was a little busier.*

Five weeks later, on 7 April, she wrote about the loneliness and the fact that young children did not fill the vacuum which three months apart was already creating.

> *I've been feeling rather lonely for you, and wishing that I could see you and talk to you just for a little. Since I've been married I feel cut off from my own family rather and my whole life and interest is centred with you and without you I don't seem to have a centre at all. The children fill up most of my time but don't satisfy me from many points of view, I feel half-empty always. But why go on? I seem to be saying this, in a different way, every letter.*

The divided loyalties, longing to be back with my father but dreading the parting from one or more of her children, is described in the next letter on 13 April.

> *I am both longing for it and dread it, the parting from the children is going to be worse this time than it ever will be again. I think they will be happy, as long as they can stay here, we don't know yet how long we shall have this house, its on a yearly basis. They are just beginning to meet a few children and it would be awful if we had to move again, from every point of view.*

She ends by reflecting on how children will move away. *But to go back to the point, ones children are bound to drift away and find their own lives, that's why its so important not to become too reliant on them. I don't expect Alan to have the slightest interest in us poor old fogeys as soon as he thinks he's a man.*

In a letter dated 6 May, she writes:

> *The country is simply lovely just now and my hay-fever hasn't started to spoil it for me! All the blossom is out and the trees are every shade of green and the grass is full of buttercups and the sun shines and shines. I don't know how*

I'm going to bear to leave it all! When we retire we must have some fruit trees and currant bushes and bees and chickens – I'm thoroughly won over to a cabbage life and feel I would be perfectly happy to be caked in mud and manure for all my days. I'm learning quite a lot too, though of course it's a mere brushing of the surface. I think you'd like it too. The Warrens up the road have a perfect place with everything, including a cow, and a wonderful work-shop for him to mess about in. I would love it. The Tea Garden has become remote and unreal to me and I feel my life out there will be the same and I can only think of what we shall do when we finally get home! I suppose I shall get into it again, the Tea Garden I mean, but I can only remember the worst parts now. What do you really feel about it now, are you liking it?

The ambivalence about staying or leaving, hoping that time would both fly until she could see my father, or stand still so she could be with her children, is shown in the same letter.

I hope we have another whole summer like last. The time will go quickly I know, I want it to although when the moment for leaving comes I shall find it one of the hardest of my life! I find the children almost more than I can manage sometimes and wish them all a million miles away – but when they are I shall hate it.

My mother did not write much in her private letters about national and international politics. She mainly did so in relation to events which led her to worry that, separated by thousands of miles, she and my father and her children would be cut off. Memories of the dangers and separations during the Second World War must have added to her fears.

The first threat was the possible blocking of the Suez Canal. On 29 May my mother wrote:

You sound a little morbid about the world situation, darling, personally I don't feel quite as bad about it, my only fear is that the Palestine affair may make me trek half way round the world to get to you. I'm afraid I'm being a complete ostrich about the "world situation", every few minutes somebody or other on the wireless tells me that I, England and the world are on the brink of the abyss, but the children have faith in life, so why not I? Even if there is going to be a war in a few years time I don't see why we should be haunted by it yet.

In a letter dated 7 June 1948 she writes of the feelings of the lost contact with my father, and her sense of inadequacy in trying to bring up three small children without him.

I don't think I have a letter to thank you for this week and wonder whats happened? I suppose you're very busy just now. What a long time it seems since I saw you, I can't think how people stay separated for years. I need personal contact so badly. I feel a little depressed at the moment, chiefly about the children who seem to be getting beyond me.... I suppose its all my fault. I'm sometimes too fierce and sometimes too lenient and I've muddled them. Its just as well I'm leaving them for a couple of years I think. I don't know why but they don't seem able to make friends here, everyone is kind and asks them out but they don't seem able to mix. I suppose it will be sorted out in time, but just now I feel I've failed miserably in some way. I wish you were here to tell me I'm silly and I know I am. I do so want them to be happy but I think I work too hard to that end. Alan is getting thoroughly spoilt I know but I'm always hitting him about, oh I don't know. I don't think I'm the sort of person who should bring up children. Oh darling, I'm losing my sense of proportion, this is such a lop-sided sort of existence. Sometimes I'm so pleased with the children and at others, like now, I feel I've failed utterly with them.

These feelings were clearly exacerbated by international threats. In the middle of 1948 the stand-off between the Soviet

Union and the West looked as if it might lead to World War III, but this time fought with nuclear weapons. My mother wrote about this in the same letter.

> *Things are so depressing just now I feel I must get some of it off my chest. By "things" I mean politics, the family are alright touch wood. This Berlin business is getting me down, I keep turning over in my mind what I will do if theres a war. I can't really believe it will come to that but I've been feeling slightly sick for days. I think I would jump into the nearest flying boat with all the children, only I know that in spite of everything you say you would be the first to rush into uniform. Would you? England would be the worst place on earth in a war now, but the point is would life anywhere be worth living if England went under? I sometimes feel it would be better to bring all the children out with me and send them to school in Shillong, everything is so terribly unsettled and likely to flare up suddenly, and I wish we could be together. It would be so awful if we couldn't get at them. And yet I don't want them out there if things are going to be alright. I just can't think what's best. If there was a war quite suddenly I think I would come out though, so be prepared! It is so awful to think of, it makes me wish I hadn't had children, one can bear anything for oneself but the awful helplessness of the young, their dependence. Personally I feel at the moment that nothing is worth an atomic war, I'd rather be a communist (alive) than a dead democrat!'*

This was a background dread that continued through the summer. Six weeks later, on 22 July, she commented that *Our summer is progressing wet and windily, and the Berlin business is at the back of every thought. I don't know what to do if there's a war, it seems so unthinkable.*

The following week she expressed real desperation at the loss of contact with my father and a feeling that they might be drifting apart. Only held together by letters, there was a real danger of a loss of love.

Darling, No letter to thank you for – I suppose you have been working hard but darling that's no excuse really because I don't believe you work till midnight every night and you could find time to scribble me a line before you got to bed.... It makes me feel terribly cut-off and sometimes I get moments of panic that you are a complete stranger and wonder how I'll ever face you again – silly I know, but letters are the only point of contact we have and it is so easy to drift apart. Of course it all boils down to the fact that you don't want to write and the effort is in itself a big daunting. I'm afraid I'm being a bit silly about it, but it makes me feel slightly sick to think that you find it a chore to write to me, as you so obviously do. It makes parting so much harder to bear and all our future partings as well as this one. It makes my letters to you an effort too, because I have lost touch. And when I get your letter I know it will start with an excuse about work and know that was an excuse and that you didn't think it worth sitting up late one night in the week, even, to write to me. Oh darling my letters seem to be a continuous moan these days, but this "cooling?? Off" makes me so miserable....

Only two days later she clearly received a letter from my father and felt restored and reassured. This gave her a chance to describe how her very strong imagination, nurtured by a childhood of rejected and insecure love, worked in his absence.

Dearest, I feel I must pour some oil on the troubled waters of our relationship! You will probably have answered my cross letter by now, in similar mood. Of course I got a letter from you the minute I posted it, and you seemed to have no idea of the storm you might have raised by not writing for a fortnight! I felt so terribly isolated and cut-off, but now you have written I feel close again so don't be too cross with me darling, but please write at least once a week. I do love you so, but my imagination works overtime as you know. It isn't that I don't trust you, but I don't trust my own

*ability to hold your interest. At least not from this distance!
Say you love me darling, you always do say it but keep on at
it. I need an awful lot of boosting.*

Three weeks later, in a letter dated 14 July, she comments
on the letter she received from my father where he responds to
her highly anxious and mildly reprimanding letter of the 22
June. She faces frankly her inferiority complex, as she calls it,
and her deep insecurity about being an object of sustained love.

*Darlingest – I have just got your letter in reply to my
angry one – you were really most restrained and I deserved
everything you said. Ah darling, don't lets quibble about
unimportant things. I love you and you love me and the
whole world falls into place because of that simple fact.
Only somehow I can't accept your loving of me, it doesn't
seem reasonable or possible, and I continually worry about
it even now in spite of everything. My formidable inferiority
complex and you will have to bear with it till the end of your
days. It isn't fair of me to keep writing you such depressed
letters but the trouble is I can't pretend with you, cant be
bright and gay if I don't feel it, and I so often don't at the
end of the day. I am happy at bottom, its only a surface
tiredness that makes me seem to be always complaining.
You have already fulfilled every promise you ever made me,
and as for the money side of it, you would be well-off
without me, so the less said about that the better! I'm writing
this in bed after a day of very bad hay-fever. I feel so love-
sick, I wish you were here to kiss me to sleep. I must stop
for to-night anyway – bless you darling.*

The absence had continued for nearly eight months, but at
least my mother felt that they would be together in a month or
so. Suddenly she heard that a boat ticket could not be obtained
for another six months.

*Darling, This is following very rapidly on my last letter,
but I have just had a letter from the Company with the very*

shattering information that I am not likely to get a passage before the new year, Feb/March they say. Apparently all the available berths on the ships sailing before then are already booked for priority cases. What on earth am I to do? I can't wait till then, or must I? The fact is that I wrote straight off to-day and asked them to see if they could book me an air passage – is this quite mad, darling, if it is please write to the board immediately and tell them so. I know we cant hope to compete financially, but I thought the board would surely advance you the money? I nearly asked them myself, but thought you might be angry! I know its only a few months difference, but I had so made up my mind that I would see you in October that this has been a fearful blow. However I can and will reconcile myself if you want me to, so please don't hesitate to cancel my air-passage if you want to and if I get one. Apparently there is no hope for unaccompanied wives nowadays – and I don't think its any good you making a fuss, because they sent me the letter from the Shipping Agents clear as crystal! Isn't it just typical. I feel murderous. I'll let you know developments.

My father agreed to the plan to fly out and the date was fixed for the middle of October. My mother now began now to feel the wrench in the other direction – joining her husband but leaving me (aged-six-and-three-quarters, and my sister Fiona, aged four-and-a-half). She wrote on 3 September trying to face the parting with courage. *I shall be seeing you in about 6 weeks time. Poor Alan is fretting terribly about it, but I think he will be quite happy in time, with his school and Robert in the holidays.*

Yet even with a flight arranged, the international situation, and her realization that she would suffer just as much when she returned to India and was deprived of two of her children, led to a long and depressed letter which summarizes the deep contradictory pain which a far-flung Empire could cause. It also alludes to a plan to leave tea and find some other job which would resolve the situation.

On 12 September she wrote to my father.

*I have been frightfully depressed all day by the news.
India looks like working itself up for a communal war and
Berlin doesn't bear thinking about. I've been milling things
round inside myself all day and got myself all of a tremble
by this evening. If only we hadn't got to be separated, any of
us, it would all be easier to bear. However the children can
be flown out at a moments notice if anything happens. I
wish we could all remove ourselves to some remote corner
of the globe and grow food and leave the rest of the world
to stew. I'm glad you are inspired with an idea to grow fruit.
I should love to have an orchard full of apples and bees,
and an enormous fruit-cage for soft fruit and a handful of
chickens. The main thing is not to put everything in one
basket, so that a late frost or heavy rain won't ruin a year's
work. I don't know a great deal about fruit, but the latest
idea is to throw away sprays and chemical solutions and pile
compost round your trees so that they're so healthy that
they withstand all bugs and blights. Daddy is hot on the
subject, he spends nearly all his time on his compost heap –
it's quite a family joke and whenever we lost anything we
accuse him of having slunk off with it to the compost! I will
try and bring out some books on the subject, and we can
have fun planning what we'll plant – the thing is, as you say,
to buy the land and plant the trees on the leave before we
retire, and leave Daddy or some-one in charge. Lets make a
real effort to save for it, the sooner we shake the dust of
Assam off our feet the better.*

As the time for leaving her children and re-meeting the
husband she had not seen for ten months approached, she
showed the same anxieties that were to be revealed in later
partings and meetings. On 25 September she wrote, *Only
about three weeks now darling, I feel excited and nervous and
worried and altogether in a muddle, but it'll be alright when I
see you I know – you will kiss me a lot won't you, because I
shall need a lot of soothing and reassuring. We arrive at 5.10
a.m on 19 October!*

In the same letter she again tried to conjure up a resolution to the problem – perhaps going to the white Empire where parents and children could live together.

> *Really no news this week. I feel like you, that we will have so much to say when we meet and nothing is worth putting on paper so soon before. Darling I feel in quite a panic at meeting you in a way. I feel that perhaps we shan't have anything to say after all, and you'll have forgotten how ugly I am and we'll have Grown Away from each other. I don't think any of these things seriously, but you do feel awfully like a stranger from here. I'm going to try and talk you into going to Canada. A young cousin of mine has just gone out (a year ago) and earns 7/- an hour as a carpenter – he is married and they have just bought a fruit farm on the "never-never" and love it all – he is not trained by the way, merely good with his hands. Anyway we'll thrash it all out and no doubt I shall be well squashed! Forgive this deadly letter darling – I do love you so and will really be able to prove it soon. Always yours. Totty.*

*

This was just the first separation. The miseries were repeated again when my mother returned at the end of 1950. I shall omit a parallel set of heart-rending letters and just encapsulate them in one poem my mother wrote in February 1951. She described this as a 'silly poem I've written to let off steam – but its true too.'

Separation

That door, which opens to the milkman and the grocer
And the paper and my bit of beef to stew,
Which welcomes the wind and lets in the sunshine
Never opens to you.

This room, which hears the news and the hum of the
    Hoover
And the clatter of cups and coal and Housewive's
    Choice,
Which recognizes the charlady's and the children
Yet does not know your voice.

There is no chair with your book half open in it,
No bed which your body has left, warm as breath
But now, my love, there is only time between us.
I am afraid of death.

Then the longing and loneliness happened again when she
returned almost a year in advance of my father in the summer
of 1954 and a whole series of letters described her anxiety,
frustration and longing to be together again.

*

The fact that my parents and we children were often
separated meant that means of long-distance communication
were particularly important. The normal form of
communication, even within Britain, and certainly to India, was
by letter. The telephone seems to have been still rather special
in this period. There was no phone in our rented house in
Broadstone and a telephone had to be specially connected to
the first house we owned, a substantial Lakeland farmhouse but
without a phone when we bought in 1955. My grandfather
notes quite often as special events the arrival or making of a
telephone call to a friend or relative.

As a result, many of the arrangements, even for holidays,
and much of the news from friends and family in other parts of
Britain came in letters and postcards. This was, in some ways,
the last great age of postal communication. A generation later
most communication was probably by the increasingly versatile
and affordable telephones, and now the internet has replaced
letters and the mobile phone is ubiquitous.

The postal service from England to Assam, which necessitated letters going by way of Calcutta and then up to the tea gardens, seems to have been both speedy and quite reliable. Letters clearly went by air, taking usually no more than a week or so to arrive. Some seem to have been lost, but there are not too many complaints about this from my parents. One example of such a complaint was on 22 January when my mother wrote *I was so sorry to get your telegram, I cant think what has happened to my letters, but I hope you're getting them by now. I only had one slight lapse, over Christmas, but certainly not 3 weeks. I think somebody must be sitting on them, as why did all those books and magazines arrive together?*

If there was particular urgency, or worries that a letter had gone astray, the alternative was the expensive but more or less instantaneous telegram or 'wire' as it was sometimes called. Two examples of this may be cited. On 2 March 1948 my mother wrote to my father in relation to their wedding anniversary on 1 March, *Thank you for your anniversary wire and it was sweet of you to send it, and it cheered me up no end.* Seven years later, when immediate decisions had to be taken about the purchase of our first house, my mother wrote on 6 February, *Got your wire yesterday, and was very relieved – it is very sweet of you darling, but I promise I will do my bit and I'm sure we shall manage alright.*

*

Just as my mother missed my father in their many months apart, so when she was with him there was the ache of being separated from one or more of her young children. And of course we missed her. Here are a few fragments which illustrate the cost of that process as seen through my mother's and grandmother's eyes in letters and a reconstructed meeting.

The first letter I have is from my grandmother to my mother, written the morning after my mother had left to fly back to India with my younger sister Anne. It is a significant document, expressing my grandmother's concern for both my mother's and our feelings as my mother faced up to two years separation from Fiona and me. It was written on 18 October 1948.

My darling Iris – You must not be hurt when I tell you that neither of the children have shed a tear – it was a brilliant notion of yours to leave the presents and Alan has lived as a conductor ever since. He turned white after hearing you on the telephone and again when your letter came this morning as we waited for the postman before he went to school. Fiona is completely undisturbed and busy all day helping. They are being incredibly good and I hope there is a good supply of books as the Wonder Tales was read last night and "Arthur and His Knights" to-night. They had a very cheery day with Mrs Byas yesterday and I painted the kitchen in their absence. Mrs Hayley did not come to-day but I expect she was very busy getting straight in her next house. Aunt Annie has died and Daddie is going off to-morrow for the funeral... The Crappers have mended the jeep and we have bought some sand paper and paint so as to scrape it down and re-paint it as Jack says it will rust away otherwise. Alan gave us one of his gentle flowing stories at lunch and Fiona bent her head down for Daddie to scratch her back and raised it covered with semolina pudding – nose, forehead and hair!! I was not as amused as I should have been I fear. I put their clothes ready on separate chairs and they dress themselves and I hope the novelty won't wear off. Such a wonderful full moon and we are winging along with you in our thoughts and Poppa misses Anne terribly and it nearly broke my heart hearing her wails on the telephone. I am going to leave the rest of the paper for the children. 19 Oct. This did not go this A.M. as there was no time for Alan to write. Fiona wrote hers unaided! She pushed her dolls pram to the Warrens with the milk bottle and it will be a ploy for her on fine days. Alan painted his jeep extremely well and as he had a reading book for home work – he read me a page and I read a page of his Comic and so in turns we got through quite a lot. M must to bed. Lots and lots of love and don't fret and be happy. Mummie.

A few days later my grandmother wrote again, this time to my father, on 24 October:

Dear Donald – I will add a few lines of birthday wishes to the children's and hope and expect you will have a very happy day and am sorry there are not presents for you from here! – Iris must not fret about the bairns here as they are supremely happy and have not been any trouble. They have been playing in the garden all day all dressed up and Alan with a frond of pampas grass fixed on his head and the rocking horse ??? ??? has been one of King Arthur's knights and Fiona the "fair maid". They have stayed up to supper and dropping with sleep have just been tucked up.

I vaguely remember the scene – the good-night from my mother accompanied by the fact that she left a large parcel for me to open in the morning. What I cannot remember is whether she had talked to me about the fact that she would be leaving for over two years either at this parting, or in the weeks before, though it seems clear that she did since there is the reference to my fretting terribly several weeks before.

Here it is perhaps worth inserting a memory of the same event, at about the same age, which my uncle Richard describes in his autobiography *The Road from Mandalay.* It reveals the fact that my grandmother had been through this with all her four children, it describes her way of handling it, and Richard's conviction that he had been building up to the event for months before. The pain also evokes a little of what I suppose I must have felt and is evidenced by the fact that I went white at hearing my mother's voice and receiving her letter.

'Billy and I went to board and had our first nights away from home, training to be apart, learning to wake and discover that were not at home. The moment had to come, the moment of parting, the Big Goodbye. It was a

September evening. I had gone to bed and sought sleep, which did not come. My mother came and we chatted for quite a time. Then she said, "Goodnight" and left. Tears kept back for so long – perhaps too long – came pouring out.

Why did she just say, "Goodnight"? Why didn't she say, "I'm leaving you now and I won't see you for two years?" Was that the best she could do? The person who always seemed to have so much to say had said far too little. I didn't understand. I knew this moment was coming; I had known it for years, but I didn't expect it to come like this. That moment I have lived a thousand times."[1]

*

It was not just the leaving. Equally painful in a strange way was the re-meeting after two years. This occurred when my mother visited me at the Dragon School after over two years absence and has been recounted in a letter she wrote to my father, included in the chapter on schools. Yet the strange, and to us now cruel, system and the miseries on both sides, the arguments and counterarguments it caused, are worth elaborating a little more.

My mother wrote a fictionalized account of her experience in about 1978, quite soon after my father's premature and sudden death.[2] In this my mother is Maria, I am William Macdonald, Doug is my father and Jess my sister Fiona. She has changed the timing of the visit to her second visit in the Easter Term, though it actually describes her November visit to me at the Dragon school.

'William was half way through his second term at Prep School before she got home to see him. She had flown

___

[1] Richard Rhodes James, *The Road to Mandalay*, (2007), 26. In one of Richard's letters at the time, it mentions that he strongly remembered that 'Goodnight' was all she said.
[2] Iris Macfarlane, *Going Back*, pp. 257ff [unpublished].

home three months before Doug so as to arrange a house for their leave, and in the first weekend of March she set off in a black straw hat decorated with daisies to visit the son she hadn't seen for nearly two years. Her stomach churned beneath the new elastic belt she had bought, and the daisies flapped in the brisk March breeze.

The door of the school house opened onto a dark hallway and the face of a distracted matron.

"William Macdonald? Goodness, he might be anywhere, do you think you could possibly find him? I'm simply run off my feet this morning."

Maria said she could, and mounted a flight of bare wooden steps and stared down a long dark passage. Three small boys were scuffling and kicking their way towards her. They all looked exactly alike, and none of them was William. She asked one of them if he knew where he was.

"William?"

"William Macdonald"

"Oh Macdonald. Well he might be outside. Or he might be in the dorm. I'm afraid I don't know."

The small boy stared at her daisies and she wondered if they had been the right choice. She walked on down the passage and looked into rooms full of boys who gazed at her politely without recognition. Would William in fact recognise her? It was so silly to be prowling about with these daisies on her head, not knowing what her own child looked like. When she had searched all the rooms and passages she went downstairs again.

Matron was nowhere to be seen, so she went outside to the playground behind the house. Thirty or so small boys were kicking balls about. They all looked alike and none of them took any notice of her. In the wind the daisies became loose and started to bang against the top of her hat. She wondered if she shouted "William" at the top of her voice he would show himself to be one of the scuttling figures, but she was afraid of disgracing him.

She went inside again to look for Matron. She peered into the first room on the right of the hall, which was a cloakroom. It smelt of sweat and gym shoes, and there was a small boy bending over a pile of these. When he straightened up and turned round she recognised him; but only just. This pinched face with the dark rings under the eyes and brown unbrushed hair bore little real resemblance to the golden-haired six year old she had left two years ago. Only his eyes above the blue smudges were recognisable.

"Darling" she cried, advancing to embrace him. He backed away, clutching a plimsoll to his chest. He looked terrified.

"Oh hullo" he muttered, "I've lost one of my shoes."

"Oh dear, well I'll help you find it."

They bent together over the rubbery heap and searched silently. When the shoe was discovered William put it with its pair in a bag hanging on a peg, and took down his blazer and cap. He had a sore on his lip, which was faintly brown; chocolate or gravy. His large teeth were buttercup yellow. He hadn't lost his baby teeth when she had left him.

Outside the wind blew stronger and carried spots of rain. Her daisies whirled like the propellers of a helicopter.

"I bought you an aeroplane" she said, handing him a parcel.

"Shall we go to the park and fly it before lunch?"

They took the aeroplane to the park but it wouldn't fly, it nose dived to their feet and eventually the rubber band broke and they put it away. It was only twelve o'clock but she suggested they go back to the hotel and have a game of ping pong before lunch. They banged the celluloid balls over the net listlessly and in silence. William's only conversation, in answer to her questions, was "I don't know" and "No not really".

"What would you like to do this afternoon?" she asked as they chewed their way through beef and cabbage.

"I don't know".

"Are there any good films on?"

"I don't really know."

After lunch they searched the pages of the local paper. Her belt was cutting into her groin and her feet, in her new shoes, seemed to have swollen. She suggested a Western they might see and he said he didn't mind, but in the cinema he relaxed and ate crisps and chocolates. She hardly saw the screen for the tears she allowed at last, in the darkness, to gather.

When it was time for her to leave him he said:

"Are you coming tomorrow?"

"Yes of course. Bring a friend out with you if you like."

"Oh I don't really know anyone" said William turning away into the cold bare darkness.

"Come early won't you, after chapel."

She walked back to the hotel and up to her room and threw herself on the bed in a storm of weeping. No damage of the Indian sun could be as dire as this. She pictured him now, teeth unbrushed, curled up in one of those icy rooms with the broken aeroplane under his pillow. She wouldn't leave him there; whatever the implications to her marriage or their finances she would take him away at the end of the term.

Next day the wind had dropped but a steady rain fell from a leaden sky. They played Knock out Whist and ping pong, they ate lunch and tea and turned over the pages of magazines, they played guessing games and more ping pong as the hours dragged past. Yet she didn't want the day to end, she dreaded the moment when she would have to leave him. When she did, and said the fatal words:

"Well goodbye then old chap" his face turned ashy white and he clung to her sleeve, his eyes enormous and his cracked lips trembling.

"Only two weeks and then it's the Easter hols and Daddy'll be home and we'll have a super time" she said. He nodded and let go of her sleeve, unable to speak.

She begged all through the summer to be allowed to take the children back. There were schools in south India, in Darjeeling, she could teach them herself if the worst came to the worst. Doug told her she was simply imagining things, he too had been miserable for his first year at Prep School but after that he'd loved every minute, hated the thought of the holidays. He and his brother both declared that Prep School days were really the happiest of your life once you'd got over the bad bit at the beginning. And boys had to learn to stand on their own feet, take a bit of roughing up, if they were to grow up normal.

By the time their leave ended William did in fact seem happier, or so she persuaded herself since Doug was adamant about leaving him at home. Jess had never been a problem, she was at a day school and genuinely contented. Doug promised her she could fly both children out the following year, and thus break the long period of separation. Only a year he said, it'll go in a flash, as they flew back....'

*

The pain of these partings and reunions continued, though perhaps never again, as my mother forecast, as bad as the first one. For my mother the absences were an echo of what she had suffered so many times in her childhood, and then again during the war when she was away from my father. They are at the heart of this account of 'Dorset Days', the times together feeling particularly precious. Fortunately, because of the warmth and care of my grandparents, and the wonderful letters my mother wrote to me weekly, I never lost faith in her love.

12. THE VIEW FROM AFAR

There have been many times in the writing about my past life when I have felt the force of L.P. Hartley's famous observation that 'the past is a foreign country'. I find myself shocked into feeling that my world of the period 1947–1955 is as foreign to me now, as Nepal was when I first went in 1968.

One concerns the lingering effects of the British Empire. When we returned to England in April 1947, I could not be aware that in that very year the dissolution of the largest Empire the world has ever known was about to occur. The fact that many generations of my family had been part of the Imperial venture, right through to my grandparents and parents, still coloured my life in numerous ways which I am only now really becoming aware of. Yet the unspoken assumptions of that Empire, its frequent quasi-racism or at least extreme paternalism, sense of destiny, imagined unity, symbols and myths strike me as strange. Photographs and letters remind us of a half-remembered world.

A hint of this feeling is worth giving in a part of one of my mother's poems written for my daughter Kate.

Legacy

I want you to have
What my grandmother gave
To me. Trinkets in amber and jade
And rows of little elephants displayed
From large to small. Buddhas in brass and stone.
But these alone
Won't do.

I want you to have too
Stories of India: the smell of musk,
Cows dragging sunset clouds back in the dusk
Their horns silver-tipped. And ankle bells
Of women bending bird-like over wells.
Parrots like candles in the rubber trees.

This is part of the legacy my mother has passed on to me in her writing. It feels strange and rare and worth passing on to others.

The fact that my parents stayed on in India for almost twenty years after Independence means that throughout my childhood, and indeed until I had almost finished my six years of study at Oxford University, I was living in parallel worlds. My parents and my grandparents lived as much in their memories of India and Burma as in their retired reality of England. I grew up with this and it deeply influenced me. At the time it seemed natural, but now it has grown strange.

Yet also it did not just disappear but surged back in a new form soon after my parents' retirement. When I went to study in Nepal, which was never part of the Empire but felt much influenced by it and where some people 'stayed on', I felt it all over again in the smells, the sights and the attitudes. Even the people with whom I worked, recruits into the Gurkhas, had played an important part in my parents' and grandparents' lives.

*

Something which had not really occurred to me before writing is the great contrast between the kind of life my grandparents and parents led in India and in England. Even after Independence, in material terms, a tea planter's life (and much more so, earlier, an Indian army officer's life) was a good one. In effect you could live the life of a minor gentleman in India or Burma, while in England, at least for my grandparents and parents, you were struggling.

In India you had numerous servants, in England, most of the time, none. In India you had horses and dogs. In England the only dog we kept was right at the end of the period surveyed here and horses and even riding lessons on a long-term basis were out of the question. In India the houses were huge and surrounded by extensive gardens, often with a paddock, swimming pool, tennis court and a garage with one or two jeeps or cars. In England my grandparents never owned a house, and my parents had a house only after they retired that they did not share with my grandparents. Throughout almost all of the period surveyed they lived in rented accommodation.

In India and Burma, holidays, trips up the river, visits to the cities and the enjoyments of life in terms of restaurants, clubs and other entertainment were within their reach. In England holidays were a real struggle, my grandparents never really went on holidays, and my parents couldn't even afford a few weeks on the Continent. In Burma and India there were balls, clubs with parties and sports, in England they seem seldom to have gone to pubs or restaurants. In Assam throughout this period there was no shortage of food, in England there was severe rationing.

The contrast was particularly pronounced at just this time. It is true that in Assam after the war the grandiose life based on huge profits and bonuses of a legendary earlier period were over, yet the good times continued to a considerable extent. If this was the case with a manager of a tea plantation, it is not difficult to imagine, especially if we look at the photographs and letters of my great-grandparents and grandparents, what it had been like for members of my family in India and Burma in the preceding two generations. In England, when they returned, as I have only now realized, there was a real slump in the relative position of the middle class. Prices were rising much faster than incomes and it was difficult to keep afloat financially in the ten years after the Second World War.

This caused a particular dissonance or frustration for my grandparents and parents. For the former, retiring in their fifties from the high standard of living and considerable position of power in India, it must have been a shock to find themselves in monetary difficulty – for a further thirty years in the case of my grandfather, forty years for my grandmother. Likewise my parents, though perhaps not in such an extreme way, dropped several rungs on the social and material ladder every time they came home on leave. There is a good deal about this in the letters. It affected me indirectly, but my parents were constantly aware of the relative poverty, as they saw it, and many of my mother's acid comments on the pretensions of others and the greater wealth of other planter friends arise out of this. She even felt uncomfortable with the other parents and the cockiness of the children when she visited me at the Dragon.

Yet something that slightly ameliorated the picture was that in the second half of the period, things were starting to improve. The year 1947, when my parents, my sisters and I returned, was very grim, with the after-effects of the worst winter of the century and heavy rationing. Not much improved for some time. It feels from the accounts as if the bottom of the dip was the year my mother spent from October 1950 to the end of 1951, my first year of the Dragon. There was a combination of awful weather, widespread disease, a crumbling Labour government, and the nightmare feeling that even five years after the war nothing seemed to be improving.

In fact, the whole of the period up to the middle of my time at the Dragon, from 1947 to 1953, seems grim. I have recently realized that when Orwell wrote and published *1984* in 1948, the background of grim material deprivation is really a reference to that year. Yet what also appears from the letters, is that when my parents returned for their third leave, my mother in June 1954, things were at last starting to improve. Suddenly the atmosphere was lighter.

My parents were still desperately worried about money, but they started to talk about and managed to purchase their first house. Food rationing was over. We moved temporarily into a centrally heated house. There were clearly the signs of that material progress which, I suspect, will be a powerful theme of the account of the later 1950s. It was only two years after the end of this period, in 1957, that Macmillan could proclaim

243

'You've never had it so good'. So this chronicle is also one of the changing expectations and the material world in the period from 1947.

*

Another element which strikes me as strange is the way in which our family was held together, and how this was mirrored through the shared bonds in the last days of the Empire. Examining the letters that passed between us, it is clear that we had constructed a small 'imagined community' in Benedict Anderson's terms. This included many people we did not personally know face to face, but trusted and felt some identity with. This community was peopled with all the virtual characters we found in children's stories, novels, radio programmes, films, and musicals. There were sportsmen, historical figures, talking animals and adventurers.

My parents and I and the middle class I was entering through my childhood and at school shared a landscape of myth, legends, jokes, and traditions which were invisible. These imagined links joined a house in Dorset, a preparatory school in Oxford, a tea plantation in Assam and anywhere else we went. We shared styles, assumptions, a similar upbringing and similar values, despite the vast distances involved.

Now this may again seem too obvious to comment on. Surely all social groups do this, indeed have to do this or they will vanish? This is true. Yet the scale on which it was done, and the methods in which the bonds were created make it special. This is not an imagined community of a town, or even the nation of Anderson's analysis. It is an imagined and largely homogenous community which stretched in those dying days of the Raj all around the globe. It is not unfamiliar to us now, of course, through the discussion of the effects of the Internet and television in creating a 'global village'. Yet this happened long before the World Wide Web or television. Letters, the wireless, the telegraph, which created the medium for continuous communication, held it together. Yet it had also existed well before the telegraph and wireless.

This is central to this study which is ultimately about a vast 'empire of the mind' which lies largely concealed at first, but becomes so obvious when you notice it. How did we learn to feel an identity with this virtual community that stretched all over the world? How did we learn to develop the shared content and shared tools of thought and feeling in our early years which would mean that wherever we were in the world we would feel and act 'British'?

*

That period, only sixty years ago, partly feels a 'foreign country' because of the huge material and technological changes that have since occurred. Watching one of the films we enjoyed at the Dragon in the early 1950's, the Ealing comedy *Passport to Pimlico*, brought home again what a different landscape that was. The ruined buildings, poverty, rationing and grimness of post-war London are quite a shock.

On the other hand, there are many things about my life in the middle of the twentieth century which seem familiar, indeed over-familiar in the sense that they seem so obvious, natural, and unremarkable that it scarcely seems worth writing them down. This is where the comparative method of anthropology, which problematizes or distances us from our own culture, is helpful. Seen from afar, from hundreds of years in the future, or from China or Japan today, it is peculiar and worthy of description.

One feature is the family system. If we look across the world, people normally interact with, live with, depend on a wide range of kin, an extended family, clan, cousins and second and third cousins, and rely much less on non-kin ties. In my middle-class family the interactions within a small pool of relatives, basically grandparents, parents and children, was intense; outside this, much of life was concerned with unrelated friends, neighbours and work colleagues.

In my growing years I never really took much interest in, or needed to know much about, my extended kin. An occasional 'Aunt Nel', or 'Uncle Ernest' or 'Cousin Jonny' would be encountered. But how exactly I was related to them I did not discover and they were really rather peripheral to our world. We met them occasionally, sometimes had presents from them, but our serious concerns – support in illness, financial worries, educational decisions, reputations – were in the hands of our immediate family, or strangers and acquaintances.

This is how it is for my own children and grandchildren. Their friends are more important than all but their closest relatives. This is how it has been in England for many centuries, as I discovered in my historical researches. We take all this as natural, for it has been so for generations. Yet for Italians or Spanish, let alone Indians or Chinese, the weak and circumscribed kin network is strange indeed.

A second strangeness, which is addressed more fully in the companion volume on the Dragon School, is the fact that even the nuclear family was not considered appropriate for the serious part of the education of a child. At first I was sent to kindergarten from six to eight, and this overlapped a good deal with home. But when I was sent away at eight to a preparatory boarding school, and later to a public school, this was all taken for granted as 'natural'. Indeed many in the middle and upper middle classes in England still take this as natural. Yet again, if we step back, it is cross-comparatively an extraordinary system and one that is more or less peculiar to the British, and those who have been strongly influenced by them, such as those in the U S or India.

That I should spend two thirds of my life between the age of eight and eighteen a long way from home in a single-sex boarding institution, interacting with strangers, is peculiar. Such a thing does happen in other forms elsewhere. Yet this English institution occurs over a longer period, takes the children further from home, and at greater expense, both in money and in the suffering of those who undergo it and often for their parents in anywhere else in the world.

A third feature which has struck me from the letters is the nature of love in this society. There are two kinds of love that shine out. One is the intensity of the romantic love between my parents. In a civilization which has produced much of the world's great poetry, drama and novels revolving about romantic love from the Anglo-Saxons down to the present, this might seem so natural as not to be worth chronicling. That my parents should be so lonely and heart-riven in their separations and long so much for each other is fully comprehensible to me and seems almost prosaic. My studies leading up to my book on *Marriage and Love in England* analysed a central feature of our psychological and social system. It is all very obvious – surely it is human nature?

Yet if we stand back from this civilization and consider husband-wife relations in the majority of societies, including those from parts of the Mediterranean through to India, China and Japan, then the comparative strangeness of what is at the core of this account strikes me as well worth documenting. All societies feel the attraction between males and females and know what romantic love is. But to base marriage upon this emotion, and then to make the husband-wife bond so deeply romantic for years after the marriage is not at all common.

Then there is the love between parents and children. Reading the letters, I am struck by the huge care and love shown by my parents for my sisters and I. There is a strong motif, which comes out most purely in some of my mother's poems, about how much they feel they are giving to us, making a sacrifice of their own lives to make ours better.

Deep love of parents for their children is almost universal. What is unusual is that this love was present so strongly despite two unusual counter-pressures. One was the previously mentioned intense love of husband and wife. My mother reassures my father constantly that her love for him trumps her love for us. Sideways, companionate, love comes first, before and exceeding the love for children. This is indeed unusual, as I have discovered most particularly in studying Japanese culture, but also in relation to most civilizations. It means that instinctively in the way we were treated from birth, we knew that in the end we were second to our parents' love for each other. They loved us, but in the end they loved each other more, just as we would put our love for the person we would meet later in our lives before our love for our parents.

This was related to the knowledge, which again my mother expresses when she says that when I grow up I will not look after her or my father later in life, that ultimately we would leave home and be independent and set up our own emotional, social and economic worlds, and never return or even be primarily responsible for her and my father.

In the majority of societies children live near their parents and support them, often operating a joint economy and one social unit until their parents die. They never 'leave' psychologically or socially. This is very different from what we find in these letters. From the first desperation of loneliness of my mother's poem 'First Parting', when she was aware that the school uniforms and entry into my kindergarten, and then even more so when I went to boarding schools, meant that I was becoming a separate and independent person. My mother even rails against this in the first months of my life in her poem 'First Illness' where she feels angry with the nurses who take me away from her –

> You are my flesh and they carried you away,
> They said "I think its wiser not to stay".
> What do they know, with their tight, bright, hospital
>   smiles
> Of the journey back through endless misty miles,
> Your lonely cot at home, and all your toys
> Drunkenly disarranged? Do they know the noise
> Of emptiness in a room that you have blessed
> With the laughter of waking and quiet breath of rest?

The separation is there from the start.

The distancing between parents and children, most vividly displayed in the boarding school experience, is most unusual and the way in which my parents still poured love, huge effort and many of their scarce resources downwards into us in the full knowledge that we could not, and would not, reciprocate this except for a very little, is amazing. They loved us against the grain, against rational calculations. If they had sent us to day school and saved our school fees and invested what they saved, their poverty-stricken old age would have been avoided.

*

Wordsworth suggested that 'the child is father of the man', suggesting that the nature of the adult is largely determined by childhood. Yet until I started writing this account I had never realized the full force of this idea. One of the great surprises has been to see how much of what I now feel and know myself to be, is shown clearly and openly in those early years. This has also emerged from the video interviews of others I have made, which show how much of the inner character which becomes obscure and overlaid later in life can be seen plainly in the first years.

I see much of the person who I now think I am beneath the surface in the little six, eight, ten, or twelve-year-old portrayed in my mother's and my own letters. This sounds roughly like psychoanalysis, yet I am not concerned with the Freudian side in particular, or in concentrating on the infant experiences. Furthermore, I am relying on contemporary evidence rather than the recalled memories elicited on the psychiatrist's couch.

What I now discover is a little boy who was filled with contradictory impulses whose resolution was sometimes self-destructive, sometimes productive. One characteristic which my mother particularly noticed was a desire to win, to compete successfully, to shine, to dominate. This could lead into bullying or theft. If thwarted it led to self-revulsion, cutting myself off from others, despair and depression. On the other hand, it could also lead to bravery, courage, determination to overcome obstacles, self-confidence to attempt the very difficult. It was both self-destructive and liberating at the same time. It was partly held in check by a contrary set of impulses, a desire to be loved, to be approved, to give others pleasure, to avoid hurting people and animals, a dislike of cruelty.

Sometimes a single event illustrates both sides working together. Desire to be able to succeed in a hobby would lead me to a short-cut, like stealing money to buy seeds for my garden, but part of the money might also be to give to my mother for a stamp to write to my father.

Thinking of Adam Smith's 'The Theory of the Moral Sentiments', I realize that I was exhibiting the central psychological ambivalence which is common to all humans – the tension between what he and others call 'self love' and 'social love'. As he explains, we need both. To survive and prosper we need enough self-love, yet to stop ourselves destroying our world through selfishness we need to co-operate, which we do out of a desire to be esteemed by others.

I think that my mother realized that, particularly without my father's presence for most of my childhood, she did not have the power to control my self-love sufficiently. She found it difficult to discipline me. The sending away to school was partly to allow others, my teachers and my peers, to keep my self-love under control, for I could not manipulate them in the way I could my mother. In most societies the parents control the children by access to vital resources. This cannot be done in the English kinship system because much wealth flows down through the generations outside the family. So school is the alternative way of exerting pressure. Then the effects of the school make the parents even more impotent.

Yet my parents also desperately wanted me to succeed, to push myself, to strive, to attempt the impossible, to be self-confident and to be impervious to pain and failure. They no doubt approved of the Dragon School motto, 'arduus ad solem', 'striving to the sun'. That was what I should try to do, but how could this be maximized without the bullying, cheating, stealing which were the negative manifestations of doing this without regard to others?

*

Another thing which surprises me is how little I knew about my parents' world when I was a child. Before I read my mother's letters I really had no idea of how lonely she was and how much she missed my father. Nor did I realize how worried both of them were about money. I had no idea of how anxious she was about the slowness of my intellectual development, my character, the difficulty of disciplining me. The whole private world of my parents (and grandparents) was invisible to me.

No doubt this is normal between parents and children, even more so in those days than now. Yet it adds to the element of discovery in this project. My mother and father have become new people to me, much more rounded and admirable. While they were alive I would have felt it an unwarranted invasion of their privacy to read and think about these letters. Now they are gone and have entrusted them to me, I feel a sense of responsibility to make their usually praiseworthy efforts on our behalf more visible.

*

I have touched on this before, but it is worth stressing something of which I was not much aware until I began to write. Many of the autobiographies dealing with childhood and boarding schools tend to treat the school and home as if they were almost entirely separate worlds. At school, home was unreal, memories of it suppressed. And at home it was the opposite.

It is possible that if I had relied just on my memory, it would have separated the world of Dorset and that of the Dragon into two compartments. Yet the letters to and from my parents and grandparents shows clearly how at school I was constantly aware both of the world of home in Dorset, but equally of the world my mother kept alive for me in Assam.

We all live most of our lives in our imagination, especially, perhaps, as children. The physical landscapes, the conversations we have, the games we play, all our life is invested with meaning by our imaginations and memories, the 'webs of significance' in Clifford Geertz's phrase, are woven round the humdrum events and transform them. A feather or tiger's tooth from Assam, a game of conkers, a football match with my young uncle, all these and innumerable other things take place within an imaginative landscape which stretches way beyond the physical and temporal location. As T.S. Eliot put it,

'Time present and time past are both perhaps present in time future, and time future contained in time past.' And the same is true of space – other spaces are present wherever we are, as well as the symbolic association we give to objects and people.

So I lived a life which interwove Assam, Dorset and the Dragon, along with all the books, comics, films, plays, songs, radio programmes, and other ways of communicating and learning about the world. Our lives, for example, were lived in the glow of books we devoured, *The Adventures of Mowgli, Swallows and Amazons, Just William* and many others. We lived in an enchanted landscape where we could step outside the present reality into other lands and other seas, as Marvell wrote, for the mind transcends the limitations of the body.

I knew all of this in a way from later experiences, or from watching my children and grandchildren playing. Yet I did not realize quite how important it all was and how interwoven all my worlds were. This is why this attempt at understanding these years has to follow the anthropological 'holistic' methodology. It needs to give an account of parallel worlds, to investigate with equal seriousness the small, apparently insignificant games or hobbies or remarks, as much as the larger, formal, events.

*

Something which overlaps with earlier discussion of my parents' sacrifice is a wider realization, looking back, of how lucky I was. Most of us can stand physical deprivation and pain much more easily than social and emotional deprivation. Reading the letters makes me realize how much I was surrounded by constant love and encouragement.

On the positive side, I was never bullied as far as I recall, either at home by any of my relatives, or at the Dragon School by older boys. I came to trust the world around me, aware of the desires and drives of others which might conflict with mine, but not (except in the case of Aunt Margery) confronted by sudden irrational anger or serious cruelty. I found that people stuck to their word, tried to see my point of view, were constructive in their criticisms. So I may have been sad and seldom smiled for a while in the absence of my parents but the dark lines under my eyes were not caused by the vindictive cruelty of others. Rather it was impersonal, the structural cruelty of a system of separation which I accepted as natural, like having my teeth out or catching measles. There was no one to hate or to fear – just a grim reality to face.

Furthermore, a strong positive love more than compensated for the negative side. My mother and father's love for each other was largely screened from me. Yet their love for us children was never in doubt. I may have sensed my mother's anxiety and sense of disappointment at my weakness, yet when I tried hard or behaved well, she was full of praise. It was clear that she was adoring and solicitous to a fault from the time of my birth. Throughout my life I knew of her hopes for me. She instilled me with confidence and ambition and stimulated my mind and imagination.

My grandparents, sisters and other relatives were also very supportive and loving. We quarreled, as family members do, and competed for resources, tangible and intangible. Yet in the end I had no doubt of their kindness, their enthusiasm and can-do, and their concern that I was well and happy. My sisters and I were for my grandparents a second chance at a real parenthood. As my grandmother wrote to my mother in February 1950, *You must **not** feel they are nuisances to us as they are a constant interest and Daddy is completely wrapped up in them...* So I had the double blessing, in effect, of two mothers and two fathers, not competing, but alternating and supporting each other.

This is what grandparents can often do to a limited extent, but the structural situation of my parents' absence for long periods made them particularly important. In them, and in Robert I was enormously fortunate and my good fortune was added to by having a younger sister, Fiona, who was very kind, intelligent and a gifted artist. Anne was also a lovely sister, though being four years younger and away in India for longer periods, we had less opportunity to get to know each other.

*

Finally, the writing, so far, has performed the major cathartic effect of making me understand and forgive, if there was anything to forgive. I understand now the structural reasons for the separation, why we were sent home and why my parents kept leaving me. My mother, a daughter of the Empire, was along with others sharing her part of the 'white man's burden'. And we as children of the Raj were sharing another part. It was not cruelty or lack of feeling, but, in a strange way, too much concern for our futures, too much altruism, too much of a sacrifice. It was the opposite of selfishness. The selfish thing would have been to have saved money, kept us with them, and sacrificed our future, as they saw it, for their present. But they, like generations of my family, did the opposite. So if I need to forgive anything, I do so, and perhaps also certain things can now be forgotten, or at least isolated and laid to rest.

AFTERWARDS

What happened after my 'Dorset Days' will, I hope, be recounted in fuller detail in subsequent accounts. Here, briefly, are the outlines, as also included in 'Dragon Days'.

In September 1955 (like Jamie and Sandy around the same time) I went on to Sedbergh School in Yorkshire, where my three uncles had also been. This was a tough northern boarding school with a tradition for rugger and running, set in magnificent country near to my relatively new home in the Lake District.

At Sedbergh I changed again. I grew by a foot, broadened out and my calf muscles expanded. I soon found that effort alone was not enough to take me to the top of sports and after the age of sixteen devoted less energy to rugger and cricket and dropped into the second stream. Instead I developed passionate hobbies, in particular fishing. I could fish both in the Lake District and Sedbergh and learnt the joys of fly-fishing, the excitement of the deep shaded pool and the struggle with sea trout.

I also learnt the guitar. These were pivotal years with the end of post-war austerity and the rise of electronic music and the start of youth culture. All was changing and I became an enthusiastic part of it, playing rock, skiffle, blues and folk in a keen, if amateurish, way. In parallel I started to love classical music.

My academic work suddenly took off too as I began to be involved in poetry, drama and history. I had wonderful teachers, especially in my last two years in the Upper Sixth, with Andrew Morgan and David Alban. They opened magic casements on the past and parallel literary worlds. There

seemed promise of university entrance and perhaps more. I
began to organize my work meticulously and to hoard my
paper archives, throwing away very little from the age of
sixteen.

The joy of living in Esthwaite Dale, Wordsworth's childhood
valley, and wandering where he had experienced the scenes
described in the 'Prelude', and then at seventeen following his
footsteps on the continental tour to Italy, added to my widening
sensibility. So did a second visit to Assam for my seventeenth
birthday, to visit my parents who were still away for the majority
of these years. I saw the horrors of Calcutta and the beauties of
tribal India and both altered my life, bringing back memories
of my infancy and the earlier visit from the Dragon school.

With my two sisters at home, our grandparents' house
became a social centre for the new pop scene and when I got
my first motorbike I started to feel the excitement of adult
freedom. The search for young love added spice and I began
to go out with girls. My grandparents, loving and energetic, gave
me a solid home environment.

In 1960 I went to Worcester College, Oxford, to read
history. If the Dragon and Sedbergh through much of their
time were purgatory, or preparation, then Oxford was paradise.
I made my own choices, had my own room and coffee set, was
treated as a young gentleman, had my first serious girl friends.
And the world of the Dragon slightly to the north of the college
fused back into my being. I tried to retain something of the
innocence and delight of pre-adulthood by reading a great deal
of poetry and children's fiction. But I also began to be
interested in international affairs and politics. The religious
enthusiasm of my last two years at Sedbergh increased for a
while and then began to fade.

Through the winter of extreme cold and the fears of the
Cuban missile crisis and the imminent end of the world, I kept
my head down and continued to work in a highly organized
and intent way. I just missed a first but did well enough to win a
county exhibition to do a doctorate in history. So I stayed on
another three years and under the superb guidance of Keith
Thomas wrote a thesis on witchcraft prosecutions in Tudor and

Stuart England. I started to attend anthropology lectures and at the end of my doctorate felt that I should add to my training by doing a two-year Master's in anthropology – which I did at the London School of Economics.

Then came the time for my final training in anthropology – intensive field research in another culture. As I had always wanted to return to the India of my infancy and two subsequent visits, and Assam was closed because of political troubles, I went to spend fifteen months in a high mountain village in Nepal. There I studied the culture, economy and demography of the Gurung peoples – original work which was turned some years later into a second doctorate at the School of Oriental and African Studies.

A year after my return in 1970 I was elected to a Research Fellowship (in history) at King's College, Cambridge, so in 1971 went to take up my Fellowship. In 1975 I started work as a Lecturer in Social Anthropology at Cambridge and subsequently became a Reader and Professor of Anthropological Science. I moved to our fenland home outside Cambridge in 1976 and have lived there ever since. I remained a Fellow of King's College for most of the period from 1971 and am now a Life Fellow.

In the forty years in Cambridge I published nineteen books and numerous articles. I taught generations of undergraduates and graduates from many countries and played my part in the administration of my department and college. Sarah and I have been involved in many research projects. We undertook the reconstruction of the history of an English village over five hundred years from original records. We made an exhibition, videodisc, database and book on the Naga peoples of the Assam-Burma border. We continued documenting the social history of the Gurung community of Nepal, using film, photographs, diaries and based on eighteen visits. We visited Japan and China at least half a dozen times each. We worked on computer retrieval systems and visual anthropology. We interviewed over 180 leading thinkers in a series of films and developed a large personal web site. The period between 1990 and 2003, in many ways the most exciting on account of my friendship with Gerry Martin, with whom I spent many hours discussing history and anthropology and co-wrote a book on glass.

Now, at the end of all this, it is time to return to the beginning. The papers I have hoarded since I was sixteen, including additional archives from my family and particularly the writings of my mother, have waited all this time to be read and absorbed. Through them I am beginning to understand something about my past and that of the various family strands that meet in me. So retirement is a mixture of sorting all these out, trips down the willowed river in our small boat, wandering through the large memory garden, and enjoying our friends, family and trips to China, Nepal, Japan and elsewhere. Sharing all of this with Sarah over the years has been my greatest pleasure.

VISUAL ESSAY

AN ALBUM OF PHOTOGRAPHS
AND DOCUMENTS

VISUAL ESSAY

The photographs reproduced here are from my collection.

COMING HOME

We arrived back in England in April 1947 and lived for some months in Oxford. Here the family, who had often met over the war years in India, were re-united. From the back left there is my uncle Robert, my father, my mother with my sister Anne, my uncles Billy and Richard. In the middle are my grandfather and grandmother, and my grandmother's mother Annie. At the front are myself and sister Fiona.

My uncle Billy on the left and my father on the right.

Our first summer in Oxford, 1947: Alan, Anne and Fiona

25 St Margaret's Road, our first home in England: Alan, 2010.

DORSET

Broadstone, Summer 1948
Billy, Robert, Violet, Will, Richard, Iris with Anne, Fiona, Alan

Alan, Fiona, Iris and Anne in summer 1948

Fiona, Granny Swinhoe, Alan, Violet, 1948-9

Alan, Robert, Richard, Fiona, Uncle Ernest 1952

Robert, grandmother, grandfather, Billy, Richard, my mother,
with Alan, Fiona and Anne in the front, spring 1951

Broadstone Summer 1951: from back left – Robert, Richard and my father. Middle: grandfather, grandmother, Billy, Anne and my mother. Fiona and Alan in front.

My grandparents

Alan and Fiona, aged ten and eight, 1952

Alan aged twelve and Uncle Richard, 1954

Uncle Robert and Alan, 1951

Uncle Alan, grand-mother Florence, and Auntie Jean, 1947.

Alan, Fiona and Anne in 1955 (aged 13, 11, 9)

HOUSE AND GARDEN

By the Way, Dorset, 1948

From the lawn in winter.

The same house in 2009.

Alan and Fiona in the large garden, 1949–50

Iris, Alan, Anne and Fiona in 1951.

A hot summer afternoon in the garden, Alan aged about twelve

The view down Corfe Mullen road, leading to Broadstone,
from the entrance drive of 'By the Way'.

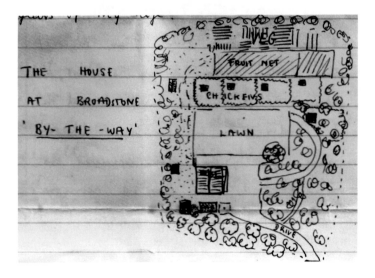

Memory map of 'By the Way' drawn by Alan at seventeen

SCHOOLS

Off to kindergarten

Off to the Dragon, accompanied by my grandmother, 1950

GAMES

'Cup Final' 1948: Robert, Fiona, Will, Alan

Football, Alan, Fiona and Robert, 1949.

Football practice, 1951

Cricket in India aged three

Cricket in Oxford aged five

Cricket in Dorset aged about eleven

BIKES

WATER WORLDS

Rubber dingy in the Cherwell, 1947, my father, grandmother,
Fiona and Alan and boat, Robert clinging.

My mother, a child, father and model boat.

Dorset coast, Alan with Fiona behind, 1948.

On 22 June 1948 my mother wrote: *I'm sending a couple of snaps taken by a man on the beach at Sandbanks – I though he was probably a fraud so didn't bother about groups of the children or making them pose but as you see he was actually a very good photographer.*

Scotland, 1949; a year on I would catch my first trout here.

With my first trout: Scotland, autumn 1950.

A trip round the harbour in about 1950: Alan and Fiona in front row, Robert back left and my grandmother back right.

Fiona and Alan, summer 1950

IMAGINED WORLDS

Robert, Alan and Fiona playing the horse-racing game, 1947

About 1946 when we were still in India and I was about four.

Alan in 1954, aged twelve

As Robin Hood, with my first bow, 1952

Tin shield and Naga spear, summer 1954.

Trying Uncle Richard's car, 1954

ASSAM LIFE

EARLY CHILDHOOD IN ASSAM

India 1944: Iris, Alan, Mac, Violet & Fiona, Billy, Robert, Will

Aged about three with a tiger which my father had shot.

Aged about three, with ayah and my friend the sweeper's son.

Aged four in Assam in 1946, with my sister Fiona aged two.

Soon after climbing this tree I broke my arm in a fall.

MY PARENTS IN ASSAM

My mother with two favourite dogs.

My father with a land-rover for the tea estate.

My mother with Miranda the deer.

My mother beside one of the rivers where my parents fished.

PARENTS

Donald Macfarlane in 1942, aged 26

Iris Macfarlane in 1949, aged 27

THE GROWING BOY

Oxford, 1947, aged about five and a half.

Alan in the year of going to the Dragon, 1950 or 1951

Aged twelve, 1954 – Dragon snake-clasp belt and aertex shirt.

At the end of Dorset Days, summer 1954

DOCUMENTS

Alans 8th birthday.   By the side of the River

Dec. 11th - 1949

My darling Alan,

This is to wish you a very happy birthday darling. I'm sure you'll have a lovely time & get some nice presents. Daddy & I & Anne are all thinking of you and wishing you many happy returns. I have started this letter sitting outside our little hut on the banks of the Deliho river. Daddy & I came up yesterday & go back the day after to-morrow. It's lovely here, I'm going to try & draw you a picture or two, as a matter of fact I've started one of the view where I'm sitting now but Daddy has just been looking over my shoulder saying it's nothing like it & an ass, anyway that's what it looks like to me! We arrived here in time for lunch yesterday, we had to leave our car & come up in boats with our luggage but it only took about twenty

of fish about. In the evening we had our
camp fire like the first night & this
morning we cleared up, burned our rubbish,
and came home - rather sad but it
was lovely to see Anne again & there was
a letter from Granny waiting for us, the
chickens had laid two eggs & all our
dahlias were out so it was really very
nice to be home. Daddy went straight to
bed after lunch just for the pleasure
of some springs & a comfortable mattress
under him! Benjy was very pleased to
see us, or me rather, but the cat didn't
take much notice.
            Well darling, my eight-year-old! –
I have lots & lots of Christmas letters to
write so must get them off.
            Hugs to Fiona & please tell
Granny I'll be writing tomorrow.
            lots of love & kisses.
                x Mummy x
                    x   o   o   o

The first and fifth page of a letter from Iris to Alan for his
eighth birthday – 1949. An early handwritten letter.

Tingalibam,
April 24th 1953

Darling Alan,

No letter from you this week, perhaps you've been too busy! I suppose you're beginning to think of the end of the hols now, depressing thought, but the summer term is the best really isnt it? The girls are just dying to come home and I think Fiona is longing to be back at school again, but they bear up pretty well and get the most out of life here. They are getting quite efficient riders and go carreering about, chasing cows and goats, they would both fall off if the horses took a step sideways as they really havent much idea of how to sit properly but they dont seem to mind being thrown from side to side. Anne usually takes a firm grip of the back of the saddle when they get into a canter and Fiona grabs any bit of the horse she can get a-hold of, very unorthodox but it keeps them on.

I have had a very depressing week and I know you will be very sad to hear that Mopsy died yesterday. She got better, but then got worse again and we tried everything but could not save her. I was heartbroken but am trying to take a sensible view of it now, we would have had to have left her next year and she might have got ill then and wouldnt have got all the attention I could give her, also she didnt like the heat at all and would have been very uncomfortable when it got really hot, so perhaps she is happier now in the Happy Hunting Grounds. I like to think so.

I havent been out anywhere this week, except for an hour on Sunday morning when we took the girls up the Kanu river, it is just right now, deep enough for them to swim in in places but not to drown in. We waded up quite a long way, Daddy and I trying to catch butterflies without much success although some lovely ones flitted past on the other side of the river, always. We did catch a Bluebottle but all the colour got rubbed off by the time we got home, I'm putting it in for you to look at. The swimming pool has been amusing the girls a lot but a large toad took possession of it a couple of days ago and scared Anne who has refused to go in since. We are cleaning it out and putting in a pump and sinking a tube well so the water will be cleaner and then we are going to put in some lime to make it blue which will also keep out the toads I hope. It still isnt too hot as we've had quite a bit of rain and on Wednesday night we had a sort of cyclone, it blew up quite suddenly with a sort of screaming noise and there were cracks and crashes all round as trees fell down, one of them just missed the bungalow and fused the lights so we were left in the pitch dark

The first typed page of a letter from my mother, 1953

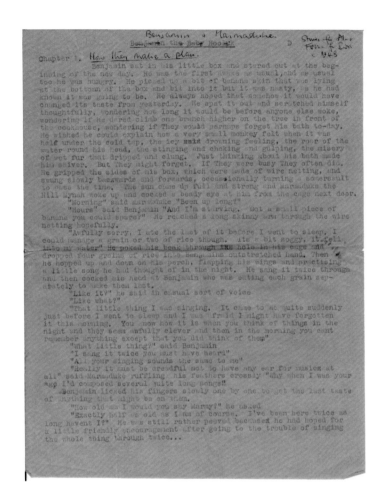

Benjamin + Marmaduke.

Benjamin the Baby Hoolik

Stories for Alan + Fiona if box < 1948

Chapter 1. How they make a plan.

Benjamin sat in his little box and stared out at the beginning of the new day. He was the first awake as usual, and as usual too he was hungry. He picked up a bit of banana skin that was lying at the bottom of the box and bit into it but it was nasty, as he had known it was going to be. He always hoped that somehow it would have changed its taste from yesterday. He spat it out and scratched himself thoughtfully, wondering how long it would be before anyone else woke, wondering if he dared climb one branch higher on the tree in front of the cookhouse, wondering if They would perhaps forget his bath to-day. He wished he could explain how a very small monkey felt when it was held under the cold tap, the icy cold drowning feeling, the roar of the water round his head, the stinging and choking and gulping, the misery of wet fur that dripped and clung. Just thinking about his bath made him shiver. But They might forget. If They were busy They often did. He gripped the sides of his box, which were made of wire netting, and swung slowly backwards and forwards, occasionally turning a somersault to pass the time. The sun came up full and strong and Marmaduke the Hill Mynah woke up and cocked a beady eye at him from the cage next door.

"Morning" said Marmaduke "Been up long?"

"Hours" said Benjamin "And I'm starving. Got a small piece of banana you could spare?" He reached a long skinny arm through the wire netting hopefully.

"Awfully sorry, I ate the last of it before I went to sleep. I could manage a grain or two of rice though. Its a bit soggy, it fell into my water" He poked his beak through the hole in his cage and dropped four grains of rice into Benjamin's outstretched hand. Then he hopped up and down on his perch, flapping his wings and practising a little song he had thought of in the night. He sang it twice through and then cocked his head at Benjamin who was eating each grain separately to make them last.

"Like it?" he said in casual sort of voice

"Like what?"

"That little thing I was singing. It came to me quite suddenly just before I went to sleep and I was afraid I might have forgotten it this morning. You now how it is when you think of things in the night and they seem awfully clever and then in the morning you cant remember anything except that you did think of them"

"What little thing?" said Benjamin

"I sang it twice you must have heard"

"All your singing sounds the same to me"

"Really it must be dreadful not to have any ear for music at all" said Marmaduke ruffling his feathers crossly "Why when I was your age I'd composed several quite long songs"

Benjamin licked his fingers slowly one by one to get the last taste of anything that might be on them.

"How old am I would you say Marmy?" he asked

"Exactly half as old as I am of course. I've been here twice as long havent I?" He was still rather peeved because he had hoped for a little friendly encouragement after going to the trouble of singing the whole thing through twice...

The start of a children's story my mother wrote in instalment in India and sent to Alan and Fiona in 1948/9.

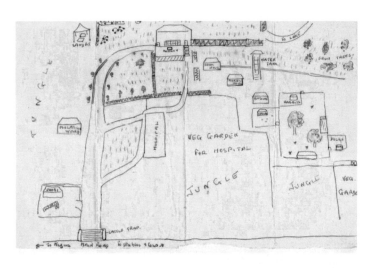

Drawing of Deopani Tea Estate – Iris for Alan - 1950

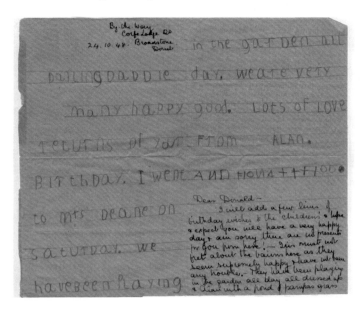

Alan to his father with addition by grandmother, 1948

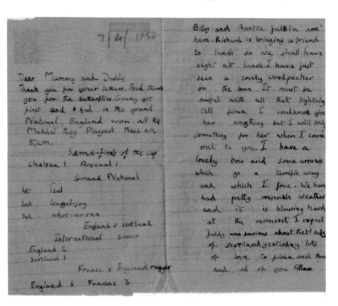

Alan to his parents, with addition by grandfather, 1952

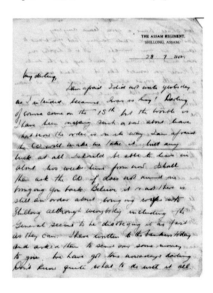

Letter from father (Mac) to mother (Iris) in 1942

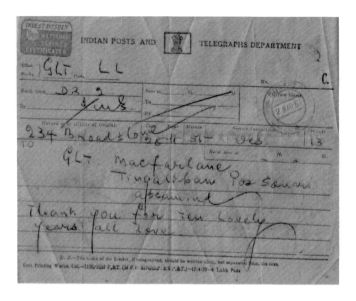

Telegram from Iris to Mac on tenth wedding anniversary, 1951

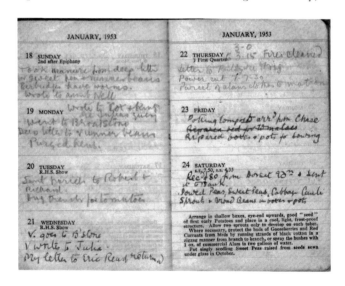

Grandfather's diary, January 1953

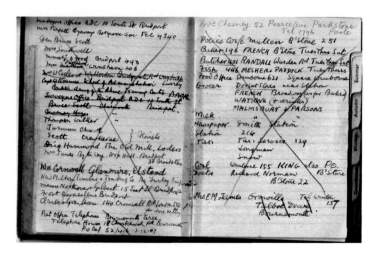

Grandfather's address book – Dorset tradesmen etc, 1950's

Returning to Sedbergh, Uncle Robert's diary

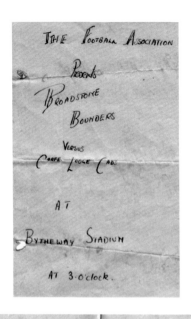

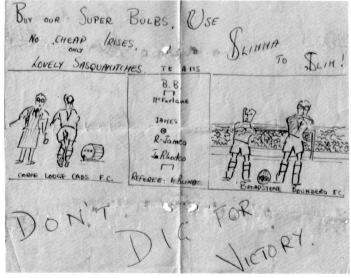

Broadstone football match - drawn by Uncle Robert

First parting.

I would not hold you. Yet I know not why
I fear to let you wander from my side.
You are so small, I guard you selfishly
For all your hurts are mine, intensified.

But I have seen you off to school, + turned
And shut the door. I would not keep you back
My grief for you is more than you have earned,
Mine is the sorrow, mine the only lack,

Yours is the world, your eyes can make it fair
I would not cloud them with a mother's fears,
I only wish, my darling, I could share
Its new, true beauty with you, through my tears

Ah no. I would not hold you. This is only
A passing weakness, weighing on my will
And yet - I never knew a day as lonely
As this which you have left for me to fill.

'First Parting', poem by Iris when Alan first went to school,
1947

ending **Feb 19th 1948**

Name *Alan Macfarlan*   Age ____ years ____ months.

Form **I**   Number of Pupils in Form ____   Average Age ____

TERMINAL EXAMINATION.

Total Marks possible ____

Total Marks gained ____   Position in Form **2nd**

Marks gained % ____

Marks gained % by Head Pupil ____

ATTENDANCE.

Possible **62** half days.   Absent ____ half days.   Late ____ times.

GENERAL REPORT.

Conduct *Excellent*

Homework

General Remarks *Alan has made good progress in the term and a half he has been with us. He is a favourite with the other children. We are very sorry he is going and feel sure he will do well where ever he is.*

(Signed) *Winifred Whittington*
CLASS MISTRESS.

GAMES MISTRESS.

DANCING MISTRESS.

S. Whittington
HEAD MISTRESS.

Report considered by ____

PARENT OR GUARDIAN.

Date ____ 193__

Next Term begins ____

REPORT for *Christmas* Term

SUBJECT.	*TERM MARK.	EXAM. MARK. %	PLACE IN FORM	SUBJECT.	TERM MARK	EXAM MARK. %	PLACE IN FORM
ENGLISH.				**SCRIPTURE.**			
Grammar				Catechism.			
Literature				**ART.**			
Composition				Model Drawing	A	18/20	2nd
Dictation				Freehand			
Recitation	A	20/20	1st	Memory			
Reading	A	18/20	2nd	Colour			
Writing	B	18/20	2nd	**MUSIC.**			
HISTORY.				Singing			
English				Sight-Reading			
European				Piano			
GEOGRAPHY.				**DOMESTIC SUBJECTS.**			
MATHEMATICS.				Needlework			
Arithmetic	A	20/20	1st	Handwork			
Mental Arithmetic				Woodwork			
Tables	A	18/20	2nd	**GENERAL KNOWLEDGE.**			
SCIENCE.				**DRILL.**			
Biology				Dancing			
LANGUAGES.							
French Grammar							
" Translation							
" Composition							
" Oral							
German				Height		ft.	in.
Latin Grammar				Weight		st.	lb.
" Translation				Chest		in. to	in.

*A = Good.
B = Fairly Good.
C = Fair to Weak.
D = Very Weak.

First school reports at kindergarten

SOUTHLANDS SCHOOL.

Report for the _Summer_ Term, 19 50

Name _Alan Macfarlane_ Age _8-7_

NO. OF ABSENCES (HALF DAYS)	12	FORM Transition	AVERAGE AGE OF FORM 7-10

SUBJECT	REMARKS	
READING	Fairly good.	LB
WRITING	Fairly good. Alan persists in forming the letter 'a' incorrectly.	LB
SPELLING	Good. Much improvement this term.	LB
ENGLISH LITERATURE ...		
COMPOSITION	Good.	LB
FRENCH		
LATIN		
HISTORY	Good.	LB
SCRIPTURE	Good.	LB
ARITHMETIC	Not very reliable, but Alan has worked	
ALGEBRA	hard throughout the term.	M.T.
GEOMETRY		
NATURE STUDY	Very good work.	JS.
GEOGRAPHY	Very good.	M.T.
HANDWORK	Good.	LB
NEEDLEWORK		
ART	Good, some work spoilt by too many minute details.	LB
DANCING		
MUSIC {		
PIANO		
VIOLIN		
PHYSICAL TRAINING ...	Good neat work. Progress in deportment quite good	JHU.
GAMES	Very good.	JAU.
GENERAL CONDUCT ...		LB

HEIGHT	ft.	in.	WEIGHT	st.	lb.	BEGINNING OF TERM.
HEIGHT	ft.	in.	WEIGHT	st.	lb.	END OF TERM.

REMARKS { A good term on the whole. Alan is a delightful little boy — quite capable. We wish him all success.

(Signed) J. Megane Barnard. High. Cert. N.S.W.

L.R.A.M.

Next Term commences _Sept. 18_, and ends _Dec 19._

JLP 2146-11-47

Last junior school report before going to the Dragon

HANDWRITING

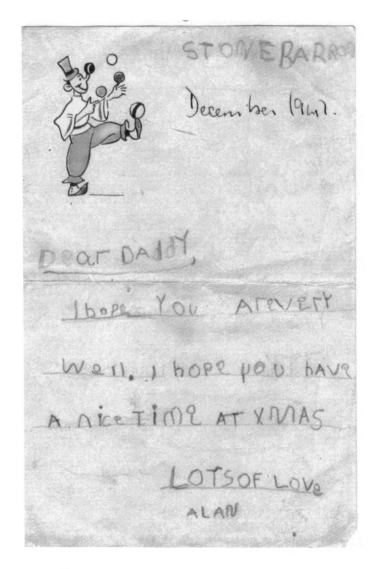

My first surviving letter; aged nearly six, December 1947

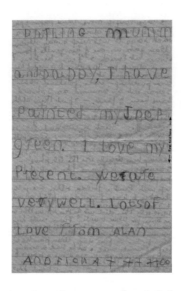

18 October 1948, a day after my mother left for India, aged six and three quarters.

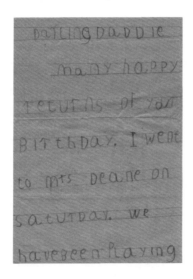

Letter on 24 October 1948 for my father's birthday

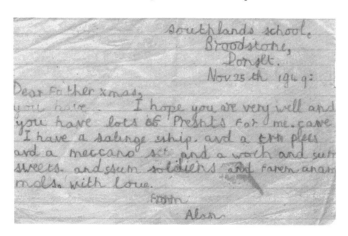

Darling mummy
and Daddy
we have 12 day
old chicks. We
are sending you a
butterfly book.
I am much better

March 1949, aged seven and a quarter

southlands school,
Broadstone,
Dorset.
Nov 25 th 1949:
Dear Father xmas,
you have.   I hope you are very well and
you have lots of Preshts for me. cave
I have a salinge ship. and a trn plees
and a meccano set and a woch and sum
sweets. and ssum soldiers and raren anam
mals. with love.
From
Alan

Letter to Father Christmas, 25 November 1949, aged nearly
eight

Croydon   July 20 1950

Dear Mummy and Daddy and Ana,
we got the lovely letter. We had
a nice Journey up from England.
I have cort a little trout and two
big ones. I am looking Forward
to when all of you come back.
What Fun we will have! I hope
we will go to Loch Morar Fishing.
we are writing because it is wet
and we can not go out to play.
we were going for a picnic but it
rains. We had a picnic in the coach

Letter from Scotland, July 1950

30 April '52
By the way
1952

Darling Mummy and Daddy

I am writing this just before going to school
Robert is taking me to Waterloo and he
will put me into the Oxford train at
paddington. I had a nice walk at Milford
on sea two days ago. Richard took Robert
and me to see the Hardcourt tennis
tournament at Bournemouth. We saw
Sedgeman win 6-0 6-1 6-0 and also
Doris Hart & Mr and Mrs Patterson. I have
been having fun with my bow and arrows also
we have had some good games of croquet
on that lawn. I hope you are all well out
there and I think of you very often. I will
write regularly from school
With lots of love from
Allan

Allan is very fit and looking grand
He seems to have enjoyed his time at
Milford. He was there for 10 days. We
think he should go there in the summer
hols but for not too long as beach nothing

Letter from Dorset, April 1952

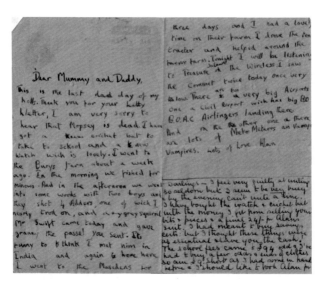

Letter from Dorset, April 1953, with addition by grandmother

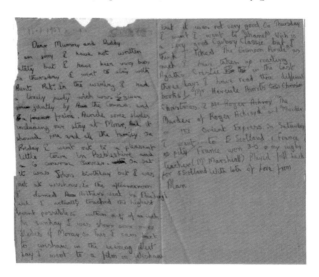

Letter from Scotland, January 1954

Friday

Dear ~~Mr~~ Mummy and Daddy,

I am so sorry as this letter will probabally not reach very soon but I think I might as well wait untill my results come and I have my papers back. I have played in three matches since ~~Swednesday~~ Wednesday. Firstly I played against Cothill in which we won by about 70 runs I only made 8 runs but while I was in the score went from 44 for 5 to about 85. On Thursday I didn't bat against Cheltenham but we won by five wickets (They scored 98 for 7) and we scored 102 for 5) Yesterday there was 2nd XI match against Salesian College. They declared (a very decently) at 120 for 6. As someone was ill I was playing. Our first few batted well, Ellis 8 Scorah 14 Axtell 32. And when I went in it was 64 for 4. Then Wilson was out for 2. and Westrup came in. We began to look as if we would draw when by a fluke I hit 10 in 3 balls then Westrup hit 3 fours. But he was out for 25 but we managed to win with ten minutes to go. I made 33 not out.

Letter from Dragon School in last summer term, July 1955

DRAWINGS AND PAINTINGS

Aged six: probably the steep hill at Charmouth

Outline drawing of Alan's fish

Aged seven: possibly the fish I caught at Oxford

My painting over the top of a drawing by another

A mill; painting over a drawing by another

July: Painting over a sketch by another

Tree and cut out baby deer (Bambi?)

Birthday card

1950 Aged eight

March: various drawings of a farm, house, zoo

August: Holiday in Scotland – Loch Morar

1952 aged ten

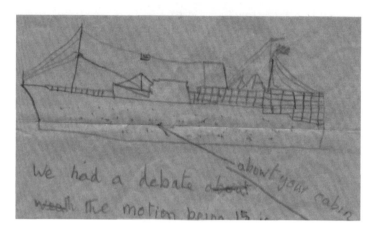

January – Parents Boat to India

1954 Aged twelve

July - the Dorset house

My sister's horse in Assam

Our pet dachshund in Assam

An uncomplimentary picture of my father

Vicky, the pet monkey in Assam

ALAN'S TOYS AND COLLECTIONS

Overviews: soldiers, animals, cars, chocolate covers etc.

Guns, search lights and dinky toys

Soldiers of the Empire

The fort made for my seventh Christmas in 1948

Games

Subuteo

Minibricks

Miniature horse racing

Collections

Chocolate covers and coins

Tiger and leopard's teeth and wild boar tusks

Wild animals

Farm animals right, ceremonial ribbons and minibricks left

AFTERWARDS

On anthropological fieldwork in Nepal in the 1990's